Anti - Inflammatory Diet Coo Beginners:

Rebalance Your Metabolism in a Healthy & Tasty Way Reducing Inflammations| Start Your Walk for a Journey to Discover Mouthwatering Recipes to Unleash Your Energy | Satyr Method

TABLE OF CONTENTS

1 INTRODUCTION

Consuming certain meals may contribute to inflammation or make it worse. Fresh, whole foods are less likely than processed or sugary foods to have this effect. The foundation of a diet that reduces inflammation is fresh produce. Plant-based diets include a significant amount of antioxidants. Free radicals can, however, be produced by some foods. Examples include foods that are repeatedly fried in hot frying oil. What are free radicals: "a specific class of unstable molecule produced throughout typical cell metabolism (chemical changes that take place in a cell). In cells, free radicals can accumulate and harm other molecules like DNA, lipids, and proteins." Trusted Food sources that are present aid the body in removing free radicals. Some body functions, such as metabolism, produce free radicals as an unavoidable byproduct. However, external factors like stress and smoking can increase the body's free radicals. Free radicals can cause cell harm. This damage can cause inflammation and play a role in certain diseases. Although the body produces some antioxidants to help remove these dangerous compounds, eating antioxidants is also advantageous. An anti-inflammatory diet favors foods strong in antioxidants over meals that encourage the production of free radicals. Oily fish, which contains omega-3 fatty acids, may aid in lowering the body's production of inflammatory proteins.

1.1 What's the immune system

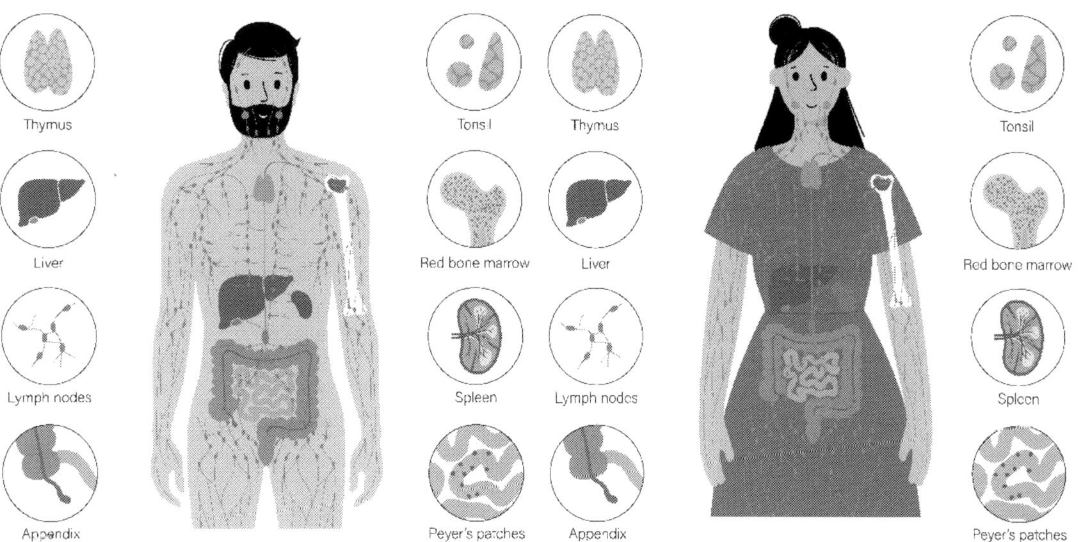

The immune system of the body is made up of a vast network of cells, organs, proteins, tissues, and other components. A fully functional immune system can distinguish healthy tissue and undesired chemicals. It will launch an intricate attack to defend the body from invaders if it identifies unwelcome material. Additionally, it detects and eliminates damaged and dead cells. However, the immune system is not always accurate. Because of a medical condition or the requirement for specific treatments, it may occasionally be unable to fight efficiently. The immune system misinterprets good tissue in autoimmune disorders (like: lupus, rheumatoid arthritis, Crohn's disease, and ulcerative colitis.) and allergies as diseased, causing an unwarranted onslaught that results in painful and occasionally severe symptoms.There are many different parts that make up the immune system, including:

- The spleen,
- White blood cells
- Thebone marrow,
- Thelymphatic system,
- The tonsils, adenoids, and appendix

White blood cells move through lymphatic and blood arteries.
Similar to how blood arteries form a network, the lymphatic system does as well. Instead of blood, lymph is what it conveys. Immune-related cells are transported by a fluid called lymph to places that require them.
Pathogen-hunting white blood cells are active all the time. Once they locate one, they start to reproduce and tell other cell types to do the same.
White blood cells are kept in the body's many lymphoid organs.

These consist of:

1. The thymus is a gland located beneath the breastbone where lymphocytes, a kind of white blood cell, develop.
2. The spleen: Immune cells congregate and function in the spleen, an organ in the upper left corner of the abdomen.
3. Bone marrow: Red and white blood cells are made in the bone marrow, a soft tissue located in the middle of the bone.
4. Lymph nodes: Lymph nodes are tiny, bean-shaped glands that can be found all throughout the body, but are most prevalent in the neck, underarms, groin, and belly. They link via lymphatic vessels. When antigens are present, immune cells assemble in lymph nodes and respond. This might cause edema
5. The tonsils, adenoids, and appendix: The lymphoid tissue is present in the tonsils, adenoids, and appendix because they serve as entry points for pathogens into the body.

1.2 What's an inflammation and what's a chronic inflammation

Your immune system is triggered when your body is exposed to a pathogen (such as viruses, bacteria, or toxic substances) or sustains damage. Inflammatory cells and cytokines are the initial responders that your immune system dispatches
These cells trigger an inflammatory response to ingest germs and other hazardous things or start mending injured tissue. The outcome could be pain, bruising, swelling, or redness. But inflammation also affects bodily functions that are not evident to the naked eye.
How does acute and chronic inflammation differ from one another?
Inflammation comes in two varieties:

- **Acute inflammation:** The body responds in a certain way to a sudden injury, such as cutting your finger. Your body sends inflammatory cells to the wound to speed up healing. The healing process is launched by these cells.
- **Chronic inflammation:** Your body releases inflammatory cells despite no external threat. In rheumatoid arthritis, for instance, inflammatory cells and chemicals attack the joint tissues, resulting in an intermittent inflammation that can gravely damage joints and cause pain and deformity.

What signs of both acute and chronic inflammation are there?

The following symptoms of acute inflammation include reddened skin at the location of the injury.

- Pain or injuries
- Swelling.
- Heat.

Compared to acute inflammation, indications of chronic inflammation may be less noticeable. Chronic inflammation may manifest as

- Stomach pain
- Chest ache
- Fatigue. (For instance, systemic lupus)
- Fever. (For example TB)
- Joint pain or stiffness (Rheumatoid arthritis, for instance)
- Mouth sores (For instance, HIV infection)
- An itchy rash (Psoriasis, for instance)

The following are the most typical causes of ongoing inflammation:

- Diseases where your body assaults good tissue, such as lupus.
- Exposure to contaminants from industry or the environment.
- Acute inflammation brought on by an untreated disease or wound

Inflammation in the body is also influenced by certain lifestyle variables. Chronic inflammation may be more likely to occur if you:

- Excessive alcohol consumption
- Unless it is due to being exceptionally muscular, have a high body mass index (BMI) that is within obesity.
- You either don't exercise enough or you exercise too frequently at your maximal effort.
- Have persistent tension.
- Smoke.

1.3 What problems can cause an inflammation

The body initiates a biological response to try to oust an invader when it finds one.

A virus, irritation, or foreign material like a thorn could be the attacker. Pathogens, which can be bacteria, viruses, or other living things, cause infections. The body occasionally views its cells or tissues as dangerous. Autoimmune conditions like type 1 diabetes can develop due to this reaction. Experts believe that inflammation may affect a variety of chronic conditions. One example is metabolic syndrome, which comprises type 2 diabetes, heart disease, and obesity. Inflammatory markers are typically seen in higher concentrations in the bodies of people with these illnesses. Acute or brief inflammation may be a sign of an illness or harm. The top five indicators of acute inflammation are listed below:

- Pain: This could be continual or only felt when one touches the wounded area.
- Increased blood flow to nearby capillaries causes the area to turn red.
- Loss of function might include difficulties breathing, moving a joint, smelling, and other parts.
- Swelling: If fluid accumulates, a condition known as edema may develop.
- The affected area might become warmer to the touch due to increased blood flow.

There aren't usually these signs. Additionally, inflammation may be "silent," manifesting no symptoms. A person may also experience fever, general malaise, and weariness. Symptoms of acute inflammation last a few days. Acute inflammation lasts between two and six weeks. Chronic inflammation can last for months or even years. It either has or may have connections to several illnesses, including:

- Cardiovascular disease and diabetes (CVD)
- Allergy and other joint conditions
- Persistent pulmonary obstruction (COPD)
- Rheumatoid arthritis and psoriasis

Depending on the illness, the symptoms may include discomfort and exhaustion.

1.4 How food can interact with inflammations

These days, discussions about nutrition frequently include the term "anti-inflammatory diet." But why exactly is inflammation harmful to us? And what connection does food have to this?

Your body typically responds to illness or injury with inflammation. White blood cells are instructed to begin mending the harm when your wounded tissue produces specific molecules. However, inflammation can also be chronic, widespread, and of moderate intensity.

This persistent inflammation may impair your health. It may increase your risk of heart disease and stroke by accelerating arterial plaque buildup. It also increases the likelihood of developing chronic conditions, including diabetes, cancer, and others.

How can your diet benefit or harm you?

Your grocery store decisions may impact your body's inflammation. However, there are several factors that scientists are aware of regarding how nutrition influences the body's inflammatory processes. Meals can influence CRP (C-Reactive Protein) levels in the blood, causing inflammation. This could be due to the release of inflammatory messengers by specific meals, such as processed sweets, which may raise the risk of chronic inflammation. With additional nutrients like fruits and vegetables, your body can combat the oxidative stress that causes inflammation.

The good news is that consuming foods that reduce inflammation frequently enhances overall health. Therefore, eating to reduce inflammation need not be complicated or restricted.

Eating more greens is a simple dietary tip for reducing inflammation. Plant-based diets contain the anti-inflammatory components your body requires. The most excellent way to start is by eating a variety of legumes, whole grains, vegetables, and fruits.

- **Place a focus on antioxidants**: They help to prevent, delay or repair various forms of cell and tissue damage. They can be found in green tea, turmeric, ginger, whole grains, beans, berries, avocados, beets, leafy greens, and lentils, in addition to other colorful fruits and vegetables.
- **Purchasing omega-3 fatty acids**: Your body's inflammatory response is controlled by omega-3 fatty acids, which may help you manage the discomfort that inflammation produces. These beneficial fats can be found in modest levels in soy, walnuts, pecans, crushed flaxseed, and fish such as salmon, tuna, and mackerel.
- **Consume less red meat**: Red meat may contribute to inflammation. Burgers, what about them? Decide on a sensible goal. A few times each week, try replacing the meat in your noon meal with fish, almonds, or soy-based protein.
- **Eat fewer prepared foods**: Pastries, fizzy beverages, and deep-fried foods cause inflammation. They could include a lot of bad fats that have been associated with inflammation. However, if you prepare a number of meals ahead of time, eating full fruits, vegetables, grains, and beans can be quick.

2 PRINCIPLES OF THE DIET

2.1 What are the principles of the Anti – Inflammatory Diet

Anti-inflammatory properties are already present in several well-known diets.
For instance, the DASH diet and the Mediterranean diet both include heart-healthy fats, fresh fruits and vegetables, fish, whole grains, and fish.
Research suggests that the Mediterranean diet, with its emphasis on plant-based foods and healthy oils, can lessen the effects of inflammation on the cardiovascular system.
Three easy rules can help them make their diet less inflammatory.

PRINCIPLE 1: EAT A WHOLE-FOOD DIET AS THE FIRST RULE

Why?
Natural foods, not those produced by humans, are what our bodies are meant to flourish on. We haven't evolved sufficiently to handle artificial foods on par with natural foods yet (evolution moves extremely slowly; it will take hundreds of years to catch up).
Our bodies are constantly in an uncomfortable little state due to ingesting foods created by humans (think biscuits, cereals, processed meats, and anything else that is sold in a pack in the grocery store). And we don't even realize it because we're so accustomed to it!
Chronic inflammation, the root cause of many diseases, causes this ongoing mild discomfort.
What?
The whole food is:

- Foods produced in the dirt, such as vegetables (incl frozen)
- Foods that have come into contact with dirt, such as pork and fowl

- Foods like dairy and eggs that are made by animals that have walked on the ground.

How?

- Start incorporating real foods into your breakfast, lunch, dinner, and snacks in place of packaged items.
- Find simple ways to prepare your regular meals without using packaged items. Consider making your own cookies. Or you can look at the natural ingredients a packaged food contains and include those into your meals.

PRINCIPLE 2: CONSUME MORE PLANT-BASED FOOD

Why?

- Natural foods are those made from plants. Natural foods are the best fuel for our bodies. It will take thousands of years for us to catch up with the evolution and be able to manage processed foods just as well as natural foods.
- Numerous essential nutrients, including vitamins, minerals, trace elements, and phytonutrients, are included in plant-based meals. These phytonutrients, potent anti-inflammatory antioxidants, are ONLY present in plants that have grown above the ground.
- Ordinarily, we don't consume enough plant-based foods. Our meal ratios for meat, carbohydrates, and plant-based diets are wildly off.

What?

- Veggie-based foods include:
- Vegetables \sFruits
- Nuts \sSeeds
- Veggies and beans
- There are grains (whole grains!), but no wheat (see the next principle)

How?

- At every meal—breakfast, lunch, supper, and snacks—including plant-based meals.
- You should have three-quarters of your lunch and dinner plates comprised of plant-based meals.
- Eat the rainbow by attempting to consume at least 3 different veggies of various hues. Vegetables that have been frozen are excellent. And if you buy fresh, avoid pre-cut, sliced, etc., purchases because cut plants lose nutrients.

PRINCIPLE 3: ELIMINATE FOODS THAT CAUSE INFLAMMATION

Why?

Inflammation is triggered by many foods. Almost all packaged foods fall under this category, but some whole foods do as well.

What?

Inflammatory foods include:

- One of the main foods that cause inflammation in people living with endometriosis is gluten, a protein found in wheat. Due to damage to the gut wall brought on by gluten sensitivity, partially digested gluten proteins can enter the circulation and cause widespread inflammation. Check the label before purchasing bread, pasta, oats, rye, barley, malt, Brewer's yeast, soy sauce, most salad dressings, vegetarian burgers, and other processed goods.
- **Sugar-containing foods:** Sugar suppresses the immune system and is very inflammatory. Avoid eating or drinking fruit juices, cake, ice cream, cake, lollipops, and biscuits.
- Ham, salami, sausages, and pre-seasoned meat items like kebabs are examples of processed meats.
- Processed snacks, such as chips and crackers
- A few oils: corn oil, soybean oil
- Trans fats: check the label because many processed goods include hydrogenated fats.
- Alcohol: Although some alcoholic beverages contain antioxidants, the alcohol content is inflammatory and will negate whatever advantages the antioxidants may have.
- Because it irritates the intestines and bowels, caffeine will make any dietary sensitivities worse.
- Dairy: If you frequently got ear infections as a kid, dairy protein could also make you feel achy.

How?

- Reviewing your current diet, determine what foods you are consuming that are on the inflammatory list above.
- First and foremost, get rid of the gluten.
- If you consume a lot of coffee, black or green tea, or chocolate, gradually reduce these items from your diet over a few weeks (to avoid caffeine withdrawal). Water or herbal teas should be used instead of coffee or tea.
- Maintain a whole-foods-based, primarily plant-based diet.

2.2 Why Anti – Inflammatory Diet is a group of diets and not a specific diet

The American diet, which prioritizes saturated fats, added sugars, refined carbohydrates, and sodium, is a prescription for chronic inflammation. Thousands of health-promoting ingredients can be found in healthy foods, including well-known ones like vitamins, minerals, fiber, and omega-3 fatty acids, as well as less well-known ones like flavan-3-oils (found in tea and cocoa) and anthocyanins (in blueberries, strawberries, raspberries and other red and purple plant foods). Inflammation is brought on by certain chemicals in the body, but it may also be prevented and treated by naturally occurring compounds found in some meals by giving the body essential nutrients. For instance:.

- **Vitamin E (found in nuts and seeds) and vitamin C (found in cauliflower, citrus, and berries)** are antioxidants that work to neutralise free radicals, which are inflammatory molecules that can enter the body through inhalation of pollutants, smoking, exposure to the sun's rays, poor diet, or even normal body metabolism.
- **The omega-3 fatty acids in fish** increase the production of molecules that reduce inflammation while suppressing the development of inflammatory substances.
- **Whole grains, fruit, legumes, and other vegetables are high in fibre**, which feeds intestinal microorganisms, which in turn produce butyrate, an anti-inflammatory fatty acid that reduces the risk of heart disease and has other advantages.

2.3 What are the anti-inflammatory diets?

People worldwide could thrive on traditional cuisines that existed before soda, chicken nuggets, cheese curls, and all of the other highly processed foods that comprise the majority of the standard American diet. A traditional diet fundamentally satisfies the parameters for an anti-inflammatory diet, despite the seeming disparity between a plate of fresh pasta covered with marinara sauce and a Chinese stir-fry. The following paragraphs summarise the DASH diet and the best anti-inflammatory eating habits worldwide.

Traditional Mediterranean diet :

Italian, Greek, Lebanese, southern French, and other Mediterranean Sea-adjacent countries' cuisines may differ, yet they frequently contain many of the same ingredients. Inflammatory disorders such as Parkinson's disease, obesity, allergies, some types of cancer, Alzheimer's disease, type 2 diabetes, stroke, and cardiovascular disease, may be prevented by adopting a Mediterranean diet, according to a study.

To follow thousands of Greek citizens aged 20 to 86 over four years, researchers selected one study from hundreds. The group most closely adhered to a Mediterranean-style diet saw a reduction of around a third in deaths from heart disease, cancer, and overall mortality rates. A traditional Mediterranean diet has the following qualities:

- Large amounts of a variety of legumes, whole grains, vegetables, and fruits make up most of the diet.
- The primary sources of fat include seeds, nuts, and olive oil.
- Fish is the primary source of animal protein. Once or twice a week, a small amount of red meat is eaten.
- Little amounts of cheese, yogurt, and scarcely any butter or cream, make up most of the dairy products.
- Wine is only allowed with meals and in small to moderate amounts.
- Only sweets often made with almonds, olive oil, and honey, are appropriate for celebrations. Walnut-stuffed figs are a popular snack.

The Traditional Diet of Okinawa :

Okinawa, a Japanese island, is renowned for having a sizable population of healthy 100-year-olds. The local diet deserves much credit.

According to the research, "the overall dietary pattern is dominated by anti-inflammatory vegetables, particularly Okinawan sweet potatoes."

He continues that they also consume the most soy in Japan and maybe the entire globe, and their diet contains little red meat and other anti-inflammatory foods like added sugar and saturated fat.
A typical Okinawan diet consists of:

- Fewer calories,
- More seaweed, and other vegetables,
- More legumes, especially soy,
- Medium amounts of seafood,
- Less dairy and meat,
- Moderate alcohol

Although this diet may seem to be similar to others, it has specific distinctive components, such as:

- It has much soy in it. The diet includes 85 grams of miso, tofu, and other daily soy products. In addition to having anti-inflammatory isoflavones, soy has also been associated with cardiovascular health.
- This area is abundant with seaweed. Even though you may only be aware of nori, the dull sushi wrapper, Okinawan cuisine employs more than a dozen other seaweed species. They are high in antioxidants, especially astaxanthin, both an antioxidant and an anti-inflammatory.
- Sweet potatoes from Okinawa are the primary source of starch. Despite its prevalence in other cuisines, frying is not the primary starch source in the traditional Okinawan diet. Just a few of the several anti-inflammatory substances contained in it include anthocyanins, the blue-violet pigment beta-carotene, and vitamins E and C.
- Little fat While there are many parallels between the Okinawan diet and the traditional Mediterranean diet, Willcox argues that the Okinawan diet is essentially distinct because it is significantly lower in fat. The standard Okinawan diet only has around 10% fat, compared to the average Mediterranean diet's 30% to 40% of good fats, primarily monounsaturated fats.

Normal Nordic Diet :
Despite the differences in their cuisines, Finland, Sweden, and Denmark all typically eat similar, healthful foods like:

- Broccoli
- Carrots
- Complete rye products (bread, muesli)
- Sauerkraut
- Berries
- Apples
- Pears \sFish \sCabbage
- Potatoes
- Canola oil is the main oil.

These meals are advantageous for lowering inflammation because they are rich in nutrients. Rye deserves special recognition since research has shown that it can reduce PSA blood sugar and C-reactive protein, a measure of inflammation (a marker for prostate cancer in men).

According to a review of the University of Eastern Finland study, persons who adhere to this diet more strictly have lower blood levels of CRP and other inflammation markers.

Fruit (berries, pears, and apples), cereals (barley, oat, and rye), diets devoid of non-lean and processed meat, and moderate alcohol use are particularly beneficial foods. The investigation also showed that a healthy Nordic diet could aid in weight loss and reduce the number of inflammatory symptoms.

Studies have been conducted in many Nordic countries assigning one group to a healthy Nordic diet while the other group continued to eat regular (and less nutrient-dense) meals. These tests were conducted with various case histories from six to 24 weeks.

Type 2 diabetes, a condition intimately connected to chronic inflammation, may also benefit significantly from a healthy Nordic diet. In a 15-year study of 57,053 middle-aged Danes, individuals whose diets were closest to the healthy Nordic pattern had a 25% reduced chance of developing type 2 diabetes in women and a 38% lower risk in men than those whose diets deviated the furthest from the paradigm.

Mexican Traditional Cuisine :

Mexico is the birthplace of another well-liked anti-inflammatory dietary regimen. A traditional Mexican diet consists primarily of:

- Fruit and vegetable plenty (including hot peppers)
- Tacos made of corn
- Rice (brown and white)
- Cheese
- Beans

Studies have suggested that a traditional Mexican diet may reduce inflammation. Those who followed a more conventional Mexican diet had an average CRP score that was 23% lower than those who did not, according to a study of 493 postmenopausal Mexican women. The National Cancer Institute provided funding for this study.

A few conditions that inflammation-related conditions are associated with defense against include high cholesterol, high blood pressure, type 2 diabetes, cardiovascular disease, and obesity. In Mexican cooking, legumes are frequently utilized. With a diet heavy on beans, how is it possible? The exceptionally high fiber content of this diet has the following impacts on the entire body, per a report published in Advances in Nutrition:

- It lowers the spike in blood sugar that occurs after eating and reduces "bad" cholesterol, which over time, aids in decreasing inflammation and type 2 diabetes, especially when red meat is replaced with beans, which reduces inflammation.
- It decreases cravings and promotes weight loss.
- Due to their high nutrient content, the Dietary Guidelines for Americans suggest that we consume beans once a week.

Dietary Methods to Reduce Blood Pressure (DASH) :
The DASH diet was developed in the 1990s to help Americans with high blood pressure (hypertension). It also completes other tasks. A 2018 meta-analysis of numerous research studies indicated that DASH significantly decreases CRP compared to the average American diet. DASH takes an anti-inflammation approach. The primary protein sources are fish, chicken, and lentils, with inflammatory foods such as sugary beverages, sweets, and red meat, consumed in moderation. The vast majority of grains are whole grains. There are also a lot of fruits and veggies. Lowering LDL cholesterol is another advantage of the DASH diet. Excessive saturated fat raises the "bad" blood cholesterol LDL, but DASH excludes foods heavy in this fat because they are also known to trigger inflammation. Palm kernel oils, palm, coconut, and high-fat dairy products, are some of these foods (butter, cream, cheese, whole milk). Instead, the menu offers low-fat or fat-free dairy products and vegetable oils such as safflower oil, olive, maize, and canola.

2.4 Foods allowed and to avoid or reduce

Studies show a lower risk of inflammatory diseases in people who consume much fish, vegetables, fruits, nuts, seeds, and healthy oils. Antioxidants and omega-3 fatty acids are two nutritional components that may have anti-inflammatory effects.

Antioxidant-rich foods include:

- Apples
- Berries (such as blueberries, raspberries, and blackberries)
- Artichokes
- Beans (such as red beans, pinto beans, and black beans)
- Dark-green vegetables with leaves (such as kale, spinach, and collard greens)
- Nuts (such as walnuts, almonds, pecans, and hazelnuts)
- The sweet potato
- Avocados
- Broccoli, Cherries
- Dark chocolate with a minimum of 70% cocoa
- Whole grains

Omega-3 fatty acids are "healthy fats" that may help ward against illnesses, including arthritis, cancer, and heart disease.

- Omega-3 fatty acid-rich foods include:
- Fatty fish (such as salmon, herring, mackerel, sardines, and anchovies)
- Flaxseed
- Meals enriched with omega-3 (including eggs and milk)
- Walnuts

Additionally, there is proof that certain herbs and spices, like ginger, turmeric, and garlic, can reduce inflammation.

Foods to exclude

Omega-6 fatty acid-rich meals are among those that promote inflammation. Omega-6 fatty acids are necessary for metabolism, which converts food into energy, as well as for the health of the brain and bones, but too much of them can lead to inflammation. Omega-6 fatty acids are prevalent in the following foods:

- Dairy items high in lactose (such as milk, cheese, butter, and ice cream)
- Meats
- Peanuts
- Margarine

If you want to reduce inflammation, keeping your omega-3 to the omega-6 fatty acid ratio in check is essential.

Foods with a high glycemic index (GI) may exacerbate inflammation. These include foods like sugar and processed carbohydrates that spike your blood glucose (sugar) level too quickly and excessively. To help minimize inflammation, stay away from processed foods, white bread, desserts, and sweets. Eat meals low in glycemic indexes (GI), such as those containing poultry, fish, whole grains, leafy greens, and non-starchy vegetables.

3 SEASONAL VEGETABLES AND FRUITS

Think of the intense red color and excellent consistency of a fully ripe, juicy summer tomato and how it tastes and feels. Dietician Lisa Hayim, RD, of New York City claims purchasing food in a season has benefits beyond merely improved flavor. She claims that purchasing vegetables in their prime season allows you to obtain more natural nutrients. When you're ready to eat your fruit, "these vital vitamins and minerals are more likely to be kept," she claims. "Fruits and vegetables in the season don't travel far to get to your kitchen". Additionally, you'll save money because shorter shipping distances for your produce mean cheaper costs for the grocery shop, which are then passed on to you at the register. Dietician Lindsey Pine from Los Angeles, California, also mentions the law of supply and demand. Prices for fruits and vegetables will decrease throughout the growing season since growers are likely to have an excess supply.

December

- Grapefruit
- Papayas
- Broccoli
- Cauliflower
- Mushrooms
- Cabbage
- Turnips
- Oranges
- Sweet potatoes
- Parsnips
- Brussels sprouts
- Rutabagas
- Kale
- Tangerines
- Leeks
- Pears

- Tangelos
- Pomegranates

January

- Oranges
- Cabbage
- Broccoli
- Turnips
- Kale
- Cauliflower
- Leeks
- Rutabagas
- Lemons
- Tangerines
- Brussels sprouts
- Tangelos
- Grapefruit
- Parsnips

February

- Parsnips
- Rutabagas
- Broccoli
- Tangelos
- Grapefruit
- Oranges
- Kale
- Brussels sprouts
- Leeks
- Tangerines
- Cabbage
- Lemons
- Cauliflower
- Turnips

March

- Radishes
- Rutabagas
- Lettuce
- Turnips
- Mushrooms
- Leeks
- Parsnips
- Pineapples
- Artichokes
- Broccoli
- Cauliflower
- Brussels sprouts

April

- Artichokes
- Spring peas
- Asparagus
- Mushrooms
- Broccoli
- Leeks
- Pineapples
- Lettuce
- Cauliflower
- Radishes
- Rhubarb

May

- Apricots
- Radishes
- Pineapples
- Swiss chard
- Strawberries
- Rhubarb
- Okra
- Spring peas
- Asparagus
- Artichokes
- Mangoes
- Cherries

- Lettuce
- Zucchini

June

- Corn
- Cantaloupe
- Kiwi
- Strawberries
- Blueberries
- Cherries
- Swiss chard
- Apricots
- Mangoes
- Peaches
- Watermelon
- Zucchini
- Lettuce

July

- Plums
- Blackberries
- Raspberries
- Cantaloupe
- Lettuce
- Mangoes
- Tomatoes
- Watermelon
- Peaches
- Cucumbers
- Green beans
- Summer squash
- Swiss chard
- Strawberries
- Peppers
- Kiwi
- Okra
- Zucchini
- Corn
- Apricots
- Blueberries
- Kohlrabi

August

- Peppers
- Summer squash
- Cantaloupe
- Corn
- Winter squash
- Zucchini
- Green beans
- Kiwi
- Plums
- Raspberries
- Cucumbers
- Apples
- Blueberries
- Eggplant
- Watermelon
- Figs
- Swiss chard
- Tomatoes
- Strawberries
- Mangoes
- Acorn squash
- Apricots
- Kohlrabi
- Lettuce
- Okra
- Peaches
- Butternut squash

September

- Acorn squash
- Eggplant
- Pomegranates
- Cauliflower
- Grapes
- Green beans
- Mushrooms
- Okra
- Spinach
- Mangoes
- Butternut squash
- Cantaloupe
- Figs
- Sweet potatoes
- Peppers
- Persimmons
- Tomatoes
- Lettuce
- Swiss chard
- Pumpkins
- Apples
- Beets

October

- Brussels sprouts
- Butternut squash
- Cabbage
- Acorn squash
- Cranberries
- Apples
- Pomegranates
- Parsnips
- Turnips
- Persimmons
- Sweet potatoes
- Grapes
- Spinach
- Leeks
- Winter squash
- Lettuce
- Mushrooms
- Broccoli
- Swiss chard
- Cauliflower
- Pumpkins
- Rutabagas
- Beets

November

- Cauliflower
- Parsnips
- Beets
- Brussels sprouts
- Tangerines
- Turnips
- Winter squash
- Oranges
- Pears
- Mushrooms
- Pomegranates
- Spinach
- Broccoli
- Sweet potatoes
- Cranberries
- Leeks
- Cabbage
- Pumpkins
- Rutabagas
- Persimmons

4 FAQ

1. **How to Recognize Excessive Inflammation**

Everyone can benefit from consuming anti-inflammatory foods and leading an anti-inflammatory lifestyle, but you can work with your doctor to determine if you have excessive inflammation. The most typical test is to measure the amount of C-reactive protein (hsCRP) in the blood.

2. **The anti-inflammatory diet: What Is It?**

The truth is that there isn't a single, established anti-inflammatory eating plan. Even more, perplexing is that what you can eat and how much of it you can have is quite flexible. Instead of strict rules (looking at you, keto), people on an anti-inflammatory diet are advised to eat more nutrients that fight inflammation and fewer things that cause it (more on that below). This means that even though they may differ, many diets, including the Mediterranean and Whole30, legally fall under the category of anti-inflammatory.

3. **What Can I Eat Now?**

A lot of delicious and healthful food. To reduce inflammation, raise your intake of whole grains, lean protein, fruits, vegetables, low-fat dairy, and healthy fats. For an anti-inflammatory breakfast, you can have whole-grain avocado toast. For lunch, you might have a Buddha bowl full of vegetables. Next, have a plate of grilled salmon and a side salad for a calming meal. Oh, and don't worry—there are lots of anti-inflammatory dessert dishes that you may enjoy. One of the finest meals for reducing inflammation is dark chocolate.

4. **What can't I eat?**

Avoid or limit your consumption of inflammatory foods like red meat, processed and fried foods, too much sugar, and items with a high glycemic index (such as white bread and pasta made from white flour). Nightshades (such as eggplant and tomatoes) and gluten can also cause inflammation in some people, but your doctor can help you figure out whether foods are a problem for you. It's up to you exactly how much you want to cut back on these items (although some people avoid them altogether).

5. **Is It Time for Me to Try an Anti-Inflammatory Diet?**

An anti-inflammatory diet may help you control your symptoms if you have a chronic inflammatory condition (like psoriasis or rheumatoid arthritis). Can it fix your health problems? No, not always. However, even if you don't have a specific illness, there are some really excellent anti-inflammatory diet advantages that you might want to take advantage of, such as increased energy,

6. How to stop or lessen unneeded inflammation

To reduce inflammation, people frequently take medicines. Ibuprofen and aspirin are examples of medications that can alter the body's chemical processes, but they are not without adverse effects. According to research, lifestyle decisions can also lessen inflammation; these decisions impact how much inflammation is present in our bodies. Adopting a balanced diet and other lifestyle habits can significantly reduce inflammation levels.

7. Reduce Inflammation Through Food

Inflammation can be influenced by what we eat; some diets are more likely to lessen pain and other disease-related symptoms. According to estimates, a balanced diet could avoid 60% of chronic diseases, including many health issues mentioned above. Eating the appropriate foods can help prevent inflammation from developing in the first place and lessen and treat the inflammation that has already started.

5 DASH DIET COOKBOOK FOR BEGINNERS

Say Goodbye to High Blood Pressure and Start Your Body & Circulatory System Improvement Journey with Tasty and Healthy Low-Sodium Recipes | Faun method

6 INTRODUCTION

Read this introduction if you're wondering how the Dash diet compares to other popular diets. We'll discuss what foods you can eat and which ones you should avoid or reduce. We'll also go over a few tips and tricks to make the diet as tasty and enjoyable as possible. And we'll cover how to implement the diet into your daily routine to maximize your results. If you're still unsure whether the Dash diet is for you, check out our review of this popular diet.

Dash diet is a low-sodium diet that focuses on eating fresh, whole, plant-based foods. U.S.D.A. recommends DASH diet and stands for Dietary Approaches to Stop Hypertension or lowering blood pressure naturally through diet without side effects from medication (as compared to medicine). This diet is recommended for those who want to learn how to lose weight naturally and effectively.

6.1 How to Make the DASH Diet Work for You

Dash diet is excellent for your health because it encourages eating lots of whole-grain foods and fresh fruits and vegetables. It also excludes many processed foods high in sodium, sugar, and fat. In addition, this diet will help you lose weight naturally.

The DASH Diet has many benefits, but how do you make it work for you? The DASH Diet encourages you to eat five or more servings of fruits and vegetables every day. Examples of fruits and vegetables you can eat include bananas, raspberries, mango, and peaches. In addition, you can choose one medium apple or half a cup of frozen peaches for more fruit options. Alternatively, you can replace the meat in your meals with a vegetable or a fruit salad.

The DASH diet allows you to eat out, but you need to be cautious about the foods you choose. Most restaurant meals are fatty, salty, and oversized. To stay within the DASH diet, you should limit your intake of salt and condiments. You can still enjoy alcohol in moderation. If you are unsure how to make the foods you eat on the DASH diet, you can find recipes online.

The DASH diet also limits your sodium intake. High sodium diets can affect otherwise healthy people. You should avoid processed foods, packaged potato snacks, and white bread. You should also limit your intake of enriched grains like white bread and pasta. Frozen meals, convenience store snacks, and fast food are all foods with high sodium. Alcohol is another food group to limit. Not only does alcohol cause hypertension, but it can also damage your liver.

6.2 Dash diet vs other diets

There are pros and cons to the DASH diet. The DASH diet is unlikely to offer any significant benefits for healthy individuals. However, individuals with heart conditions or high blood pressure may benefit from a DASH-based diet. People on this diet should not use salt in their cooking but instead, add a few tablespoons of spices to their dishes. They should also limit the amount of salt in their beverages, as it increases the amount of sodium in their blood.

The DASH diet is also known for its focus on fruits and vegetables. The diet promotes eating various lean meats, whole grains, vegetables, and low-fat dairy foods. The DASH diet also encourages using many vegetable oils, including olive, canola, and margarine, instead of oily cooking oils. Those who follow the DASH diet should replace high-calorie salad dressings with low-fat alternatives.

One of the benefits of the DASH diet is its potential for lowering blood pressure without medication. It's low-sodium diet combined with increased intake of whole grains, vegetables and fruits, and lean protein reduces systolic blood pressure by 8-14 points. These reductions in blood pressure may also help lower risk of cardiovascular disease. In addition, DASH diet promotes an increased intake of fruits, vegetables, whole grains, fish, poultry, and nuts.

The DASH diet is not for everyone. For example, it is not for everyone and requires a calorie-restricted diet. Diets with low-fat components may be the most suitable choice for some people. While it may be hard for some people to follow the DASH diet, it does have other benefits. It may even lower your risk of developing cancer.

The DASH diet requires significant changes in a person's diet and is hard to follow. It limits salt and fat intake significantly. It also requires significant cuts in precooked foods. As a result, many people have trouble following the DASH diet. And even if you do manage to stick to the diet, you are unlikely to see any results in the long run. You'll need to see your doctor regularly to check on the results of the DASH diet.

6.3 Tips and tricks of the diet for limiting sodium

To minimize sodium intake on the Dash Diet, check each food's nutritional content. For example, avoid poultry packed with a sodium solution when choosing your dinners. You can also try replacing the sodium in meat and poultry with herbs and citrus. Also, note down your serving size, and check the nutritional facts of each food. Finally, cook your food at a lower temperature to avoid excess sodium.

Aim to cook at home more often. Using fresh ingredients and cooking from scratch is a great way to limit sodium. Avoid going out to eat and try to cook at home more often. Taking a food log is helpful in monitoring sodium intake. It can take about a week to calculate your daily intake. To make it easier, try to cook dinner at least once a week. To cut down on eating out, use recipes that are low in sodium and avoid using saltshakers.

Look for packaged food with a Nutrition Facts label. Choose foods with less than 2,300 milligrams of sodium per serving. When you are eating out, choose unsalted or no-salt-added products. Try to ensure fruits and vegetables cover at least half of plate. These foods are natural sources of fiber and are low in sodium. It also helps you lose weight, which is great for your overall health.

Another tip to limit sodium on the DASH Diet is to eat more fruits and vegetables. Fruits and vegetables are a great way to increase your intake of fibre and potassium. As you can see, eating more fruits and vegetables increases your blood potassium level and triggers the kidneys to eliminate extra sodium and fluid from the body. This helps lower blood pressure and reduces your risk of a heart attack.

6.4 Foods allowed and foods to avoid or reduce

A DASH diet aims to lower blood pressure by reducing sodium in the body. According to the National Institute of Health, sodium intake should not exceed 2,300 milligrams per day. High blood pressure is the silent killer. Most people don't experience symptoms for decades, and it often does not cause any other symptoms unless it becomes complicated. This diet also promotes weight loss. There are some foods you should avoid when eating the DASH diet, but don't worry, there are recipes available that are heart-healthy and delicious.

A good example of what you should limit on the DASH diet is red meat. The DASH diet encourages the consumption of fruits, whole grains, vegetables, lean meats, and low-fat dairy products. You should cut back on red meat because it is high in saturated fat and has been linked to coronary heart disease. Therefore, it's best to cut down on meat intake by a half or third at each meal.

6.5 Tacking weight loss

While many people associate the DASH diet with losing weight, that isn't the case. Instead of weight loss, this plan teaches you how to make healthier food choices for life. Written by Ashley Mateo, RRCA-certified running coach, the Dash diet isn't a crash diet. Instead, it's an exercise plan that focuses on heart-healthy foods from your local grocery store. These include whole grains, lean proteins, and low-fat dairy. The DASH diet is also free of sodium and saturated fat, which are common on other diets.

While many people think of this diet as low-fat and high-protein, this is not the case. Numerous individuals have high blood pressure and a heart issue, thus the DASH diet emphasises lowering the risk of high blood pressure and cholesterol. Using the Lose It! app to monitor your progress is a great tool to help you stick to your goals. Just be careful to adhere to the suggested serving amounts and avoid overindulging in carbohydrates.

The DASH Diet focuses on whole, unrefined foods that are as close to their natural state as possible. It emphasizes lean proteins such as chicken, fish, and beef, as well as low-fat dairy products. You should also have a large amount of veggies, between four and five servings every day.One serving size equals half a cup of raw vegetables or one cup of cooked vegetables.

While the DASH diet does not require calorie counting, it does recommend a specific number of servings of specific foods. You can easily reach this target by adjusting your daily calorie goal. To maximize your weight loss efforts, the DASH diet encourages the eating of 6 servings of lean meat, poultry, and fish each day. The standard serving sizes are 500-600kJ. The DASH Diet is ideal for those with a higher energy requirement, but this plan isn't for everyone.

While the DASH Diet was originally developed to treat hypertension, it has been found to be effective at boosting weight loss. It's goal is to reduce sodium, fats, and refined sugars, which are the main causes of hypertension. Currently, one in three adults in the US suffer from high blood pressure, and it's one of the leading causes of heart disease. In addition, the DASH Diet is less restrictive than other weight loss programs.

6.6 FAQs

Q. Should I count calories?
A. No. The DASH Diet is rich in whole food and low in saturated fat, so calorie counting isn't necessary.
Q. Will the DASH Diet make me constipated?
A. No. The high-fiber content ensures you'll be as regular as ever, while the low-sodium diet will reduce problems from excess sodium.
Q. Which fruits and vegetables are best for me?
A. All fresh produce is good for you and should be included in your diet. It's best to select the highest-quality foods you can afford.
Q. Can I have any "bad" foods on the DASH Diet?
A. No, although it may seem hard at first there are no "bad" foods as long as they are consumed in the right quantity and proportion to other food groups.
Q. Should I start with phase 1?
A. No. People who are healthy and eat a very healthy diet can go straight to phase 2 of the DASH Diet.
Q. Which phase should I pick?
A. The first phase is for beginners, so if you're healthy and have been eating a healthy diet for many years you can skip phase 1 and move straight to phase 2, but it's important that you try at least one meal of both phases to see which you feel best on.
Q. Is it possible to drink coffee?
A. Yes, as long as there is no added sugar or creamer.
Q. What about alcohol?
A. Alcohol has many health benefits and is fine to have up to one or two drinks a day but going over this amount can be dangerous for your health. Don't go over the safe limits that are set for you in phase 2 of the DASH Diet.
Q. How long does it take to get used to the DASH Diet?
A. As long as you don't add more fat, sugar, or salt to your diet it will be very easy to adapt. Some people take only a few days to get used to the diet, while others take longer.
Q. Can I go on the DASH Diet if I have a history of heart disease?
A. Yes, as long as you follow all the recommendations of the DASH Diet in terms of healthy fats and low sodium.
Q. What about my sleep patterns?
A. I don't think it's important to determine how well you sleep every night, as long as you don't try to force yourself to get more than six hours a night, as this may be counter-productive if your body is telling you, it needs more sleep than this.
Q. Should I exercise?
A. Yes, it's very important to exercise on a daily basis for at least thirty minutes if you can.
Q. How will the DASH Diet benefit me physically?
A. Studies have shown that the DASH Diet cuts down your risk of stroke and heart disease.
Q. How will the DASH Diet benefit me mentally?
A. The DASH Diet will reduce your risk of developing Alzheimer's and other mental disorders by cutting the risk of heart disease.

Q. How will the DASH Diet benefit me financially?
A. The DASH diet will save you money as you won't need to buy any processed foods or other unhealthy extras that may come with them.

7 BREAKFASTS

7.1 Millet Cream

Serves: 4 | Preparation Time: 10 minutes | Cooking Time: 30 minutes

Ingredients:

- low-fat milk - 14 oz.
- millet - 1 c.
- liquid honey - 1 tsp.
- vanilla extract -½ tsp.

Procedure:

1. Using a medium high source of heat, set a pot in place. Add in the milk and let simmer. Mix in vanilla extract and millet and let cook for about 30 minutes as you stir constantly.
2. Apply a topping of honey to the ready millet cream.

Nutrition per serving:

989 calories, 5.9g protein, 37.9g carbs, 200mg sugars, 2.1g fat, 189mg sodium.

7.2 The Amazing Feta Hash

Serves: 6 | Preparation Time: 10 minutes | Cooking Time: 25 minutes

Ingredients:

- hash browns - 16 oz.
- low-fat feta, crumbled - 2 oz.
- olive oil - 1 tbsp.
- beaten eggs - 4
- soy milk - 1/3 c.
- chopped yellow onion - 1

Procedure:

1. Using a medium high source of heat, set a pan in place. Add in your oil and heat before mixing in hash browns. Allow to sauté for approximately 5 mins.
2. Toss in the remaining ingredients with the exception of cheese. Let your mixture cook for an additional 5 minutes.
3. Add sprinkles of cheese to top. Set pan in your oven. Cook for 15 minutes at 390°F.

Nutrition per serving:

303 calories, 8.2g protein, 29.6g carbs, 17.1g fat, 2.87g fiber, 120mg cholesterol, 415mg sodium, 525mg potassium.

7.3 Sausage Casserole

Serves: 4 | Preparation Time: 10 minutes | Cooking Time: 35 minutes

Ingredients:

- beaten eggs - 2
- chopped onion - 1
- chopped chili pepper - 1
- olive oil - 1 tbsp.
- ground sausages - 1 c.
- chili flakes - 1 tsp.

Procedure:

1. Using a pan, mix in sausages, onion, and olive oil.
2. Mix in the remaining ingredients. Let your mixture roast for approximately 5 minutes before transferring to oven.

3. Place in the oven preheated to attain 370°F and allow to bake through for 25 minutes.

Nutrition per serving:

74 calories, 3.3g protein, 2.8 g carbs, 5.9g fat, 0.52g fiber, 84mg cholesterol, 35mg sodium, 75mg potassium.

7.4 Apples and Raisins Bowls

Serves: 4 | Preparation Time: 5 minutes | Cooking Time: 15 minutes

Ingredients:

- blackberries - 1 c.
- ground cardamom - 1 tsp.
- coconut milk - 1 ½ c.
- raisins - ¼ c.
- peeled, cored and cubed apples - 2
- coconut cream - 1 c.

Procedure:

1. Using a pot, pour in your coconut milk and let boil.
2. Stir in all the other ingredients.
3. Set heat to medium high and allow to simmer for 15 minutes.

Nutrition per serving:

266.1 calories, 2.61g protein, 14.4g carbs, 15.6g fat, 5.3g fiber, 0mg cholesterol, 65mg sodium, 374mg potassium

7.5 Dill Omelet

Serves: 6 | Preparation Time: 10 minutes | Cooking Time: 6 minutes

Ingredients:

- low-fat milk -2 tbsps.
- white pepper - ¼ tsp.
- beaten eggs - 6
- chopped dill - 2 tbsps.
- avocado oil - 1 tbsp.

Procedure:

1. Using a skillet, heat avocado oil.
2. Using a bowl, mix the other ingredients.
3. Transfer the egg mixture to the hot oil. Allow your omelet to cook for 6 minutes.

Nutrition per serving:

71 calories, 6g protein, 1.4g carbs, 4.8g fat, 0.3g fiber, 164mg cholesterol, 66mg sodium, 109mg potassium.

7.6 Cheese Hash Browns

Serves: 6 | Preparation Time: 10 minutes | Cooking Time: 30 minutes

Ingredients:

- olive oil - 1 tsp.
- beaten eggs - 3
- hash browns - 2 c.
- shredded vegan mozzarella - 3 oz.

Procedure:

1. Set a pan in a pan. Add in olive oil and heat. Mix in your hash browns.
2. Allow 5 minutes of roasting as you occasionally stir.
3. Pour your eggs over the roasted hash browns. Set in your oven preheated at 380°F.
4. Allow the mixture to bake for 20 minutes. Enjoy.

Nutrition per serving:

212 calories, 4.9g protein, 21.8g carbs, 12.4g fat, 1.6g fiber, 83mg cholesterol, 316mg sodium, 328mg potassium.

7.7 Tomato and Spinach Eggs

Serves: 4 | Preparation Time: 10 minutes | Cooking Time: 20 minutes

Ingredients:

- low-fat milk - ½ c.
- whisked eggs - 8
- freshly chopped spinach - 1 c.
- chopped red onion - 1
- canola oil - 1 tbsp.
- cubed cherry tomatoes - 1 c.

Procedure:

1. Using a medium high source of heat, set a pan in place, add in oil and heat. Stir in onion and let cook for approx. 3 minutes.
2. Add in spinach and tomatoes. Stir well and let continue cooking for an additional 2 minutes.
3. Toss in eggs mixed with milk.
4. Transfer to a pan and place in your oven preheated at 390°F and cook for 15 more minutes.
5. Set in serving plates and enjoy.

Nutrition per serving:

202 calories, 15.4g protein, 7.2g carbs, 12.5g fat, 1.5g fiber, 332mg cholesterol, 218mg sodium, 354mg potassium

7.8 Scallions and Sesame Seeds Omelet

Serves: 4 | Preparation Time: 5 minutes | Cooking Time: 10 minutes

Ingredients:

- whisked eggs - 4
- olive oil - 1 tbsp.
- sesame seeds - 1 tsp.
- chopped scallions - 2
- chopped cilantro - 1 tbsp.

Procedure:

1. Place a pan over a medium high source of heat. Add in oil and heat. Add in scallions and stir. Sauté for 2 minutes.
2. Mix in the remaining ingredients. Toss and spread the omelet to your pan. Cook until well done on one side for 3 minutes.
3. Flip and continue cooking the other side for 2 additional minutes.

Nutrition per serving:

101 calories, 5.9g protein, 1.4g carbs, 8.3g fat, 0.5g fiber, 164mg cholesterol, 63mg sodium, 97mg potassium

7.9 Omelet with Peppers

Serves: 4 | Preparation Time: 10 minutes | Cooking Time: 15 minutes

Ingredients:

- beaten eggs - 4
- margarine - 1 tbsp.
- chopped bell peppers - 1 c.
- chopped scallions - 2 oz.

Procedure:

1. Using a skillet, toss in margarine and heat well until melted.
2. Using a mixing bowl, add scallions, eggs, bell peppers and mix well.
3. Set your egg mixture in your hot skillet and allow the omelet to roast for about 12 minutes.

Nutrition per serving:

102 calories, 6.1g protein, 3.7g carbs, 7.3g fat, 0.8g fiber, 164mg cholesterol, 98mg sodium, 156mg potassium.

7.10 Artichoke Eggs

Serves: 4 | Preparation Time: 5 minutes | Cooking Time: 20 minutes

Ingredients:

- beaten eggs - 5
- chopped low-fat feta - 2 oz.
- chopped yellow onion - 1
- canola oil - 1 tbsp.
- chopped cilantro - 1 tbsp.
- chopped artichoke hearts, canned - 1 c.

Procedure:

1. Using the oil, grease 4 ramekins.
2. Mix all the remaining ingredients and divide the mix between the prepared ramekins.
3. Preheat your oven to 380F and allow to bake for approximately 20 minutes.

Nutrition per serving:
176 calories, 10 protein, 7.6g carbs, 12g fat, 2.7g fiber, 219mg cholesterol, 256mg sodium, 238mg potassium.

7.11 Bean Casserole

Serves: 8 | Preparation Time: 10 minutes | Cooking Time: 30 minutes

Ingredients:

- chopped white onions - ½ c.
- beaten eggs - 5
- chopped bell pepper - ½ c.
- red kidney beans (cooked) - 1 c.
- low-fat shredded mozzarella cheese - 1 c.

Procedure:

1. Using a casserole mold, spread the kidney beans and add in bell pepper and onions.
2. Mix cheese and eggs and transfer to the beans mixture.
3. Allow to bake at a heat of 380°F for about 30 minutes.

Nutrition per serving:
143 calories, 12.6g protein, 17g carbs, 3.2g fat, 4.5g fiber, 107mg cholesterol, 163mg sodium, 376mg potassium.

7.12 Strawberry Sandwich

Serves: 4 | Preparation Time: 5 minutes | Cooking Time: 0 minutes

Ingredients:

- low-fat yogurt - 4 tbsps.
- sliced strawberries - 4
- whole-wheat bread slices - 4

Procedure:

1. Spread the bread with yogurt and then top with sliced strawberries.

Nutrition per serving:
84 calories, 4.6g protein, 13.6g carbs, 1.2g fat, 2.1g fiber, 1mg cholesterol, 143mg sodium, 124mg potassium.

8 SALADS

8.1 Shrimp and Veggie Salad

Serves: 4 | Preparation Time: 10 minutes | Cooking Time: 0 minutes

Ingredients:

- halved cherry tomatoes - 2 c.
- Cracked black pepper - 1
- freshly trimmed asparagus spears - 12 oz.
- cooked frozen and peeled shrimp - 16 oz.
- Cracker bread - 1
- watercress - 4 c.
- bottled light raspberry - ½ c.

Procedure:

1. Using a large skillet, add asparagus in some boiled lightly salted water. Allow to cook for approximately 3 minutes while covered. Drain using a colander. Use cold running water to cool.
2. Set the asparagus ~~in~~ on 4 dinner plates; add a topping of cherry tomatoes, shrimp and watercress. Drizzle over with raspberry.
3. Add sprinkles of cracked black pepper and enjoy alongside cracker bread.

Nutrition per serving:
Calories 155.5, Fat 1.4 g, Carbs 15 g, Protein 22 g, Sodium: 346 mg, Potassium: 714mg

8.2 Salmon and Spinach Salad

Serves: 4 | Preparation Time: 10 minutes | Cooking Time: 0 minutes

Ingredients:

- drained and flaked canned salmon - 1 c.
- grated lime zest - 1 tbsp.
- lime juice - 1 tbsp.
- fat-free yogurt - 3 tbsps.
- baby spinach - 1 c.
- drained and chopped capers - 1 tsp.
- chopped red onion - 1
- pepper – ¼ tsp.

Procedure:

1. Using a bowl, add salmon, zest, lime juice and other ingredients
2. Toss well and serve

Nutrition per serving:

Calories 155.5| Fat 1.4 g| Carbs 15 g| Protein 22 g | Sodium: 366mg| Potassium: 544mg

8.3 Corn Salad

Serves: 6 | Preparation Time: 10 minutes | Cooking Time: 2 hours|

Ingredients:

- prosciutto, sliced into strips - 2 oz.
- olive oil - 1 tsp.
- corn - 2 c.
- salt-free tomato sauce - 1/2 c.
- minced garlic - 1 tsp.
- chopped green bell pepper - 1

Procedure:

1. Using a Slow Cooker, add oil to grease.
2. Add corn, tomato sauce, garlic, prosciutto, bell pepper to the Slow Cooker as you stir.
3. Set the lid in place and cook for 2 hours on HIGH setting.

Nutrition per serving:

Calories 158.5, Fat 1.4 g, Carbs 15 g, Protein 23 g, Sodium 332mg, Potassium 501mg

8.4 Watercress Salad

Serves: 4 | Preparation Time: 5 minutes| Cooking Time: 4 minutes

Ingredients:

- Chopped asparagus - 2 c.
- cooked shrimp - 16 oz.
- torn watercress - 4 c.
- apple cider vinegar - 1 tbsp.
- olive oil - ¼ c.

Procedure:

1. Combine watercress, shrimp, asparagus, and olive oil in the mixing bowl.

Nutrition per serving:

264 calories| 28.3g protein| 4.5g carbs| 14.8g fat| 1.8g fiber| 239mg cholesterol| 300mg sodium| 393mg potassium.

8.5 Tuna Salad

Serves: 4 | Preparation: 15minutes | Cooking: 0 minutes

Ingredients:

- low-fat Greek yogurt - ½ c.
- canned tuna - 8 oz.
- freshly chopped parsley - ½ c.
- cooked corn kernels - 1 c.
- ground black pepper - ½ tsp.

Procedure:

1. Combine kernels, tuna, black pepper, and parsley.
2. Mix in yogurt and ensure you stir properly to get a homogenous salad.

Nutrition per serving:

173 calories, 17.7g protein, 13.7g carbs, 5.6g fat, 1.3g fiber, 19.3mg cholesterol, 57mg sodium, 393mg potassium.

8.6 Watermelon Salad

Serves: 6 | Preparation Time: 18 minutes | Cooking Time: 0 minutes

Ingredients:

- sea salt - ¼ tsp.
- black pepper - ¼ tsp.
- balsamic vinegar - 1 tbsp.
- quartered & seeded cantaloupe - 1
- small & seedless watermelon - 12
- fresh mozzarella balls, - 2 c.
- fresh and torn basil - 1/3 c.
- olive oil - 2 tbsps.

Procedure:

1. Scoop out balls of cantaloupe and put them in a colander over a bowl.
2. With a melon baller, slice the watermelon.
3. Allow your fruit to drain for ten minutes, and then refrigerate the juice.
4. Wipe the bowl dry, and then place your fruit in it.
5. Stir in basil, oil, vinegar, mozzarella and tomatoes before seasoning.
6. Mix well and enjoy.

Nutrition per serving:

Calories: 218, Protein: 10g, Fat: 13g, Sodium: 59mg, Potassium: 43mg.

8.7 Orange Celery Salad

Serves: 6 | Preparation Time: 16 minutes | Cooking Time: 0 minutes

Ingredients:

- fresh lemon juice - 1 tbsp.
- olive brine - 1 tbsp.
- olive oil - 1 tbsp.
- sliced red onion - ¼ c.
- fine sea salt - ¼ tsp.
- green olives - ½ c.
- peeled & sliced oranges - 2
- black pepper - ¼ tsp.
- celery stalks, sliced diagonally in ½ inch slices - 3

Procedure:

1. Using a shallow bowl, add in oranges, onion, olives, and celery.
2. Stir together oil, lemon juice & olive brine, pour this over your salad.
3. Add pepper and salt for seasoning and enjoy

Nutrition per serving:

Calories: 65, Protein: 2g, Fat: 0.2g, Sodium: 43mg, Potassium: 123mg.

8.8 Lettuce & Cucumber Salad

Serves: 4 | Preparation Time: 20 minutes | Cooking Time: 0 minutes

Ingredients:

- chopped romaine lettuce - 2 c.
- cooked corn kernels - 1 c.
- canola oil - 1 tbsp.
- cooked green beans, chopped roughly - ½ pound
- chopped cucumber - 1 c.

Procedure:

1. Using a salad bowl, add in the above ingredients and mix. Set on serving plates and serve

Nutrition per serving:

88 calories, 2.7g protein, 13.2g carbs, 4.2g fat, 3.4g fiber, 0mg cholesterol, 12mg sodium, 302mg potassium.

8.9 Seafood Arugula Salad

Serves: 4 | Preparation Time: 15 minutes | Cooking Time: 0 minutes

Ingredients:

- olive oil - 1 tbsp.
- cooked shrimps - 2 c.
- chopped cilantro - 1 tbsp.

Procedure:

1. Using a salad bowl, mix in all the above ingredients. Shake well to have a well combined mixture.

Nutrition per serving:

62 calories, 6.7g protein, 0.3g carbs, 3.8g fat, 0.2g fiber, 124mg cholesterol, 217mg sodium, 21mg potassium.

9 SOUPS

9.1 Lemon & Garlic Soup

Serves: 3 | Preparation Time: 10 minutes | Cooking Time: 0 minutes

Ingredients:

- chopped and pitted avocado - 1
- chopped cucumber - 1
- coconut aminos - ½ c.
- bunches spinach - 2
- chopped watermelon - 1 ½ c.
- chopped cilantro - 1 bunch
- Juice of 2 lemons
- lime juice - ½ c.

Procedure:

1. In a blender, add in avocado and cucumber and pulse carefully.
2. Add in spinach, cilantro, and watermelon. Blend well.
3. Mix in coconut aminos, lime juice and lemon juice and pulse again.
4. Set in soup bowls and enjoy.

Nutrition per serving:

Calories: 101, Fat: 7.3g, Carbs: 6.2g, Protein: 3.1g, Sodium: 228mg, Potassium: 1946 mg

9.2 Healthy Cucumber Soup

Serves: 4 | Preparation Time: 14 minutes | Cooking Time: 0 minutes

Ingredients:

- minced garlic - 2 tbsps.
- peeled and diced English cucumbers - 4 c.
- diced onions - ½ c.
- lemon juice - 1 tbsp.
- vegetable broth - 1 ½ c.
- sunflower seeds - ½ tsp.
- red pepper flakes - ¼ tsp.
- diced parsley - ¼ c.
- plain Greek yogurt - ½ c.

Procedure:

1. Add the listed ingredients to a blender and blend to emulsify (keep aside ½ cup of chopped cucumbers).
2. Blend until smooth.
3. Divide the soup amongst 4 servings and top with extra cucumbers.
4. Enjoy chilled!

Nutrition per serving:

Calories: 371, Fat: 36g, Carbs: 8g, Protein: 4g, Sodium: 240 mg, Potassium: 458 mg

9.3 Amazing Pumpkin Soup

Serves: 4 | Preparation Time: 5 minutes | Cooking Time: 25 minutes

Ingredients:

- halved, deseeded, peeled & cubed pumpkin - 1
- coconut milk - 1 c.
- chicken broth - 2 c.
- Pepper & thyme - ¼ tsp. each
- roasted seeds - ¼ c.

Procedure:

1. Using a crockpot, add in all the above ingredients except roasted seeds and set the lid in place.
2. Allow to cook on low for 25 minutes.
3. Set in a blender. Process well to obtain a smooth puree.
4. Add roasted seeds to garnish. Enjoy

Nutrition per serving:
Calories: 61, Fat: 2.2g, Net Carbs: 10.3g, Protein: 3.2g, Sodium: 254mg, Potassium: 505mg

9.4 Coconut Avocado Soup

Serves: 4 | Preparation Time: 5 minutes | Cooking Time: 5-10 minutes

Ingredients:

- vegetable stock - 2 c.
- Thai green curry paste - 2 tsps.
- Pepper – ¼ tsp.
- chopped avocado - 1
- chopped cilantro - 1 tbsp.
- Lime wedges
- coconut milk - 1 c.

Procedure:

1. Add milk, curry paste, avocado, pepper to blender and blend.
2. Set a pan over a medium high source of heat.
3. Place the mixture on your pan and heat before simmering for 5 minutes.
4. Stir in seasoning, cilantro and simmer for 1 minute.
5. Enjoy!

Nutrition per serving:
Calories: 250, Fat: 30g, Net Carbs: 2g, Protein: 4g, Sodium: 42mg, Potassium: 487mg

9.5 Pumpkin & Garlic Soup

Serves: 4 | Preparation Time: 10 minutes | Cooking Time: 6 hours

Ingredients:

- pumpkin chunks - 1 pound
- diced onion - 1
- vegetable stock - 2 c.
- crushed garlic - 1 tsp.
- coconut cream - 1 2/3 c.
- almond butter - ½ stick
- crushed ginger - 1 tsp.
- Pepper - ¼ tsp.

Procedure:

1. In a slow cooker, add all ingredients. Mix well and cook for 6 hours on HIGH setting.
2. Transfer the mixture to your immersion blender and puree your soup. Enjoy!

Nutrition per serving:
Calories: 234, Fat: 20g, Carbs: 11.2g, Protein: 2.1g, Sodium: 326mg, Potassium: 1321mg

9.6 Minty Avocado Soup

Serves: 4 | Preparation Time: 10 minutes | Cooking Time: 0 minutes

Ingredients:

- ripe avocado - 1
- chilled coconut almond milk - 1 c.
- romaine lettuce leaves - 2
- fresh mint leaves - 20
- lime juice - 1 tbsp.
- Sunflower seeds, to taste

Procedure:

1. Turn on your slow cooker and add all the ingredients into it.
2. Mix them in a food processor.
3. Make a smooth mixture.
4. Allow it chill for approximately 10 minutes.
5. Enjoy!

Nutrition per serving:
Calories: 280, Fat: 26g, Carbs: 12g, Protein: 4g, Potassium: 414mg, Sodium: 74mg

9.7 Celery, Cucumber and Zucchini Soup

Serves: 2 | Preparation Time: 10 minutes | Cooking Time: 0 minutes

Ingredients:

- chopped celery stalks - 3
- cubed cucumber - 7 oz.
- olive oil - 1 tbsp.

- fresh 30% low fat cream - 2/5 c.
- chopped red bell pepper - 1
- chopped dill - 1 tbsp.
- cubed zucchini - 10 ½ oz.
- Sunflower seeds and pepper, to taste

Procedure:

1. Juice the veggies.
2. Add in fresh cream and olive oil. Mix well.
3. Add pepper and sauce for seasoning.
4. Garnish with dill.
5. Enjoy while chilled.

Nutrition per serving:

Calories: 325, Fat: 32g, Carbs: 10g, Protein: 4g, Sodium: 477mg, Potassium: 1138mg

9.8 Vegetable Barley & Turkey Soup

Serves: 3 | Preparation Time: 10 minutes | Cooking Time: 23 minutes

Ingredients:

- canola oil - 1 tbsp.
- carrots - 5
- onion - 1
- quick-cooking barley - 2/3 c.
- reduced-sodium chicken broth - 6 c.
- cooked & cubed turkey breast - 2 c.
- fresh baby spinach - 2 c.
- pepper - ½ tsp.

Procedure:

1. Using an expansive pot set over a medium high source of heat, add oil and heat.
2. Add in your onion and carrots. Mix well before cooking for 5 minutes to ensure the carrots become delicate.
3. Add in broth and barley and allow to boil. Reduce the heat and let simmer for 15 minutes to make the grains delicate.
4. Add in pepper, spinach, and turkey. Combine well and heat for 3 minutes until well done.

Nutrition per serving:

Calories 209, Fat 5g, Carbs 24g, Sugars 4.3g, Protein 2.4g, Sodium 937mg, Potassium 2397mg

9.9 Tomato Green Bean Soup

Serves: 4 | Preparation: 10 minutes | Cooking: 35 minutes

Ingredients:

- chopped onion - 1 c.
- chopped carrots - 1 c.
- butter - 2 tsps.
- reduced-sodium chicken broth - 6 c.
- fresh green beans - 1 pound
- garlic clove - 1
- diced fresh tomatoes - 3 c.
- minced fresh basil - ¼ c.
- salt - ½ tsp.
- pepper - ¼ tsp.

Procedure:

1. Using a vast pot, add in carrots and onion and sauté in a spread for 5 minutes.
2. Blend in the broth, beans, and garlic; heat to the point of boiling.
3. Decrease heat; spread and stew for 20 minutes or until vegetables are delicate.
4. Blend in the tomatoes, basil, salt, and pepper. Spread and stew 5 minutes longer.

Nutrition per serving:

Calories 58, Fat 1g, Carbs 10g, Sugars 5g, Protein 4g, Sodium 203mg, Potassium 832mg

9.10 Mushroom Barley Soup

Serves: 4 | Preparation Time: 15minutes | Cooking Time: 45 minutes

Ingredients:

- canola oil - 1 tbsp.
- onions - 1½ c.
- carrots - ¾ c.
- dried thyme - 1 tsp.

- black pepper - 1/8 tsp.
- garlic - ½ tsp.
- vegetable stock - 8 c.
- sliced mushrooms - 1 c.
- pearl barley - ¾ c.
- dry sherry - 3 oz.
- potato - ½
- chopped green onions - ¼ c.

Procedure:

1. Using a stock pot, add in oil and heat. Mix in onions, carrots, pepper, thyme, mushrooms, and garlic. Sauté the mixture until onion is translucent for 5 minutes.
2. Mix in veggie stock and barley. Allow the mixture to heat until it boils.
3. Reduce heat and let simmer for approximately 20 minutes until barley becomes tender.
4. Mix in potato and sherry and continue simmering until potato becomes well-cooked for about 15 minutes.
5. Add green onions to garnish.
6. Enjoy

Nutrition per serving:

Calories 129, Fat 5.6g, Carbs 18.2g, Sugars 2.2g, Protein 3.3g, Sodium 22mg, Potassium 562mg

10 FISH AND SHELLFISH

10.1 Cilantro Halibut

Serves: 4 | Preparation time: 10 minutes | Cooking time: 15 minutes

Ingredients:

- chopped shallots - 2
- olive oil - 1 tbsp.
- boneless halibut fillets - 4
- chopped cilantro - 1 tbsp.
- lemon juice - 2 tsps.

Procedure:

1. Apply oil to a pan for greasing. Set your fish inside before topping with cilantro, lemon juice and shallot.
2. Set in oven preheated at 365°F. Bake until done for 15 minutes.

Nutrition per serving:

365 calories, 61.3g protein, 3.6g carbs, 10.4g fat, 1g fiber, 93g cholesterol, 171mg sodium, 1502mg potassium

10.2 Shallot and Salmon Mix

Serves: 4 | Preparation time: 10 minutes | Cooking time: 15 minutes

Ingredients:

- olive oil - 2 tbsps.
- boneless salmon fillets - 4
- chopped shallot - 1
- water - ½ c.
- chopped parsley - 2 tbsps.

Procedure:

1. Set a pan over a medium high source of heat. Add oil and heat. Mix in shallot and allow to sauté for 4 minutes.
2. Mix in water, parsley and salmon.
3. Set the lid in place and allow to cook for 11 minutes while heat is set to medium.

Nutrition per serving:

369 calories, 37.3g protein, 3.6g carbs, 24g fat, 1.7g fiber, 78g cholesterol, 97mg sodium, 806mg potassium

10.3 Limes and Shrimps Skewers

Serves: 4 | Preparation Time: 15 minutes | Cooking Time: 6 minutes

Ingredients:

- peeled shrimps - 1 pound
- lime - 1
- lemon juice - 1 tsp.
- white pepper - ½ tsp.

Procedure:

1. Cut the lime into wedges.
2. Sprinkle lemon juice and pepper on shrimp.
3. Individually thread the lime and lime wedges onto the wooden skewers.
4. Preheat the grill to 400F.
5. Put the shrimp skewers in grill. Cook each side for 3 minutes until the shrimps become light pink.

Nutrition per serving:

141 calories| 26g protein| 3.7g carbs| 2g fat| 0.6g fiber| 239mg cholesterol| 277mg sodium| 214mg potassium.

10.4 Tuna and Pineapple Kebob

Serves: 4 | Preparation Time: 10 minutes | Cooking Time: 8 minutes

Ingredients:

- tuna fillet - 12 oz.
- peeled pineapple - 8 oz.
- olive oil - 1 tsp.
- ground fennel - ¼ tsp.

Procedure:

1. Tuna and pineapple should be cut into bite-sized pieces.
2. Sprinkle ground fennel and olive oil over the mixture.
3. String them in the skewers and place them in preheated oven to 400F grill.
4. The skewers (also named kebobs) need to be cooked for 4 minutes on each side.

Nutrition per serving:

347 calories, 18.2g protein, 7.5g carbs, 27.6g fat, 0.8g fiber, 0mg cholesterol, 1mg sodium, 64mg potassium.

10.5 Coconut Cod

Serves: 4 | Preparation Time: 10 minutes | Cooking Time: 25 minutes

Ingredients:

- coconut shred - 2 tbsps.
- boneless cod fillets - 4
- chopped red onion - 1
- olive oil - 2 tbsps.
- coconut milk - ¼ c.

Procedure:

1. Set a pan over a medium high source of heat. Add in oil and heat. Mix in onion and let cook for 5 minutes.
2. Mix in fish plus the other ingredients. Cook for an additional 20 minutes.

Nutrition per serving:

207 calories, 23.5g protein, 11.6g carbs, 8.4g fat, 3.5g fiber, 40g cholesterol, 135mg sodium, 399mg potassium

10.6 Ginger Sea Bass

Serves: 4 | Preparation Time: 10 minutes | Cooking Time: 20 minutes

Ingredients:

- grated ginger - 1 tbsp.
- olive oil - 2 tbsps.
- boneless sea bass fillets - 4

Procedure:

1. Rub the sea bass fillet with ginger and sprinkle with olive oil.
2. Set the fish in a tray. Preheat oven to 365F. Bake for about 20 minutes.

Nutrition per serving:

191 calories, 24g protein, 1g carbs, 9.7g fat, 0.2g fiber, 54g cholesterol, 89mg sodium, 353mg potassium

10.7 Baked Cod

Serves: 2 | Preparation Time: 10 min | Cooking Time: 20 minutes

Ingredients:

- cod fillet - 10 oz.
- Italian seasonings - 1 tsp.
- margarine - 1 tbsp.

Procedure:

1. Rub the baking pan with margarine.
2. Then chop the cod and sprinkle with Italian seasonings.
3. Set the fish in baking pan and use a foil to cover.
4. Bake the meal at 375F for 20 minutes.

Nutrition per serving:

170 calories, 25.1g protein, 0.3g carbs, 7.6g fat, 0g fiber, 70mg cholesterol, 155mg sodium, 4mg potassium.

10.8 Five-Spices Sole

Serves: 3 | Preparation Time: 10 minutes| Cooking Time: 11 minutes

Ingredients:

- sole fillets - 3
- five-spice seasonings - 1 tbsp.
- coconut oil - 1 tbsp.

Procedure:

1. Rub the sole fillets with seasonings.
2. Using a skillet, add in coconut oil and heat for 2 minutes.
3. Place sole fillets in hot oil and cook each side for 4.5 minutes.

Nutrition per serving:

204 calories, 31.8g protein, 1g carbs, 6.5g fat, 2.2g fiber, 86mg cholesterol, 133mg sodium, 437mg potassium.

10.9 Parsley Shrimp

Serves: 4 | Preparation Time: 10 minutes | Cooking Time: 10 minutes

Ingredients:

- peeled and deveined shrimp - 1 pound
- Juice of 1 lemon
- olive oil - 1 tbsp.
- chopped parsley - a bunch

Procedure:

1. Using a pan set over a medium high source of heat, add oil and allow to heat. Mix in shrimp and let each side cook for 3 minutes.
2. Mix in parsley and lemon juice before cooking for 4 more minutes.

Nutrition per serving:

190 calories, 26.2g protein, 8.3g carbs, 5.5g fat, 0.7g fiber, 239g cholesterol, 279mg sodium, 267mg potassium

10.10 Tender Salmon with Chives

Serves: 4 | Preparation Time: 10 minutes | Cooking Time: 20 minutes

Ingredients:

- chopped yellow onion - 1
- chili powder - 1 tsp.
- olive oil - 2 tbsps.
- water - ¼ c.
- skinless and boneless salmon fillets - 4
- chopped chives - 2 tbsps.

Procedure:

1. Set a pan over a medium source of heat. Add oil and heat. Mix in onion and sauté for 3 minutes.
2. Set in salmon and allow each side to cook for 5 minutes.
3. Mix in chili powder, chives and water before cooking for 12 more minutes.

Nutrition per serving:

317 calories, 35.1g protein, 3.7g carbs, 18.7g fat, 1.1g fiber, 78g cholesterol, 169mg sodium, 749mg potassium

10.11 Fennel and Salmon

Serves: 4 | Preparation Time: 5 minutes | Cooking Time: 15 minutes

Ingredients:

- skinless and boneless salmon fillets - 4
- chopped fennel bulb - 1
- water - ½ c.
- olive oil - 2 tbsps.
- lemon juice - 1 tbsp.
- chopped cilantro - 1 tbsp.

Procedure:

1. Set a pan over a medium high source of heat. Add in oil and heat. Mix in fennel before cooking for about 3 minutes.
2. Set in the fish. Cook each side for 4 minutes until browned.
3. Mix in remaining ingredients and allow to cook for an extra 8 minutes.

Nutrition per serving:

317 calories, 35.4g protein, 4.9g carbs, 18.1g fat, 2g fiber, 78g cholesterol, 127mg sodium, 948mg potassium

10.12 Cod and Asparagus

Serves: 4 | Preparation Time: 10 minutes | Cooking Time: 25 minutes

Ingredients:

- olive oil - 1 tbsp.
- chopped red onion - 1
- boneless cod fillets - 1 pound
- trimmed asparagus - 1 bunch

Procedure:

1. Place the cod in the tray and sprinkle it with olive oil and red onion.
2. Add asparagus.
3. Bake the fish for 25 minutes at 365F.

Nutrition per serving:

298 calories, 27.4g protein, 7.2g carbs, 19.1g fat, 2.6g fiber, 50g cholesterol, 111mg sodium, 268mg potassium

11 VEGETARIAN PLATES

11.1 Roasted Brussels Sprouts

Serves: 4 | Preparation Time: 5 minutes | Cooking Time: 35minutes

Ingredients:

- halved trimmed Brussels sprouts - 1½ pounds
- olive oil - 2 tbsps.
- salt - ¼ tsp.
- freshly ground black pepper - ½ tsp.

Procedure:

1. Preheat your oven to attain 400°F. Using a mixing bowl, mix in Brussels sprouts and olive oil. Toss well to evenly coat.
2. Set brussel sprouts to a large baking sheet. Flip them over, so the cut-side faces down with the flat part touching the baking sheet. Sprinkle pepper and salt to the mixture.
3. Bake within 30 minutes to ensure the brussel sprouts become crispy and lightly charred to the outside while toasted to the bottom side. Serve.

Nutrition per serving:

Calories: 134, Fat: 8g, Sodium: 189mg, Carbs: 15g, Protein: 6g, Potassium: 662mg

11.2 Chunky Black-Bean Dip

Serves: 2 | Preparation Time: 5 minutes | Cooking Time: 1 minutes

Ingredients:

- drained black beans, with liquid reserved - 1 (15 oz.) can
- chipotle peppers in adobo sauce - ½ can
- plain Greek yogurt - ¼ c.
- ground black pepper - ¼ tsp.

Procedure:

1. Using a blender, add in chipotle peppers, yogurt and beans. Mix well before processing to obtain a smooth consistency. Mix in part of reserved bean liquid (a tablespoon at a moment) to obtain a thinner consistency.
2. Add black pepper for seasoning and enjoy.

Nutrition per serving:

Calories: 70, Fat: 1g, Sodium: 159mg, Carbs: 11g, Protein: 5g, Potassium: 281mg

11.3 Greek Flatbread with Spinach, Tomatoes & Feta

Serves: 2 | Preparation Time: 15 minutes | Cooking Time: 9 minutes

Ingredients:

- fresh and coarsely chopped baby spinach - 2 c.
- olive oil - 2 tsps.
- naan or flatbread - 2 slices
- sliced black olives - ¼ c.
- sliced plum tomatoes - 2
- Italian seasoning blend (salt-free) - ½ tsp.
- crumbled feta - ¼ c.

Procedure:

1. Preheat oven to attain 400°F. Using a skillet set in place over the medium high heat, add in 3 tbsps. water and heat. Mix in spinach, and steam for 2 minutes to

wilt while covered. Drain any water in excess before placing aside.

2. Drizzle flatbreads with oil. To each of the flatbread, add olives, seasoning, spinach, feta and tomatoes to top. Bake until browned for 7 minutes. Slice in 4 pieces and enjoy.

Nutrition per serving:
Calories: 410, Fat: 16g, Carbs: 53g, Fiber: 7g, Protein: 16g , Sodium: 622mg, Potassium: 521mg

11.4 Black-Bean and Vegetable Burrito

Serves: 4 | Preparation Time: 15 minutes | Cooking Time: 15 minutes

Ingredients:

- olive oil - ½ tbsp.
- chopped red or green bell peppers - 2
- diced zucchini or summer squash - 1
- chili powder - ½ tsp.
- cumin - 1 tsp.
- ground black pepper – ¼ tsp.
- drained and rinsed black beans - 2 (14 oz.) cans
- halved cherry tomatoes - 1 c.
- whole-wheat tortillas - 4 (8-inch)
- Optional for **Serving:** spinach, chopped scallions, sliced avocado, or hot sauce

Procedure:

1. Set a sauté pan on a medium high source of heat. Add in oil and heat. Mix in bell peppers and sauté for 4 minutes until crisp and tender. Add the zucchini, chili powder, cumin, and black pepper, and continue to sauté for 5 minutes until vegetables become tender.
2. Add the black beans and cherry tomatoes and cook within 5 minutes. Divide between 4 burritos and serve topped with optional ingredients as desired. Enjoy immediately.

Nutrition per serving:
Calories: 311, Fat: 6g, Sodium: 199mg, Carbs: 52g, Protein: 19g, Potassium: 329mg

11.5 Red Beans and Rice

Serves: 2 | Preparation Time: 5 minutes | Cooking Time: 30 minutes

Ingredients:

- dry brown rice - ½ c.
- water - 1 c. plus extra ¼ c.
- drained red beans - 1 (14 oz.) can
- ground cumin - 1 tbsp.
- Juice of 1 lime
- fresh spinach - 4 handfuls
- Optional toppings: Greek yogurt, avocado, chopped tomatoes, onions

Procedure:

1. Using a pot, mix rice plus water and let boil. Cover and lower your heat to a low simmer. Cook within 20 to 25 minutes or as per the directions on the package.
2. Meanwhile, add the beans, ¼ c. water, lime juice, and cumin to a medium skillet. Simmer within 5 to 7 minutes.
3. Once the liquid is reduced considerably, remove from the heat. Mix in spinach and allow to wilt for 3 minutes while covered. Add in beans and mix well. Enjoy alongside rice with toppings of your choice.

Nutrition per serving:
Calories: 232, Fat: 2g , Sodium: 210mg, Carbs: 41g , Protein: 13g, Potassium: 367mg

11.6 Veggie Pita Rolls

Serves: 2 | Preparation Time: 30 minutes| Cooking Time: 0 minutes

Ingredients:

- shredded romaine lettuce - 1 c.
- chopped cucumber - ½ c.

- chopped red onion - 1
- olive oil - 1 tbsp.
- black pepper – ¼ tsp.
- prepared hummus - ¼ c.
- chopped and seeded bell pepper - 1
- chopped and seeded tomato - 1
- finely minced garlic clove - 1
- fresh lime juice - ½ tbsp.
- warmed whole-wheat pita breads - 2

Procedure:

1. Using a bowl, mix in the above ingredients with exception of pitas and hummus. Toss gently and ensure they are well coated. Place each pita bread onto serving plates.
2. Spread 2 tbsp. of hummus over a pita bread evenly. Top with salad and roll the pita bread.
3. Repeat with remaining pita bread, hummus and salad.

Nutrition per serving:

Calories: 334, Fat: 12g, Carbs: 51.6g, Fiber: 9g, Sugar: 6.9g, Protein: 10.5g, Sodium: 400mg, Potassium: 587mg

11.7 Veggies Stuffed Bell Peppers

Serves: 4 | Preparation Time: 15 minutes | Cooking Time: 25 minutes

Ingredients:

- fresh shiitake mushrooms - ½ lb.
- peeled garlic cloves - 2
- olive oil - 2 tbsps.
- black pepper – ¼ tsp.
- celery stalk - 1 c.
- unsalted walnuts - ½ c.
- Pinch of salt
- halved and deseeded bell peppers - 4

Procedure:

1. Preheat oven to attain 400 °F. Grease your baking sheet.
2. Using a food processor, mix in oil, salt, mushrooms, celery, garlic, walnuts, pepper and pulse to finely chop. Stuff bell peppers with the mushroom mixture.
3. Set them onto the prepared baking sheet. Bake until slightly brown for about 25 minutes. Enjoy while warm.

Nutrition per serving:

Calories: 213, Fat: 16.7g, Carbs: 13.7g, Fiber: 3.7g, Sugar: 7g, Protein: 7g , Sodium: 160mg, Potassium: 456mg

11.8 Rosemary Endives

Serves: 4 | Preparation Time: 10 minutes | Cooking Time: 20 Minutes

Ingredients:

- olive oil - 2 tbsps.
- dried rosemary - 1 tsp.
- halved endives - 2
- black pepper - ¼ tsp.
- turmeric powder - ½ tsp.

Procedure:

1. Using a baking pan, mix all ingredients as you toss for maximum coating. Set in your preheated oven to attain 400 °F and let bake well for 20 minutes.
2. Enjoy.

Nutrition per serving:

Calories: 66, Fat: 7.1 g, Carbs: 1.2 g, Protein: 0.3 g, Sugars: 1.3 g, Sodium: 113 mg, Potassium: 411mg

11.9 Easy Chickpea Veggie Burgers

Serves: 4 | Preparation Time: 10 minutes | Cooking Time: 20 minutes

Ingredients:

- drained and rinsed chickpeas - 1 (15 oz) can
- onion powder - 1 tsp.
- thawed and frozen spinach - ½ c.

- rolled oats - ⅓ c.
- garlic powder - 1 tsp.

Procedure:

1. Set your oven to preheat to attain 400°F. Set a parchment paper to your baking sheet.
2. Using a mixing bowl, add half of the beans and mash until fairly smooth.
3. In a blender, add the remaining beans, spinach, oats, and spices. Blend until puréed. Add mixture to the bowl of mashed beans and stir until well combined.
4. Divide in 4 equal sections and form patties. Bake for 7 to 10 minutes. Carefully flip and bake until crusty on the outside for extra 10 minutes.
5. Place on a whole grain bun with your favorite toppings.

Nutrition per serving:

Total Calories: 118, Total Fat: 1g, Saturated Fat: 0g, Cholesterol: 7mg, Sodium: 108mg, Potassium: 583mg, Total Carbs: 21g, Fiber: 7g, Sugars: 0g, Protein: 7g

11.10 Baked Sweet Potatoes with Cumin

Serves: 4 | Preparation Time: 15 minutes | Cooking Time: 20 minutes

Ingredients:

- sweet potatoes - 4
- Freshly ground black pepper – ¼ tsp.
- diced red onion - ½
- low-fat or nonfat plain Greek yogurt - ½ c.
- olive oil - 1 tsp.
- diced and cored red bell pepper - 1
- ground cumin - 1 tsp.
- drained and rinsed chickpeas - 1 (15 oz.) can

Procedure:

1. Prick the potatoes using a fork and cook potato on setting of the microwave for 10 minutes until well cooked and potatoes become soft.
2. Using a bowl, add in black pepper and yogurt and combine. Set a pot over a medium source of heat, add in oil and heat. Add in cumin, bell pepper, onion and an extra black pepper to enhance the taste.
3. Add in the chickpeas, stir well to combine, and allow the mixture to cook for 5 minutes. Slice potatoes midway lengthwise down and top each half with a portion of the bean mixture followed by 1 to 2 tbsps. of the yogurt. Serve immediately.

Nutrition per serving:

Calories: 264, Fat: 2g, Sodium: 124mg, Carbs: 51g, Protein: 12g, Potassium: 78mg.

11.11 White Beans with Spinach and Pan-Roasted Tomatoes

Serves: 2 | Preparation Time: 15 minutes | Time: 11 minutes

Ingredients:

- olive oil - 1 tbsp.
- halved plum tomatoes - 4
- frozen spinach, defrosted and squeezed of excess water - 10 oz.
- thinly sliced garlic cloves - 2
- water - 2 tbsps.
- black pepper, freshly ground - ¼ tsp.
- drained white beans - 1 can
- Juice from 1 lemon

Procedure:

1. Add and heat oil in your nonstick skillet set over a medium high source of heat. Add tomatoes, the cut-side should face down, and let cook within 5 minutes.

You then flip to the second side and cook within 1 more minute. Set on a plate.

2. Lower your heat towards medium setting and mix in spinach, pepper, water, and garlic. Cook as you toss for 3 minutes to ensure the spinach is cooked through.
3. Take back the tomatoes to your skillet, add the white beans and lemon juice, toss well until heated for 2 minutes.

Nutrition per serving:

Calories: 293, Fat: 9g, Sodium: 267mg, Carbs: 43g, Protein: 15g, Potassium: 78mg.

11.12 Black-Eyed Peas and Greens Power Salad

Serves: 2 | Preparation Time: 15 minutes | Cooking Time: 6 minutes

Ingredients:

- olive oil - 1 tbsp.
- Juice of ½ lemon
- chopped purple cabbage - 3 c.
- baby spinach - 5 c.
- Salt – ¼ tsp.
- shredded carrots - 1 c.
- drained black-eyed peas - 1 can
- Ground black pepper – ¼ tsp.

Procedure:

1. In a medium pan, add oil and cabbage and sauté for 2 minutes while on the medium heat setting. Add in your spinach, cook for 4 minutes while covered until the greens become wilted. Once done, transfer to a bowl.
2. Mix in peas, carrots, juice, pepper and salt as you toss well.

Nutrition per serving:

Calories: 320, Fat: 9g, Sodium: 351mg, Potassium: 544mg, Carbs: 49g, Protein: 16g.

11.13 Butternut-Squash Macaroni and Cheese

Serves: 2 | Preparation Time: 15 min | Cooking Time: 20 minutes

Ingredients:

- ziti macaroni, whole-wheat - 1 c.
- olive oil - 1 tbsp.
- cubed butternut squash, peeled - 2 c.
- nonfat divide milk - 1 c.
- black pepper - ¼ tsp.
- Dijon mustard - 1 tsp.
- shredded low-fat cheddar cheese - ¼ c.

Procedure:

1. Cook your pasta al dente using a pot with boiling water. Drain pasta and place aside. Using a saucepan set on a medium high source of heat, mix ½ c. milk and butternut squash. Add black pepper for seasoning. Allow to simmer. Reduce heat intensity and continue cooking for 10 minutes.
2. Using a blender, mix in Dijon mustard and squash. Purée well to obtain a smooth consistency. Meanwhile, using a sauté pan set on medium heat, mix in olive oil, the squash purée and the rest of the milk. Simmer for 5 minutes before stirring in the cheese.
3. Add in your pasta as you stir. Enjoy right away.

Nutrition per serving:

Calories: 373, Fat: 10g, Sodium: 193mg, Carbs: 59g, Protein: 14g, Potassium: 56mg.

11.14 Pasta with Peas & Tomatoes

Serves: 2 | Preparation Time: 15 minutes | Cooking Time: 15 minutes

Ingredients:

- whole-grain pasta of choice - ½ c.
- water - 8 c. plus ¼ for finishing

- frozen peas - 1 c.
- olive oil - 1 tbsp.
- halved cherry tomatoes - 1 c.
- Ground black pepper - ¼ tsp.
- dried basil - 1 tsp.
- grated Parmesan cheese (low-sodium) - ¼ c.

Procedure:

1. Cook your pasta accordingly until al dente. Add the water to the same pot you used to cook the pasta, and when it's boiling, add the peas. Cook within 5 minutes before draining and setting aside until ready.
2. Using a nonstick skillet set over medium source of heat. Pour in oil and heat. Mix in cherry tomatoes, set lid in place and allow the tomatoes to soften for 5 minutes as you occasionally stir.
3. Add in basil and black pepper for seasoning. Toss in peas, pasta, and ¼ cup of water, stir and remove from heat. Enjoy with a topping of Parmesan.

Nutrition per serving:

Calories: 266, Fat: 12g, Sodium: 320mg, Carbs: 30g, Protein: 13g, Potassium: 67mg.

11.15 Healthy Vegetable Fried Rice

Serves: 4 | Preparation Time: 15 minutes | Cooking Time: 10 minutes

Ingredients:

For sauce:

- garlic vinegar - 1/3 c.
- dark molasses - 1½ tbsps.
- onion powder - 1 tsp.

For the fried rice:

- olive oil - 1 tsp.
- lightly beaten whole eggs - 2 + 4 egg whites
- frozen mixed vegetables - 1 c.
- frozen edamame - 1 c.
- cooked brown rice - 2 c.

Procedure:

1. To prepare sauce, mix the garlic vinegar, molasses, and onion powder in a glass jar. Shake well.
2. Using a skillet set over a medium high source of heat, add in oil and heat. Set in eggs and egg whites, cook for 1 minute until the eggs set.
3. Use a spoon to break eggs into small pieces. Mix in edamame and mixed vegetables. Cook as you stir for approximately 4 minutes.
4. Mix in the sauce and brown rice to your veggie-egg mixture and cook until well done for 5 minutes. Serve immediately.

Nutrition per serving:

Calories: 210, Fat: 6g, Sodium: 113mg, Carbs: 28g, Protein: 13g, Potassium: 78mg.

11.16 Cast Iron Roots and Grain

Serves: 4 | Preparation Time: 10 minutes | Cooking Time: 30 minutes

Ingredients:

- olive oil - 2 tbsps.
- honey - 2 tsps.
- sliced rainbow carrots - 2 c.
- sliced beets - 1 c.
- chopped turnips - 1 c.
- sliced onion - 1 c.
- fresh tarragon - 1 tbsp.
- dried lavender - 1 tsp.
- low sodium vegetable broth - 4 c.
- bulgur - 1 ½ c.

Procedure:

1. Set a cast iron skillet over a medium high source of heat and heat well.
2. Using a bowl, combine the beets, turnips, carrots, and onion. Drizzle over the honey and olive oil. Add tarragon and

lavender for seasoning. Toss well to ensure well coated.

3. Add the vegetables to your skillet and cook until slightly tender, approximately 10 minutes.
4. Mix in vegetable broth and allow to boil.
5. Mix in the bulgur and reduce your heat to low. Simmer for 15 minutes while covered until bulgur becomes tender.

Nutritional Information:

Calories 312.1, Total fat 7.6 g, saturated fat 1.0 g, Sodium 241.4 mg, potassium 593.8 mg,Total carbs 56.4 g, dietary fiber 13.9 g, Sugars 10.8 g, protein 7.9 g

11.17 Easy Beet and Goat Cheese Risotto

Serves: 4 | Preparation Time: 10 minutes | Cooking Time: 30 minutes

Ingredients:

- olive oil - ¼ c.
- diced beets - 1 ½ c.
- diced red onion - 1 c.
- chopped spinach - 2 c.
- Arborio rice - 1 c.
- low sodium vegetable broth - 2 c.
- chopped fresh rosemary - 2 tsps.
- goat cheese - ½ c.
- chopped walnuts - ¼ c.

Procedure:

1. Using a saucepan set over a medium source of heat, add olive oil and heat.
2. Add in onions and beets. Sauté until tender, approximately 5 minutes.
3. Mix in spinach and cook for 3 more minutes.
4. Add in rice and continue cooking as you stir for 3 minutes, to lightly toast the rice.
5. Next, add the vegetable broth and rosemary. Increase the heat to ensure the broth boils.
6. Reduce your heat intensity to low, and continue cooking as you stir occasionally, until the rice has a soft but firm texture.
7. Take out from the heat and stir in goat cheese.
8. Garnish with chopped walnuts for serving.

Nutritional Information:

Calories 412.5, Total fat 29.2 g, saturated fat 6.0 g, Sodium 257.3 mg, potassium 352.7 mg, Total carbs 26.7 g, dietary fiber 4.5 g, Sugars 16.9 g, protein 11.1 g

11.18 Mushroom and Eggplant Casserole

Serves: 4 | Preparation Time: 10 minutes | Cooking Time: 30 minutes

Ingredients:

- sliced eggplant - 1 pound
- olive oil - 1 tbsp.
- chopped yellow onion - 1 c.
- crushed and minced cloves garlic - 3
- oregano - 1 tsp.
- black pepper - ½ tsp.
- sliced mushrooms - 3 c.
- tomato sauce (low sodium) - 1 c.
- cooked brown rice - 2 c.
- low fat mozzarella cheese - 1 c.
- grated asiago cheese - ½ c.
- fresh chopped basil - ¼ c.

Procedure:

1. Preheat your oven to attain 375°F.
2. Using a nonstick skillet set on medium high heat intensity, pour in olive oil and heat.
3. Mix in the eggplant and cook each side for 3 minutes. Place aside.
4. Add in the garlic, oregano, onion, and black pepper to the pan. Sauté for 4 minutes until onions become tender. Add the mushrooms and cook an additional 3 minutes.

5. Lightly oil an 8x8 baking dish and spread along the bottom a thin layer of tomato sauce.
6. Make layers of eggplant, rice, mozzarella, and mushrooms, repeating until all ingredients have been used.
7. Make the final layer mozzarella topped with asiago cheese and fresh basil.
8. Set in your oven and bake for 20 minutes.

Nutritional Information:

Calories 377.7, Total fat 16.1 g, saturated fat 8.2 g, Sodium 383.0 mg, potassium 604.4 mg, Total carbs 41.1 g, dietary fiber 6.2 g, Sugars 4.5 g, protein 19.6 g

12 VEGAN PLATES

12.1 Vegetarian Black Bean Pasta

Serves: 6 | Preparation time: 15 minutes | Cooking time: 20 minutes

Ingredients

- sliced Portobello baby mushrooms - 1 ¾ c.
- Olive oil - 1 tsp.
- Diced tomatoes with juices - 1 (15 oz.) can
- minced garlic clove - 1
- Whole wheat fettuccine - 9 oz.
- Baby spinach - 2 c.
- Dried rosemary - 1 tsp.
- rinsed Black beans - 1 (15 oz.) can
- Dried oregano - ½ tsp.

Procedure:

1. Cook pasta as per the pack's instructions.
2. Set a skillet over a medium source of heat. Add oil and heat. Mix in mushrooms to sauté and cook for 6 minutes.
3. Add in garlic and continue cooking for 1 minute.
4. Mix in the remaining ingredients, toss well and enjoy.

Nutrition for 1 ¼ cups:

Calories 255, Fat 3 g, Sugar 4 g, Protein 12 g, Sodium 230 mg, Carbs 45 g

12.2 Eggplant Parmesan

Serves: 6 | Preparation time: 15 minutes | Cooking time: 1 hour & 40 minutes

Ingredients:

- eggs - 2
- Water - 2 tbsps.
- whole-wheat panko breadcrumbs - 1 c.
- torn fresh basil - ¼ c.
- Parmesan cheese - ¼ c.
- eggplants sliced into ¼" thick slices - 2 pounds
- Italian seasoning - 1 tsp.
- Mozzarella cheese, low-fat - 1 c.
- minced garlic cloves - 2
- Black pepper - ½ tsp.
- Tomato sauce, unsalted - 1 (24 oz.) jar
- Red pepper flakes - ½ tsp.

Procedure:

1. Let your oven preheat to attain 400 F.
2. Oil spray a baking dish.
3. Using a bowl, add in egg and water and whisk.

4. Using a dish, add parmesan, Italian seasoning and bread crumbs.
5. Coat eggplant in whisked egg, then in bread crumbs, press to adhere.
6. Set breaded eggplant on the prepared baking sheet. Oil spray your eggplant on both sides.
7. Bake for half an hour, switch racks after flipping the eggplant in the upper and third rack.
8. Sprinkle pepper.
9. Using a bowl, add in garlic, tomato sauce, red pepper, and basil. Mix.
10. In the baking dish, add half a cup of the sauce, place the eggplant slices, add one cup of sauce on top, sprinkle parmesan on top.
11. Bake for 30 minutes, cool for about 5 minutes. Enjoy.

Nutrition per serving:

Calories 241, Fat 9 g, Sugar 9 g, Protein 14 g, Sodium 487 mg, Carbs 28 g

12.3 Spinach Soufflés

Serves: 4 | Preparation time: 15 minutes | Cooking time: 1 hour & 20 minutes

Ingredients

- egg whites - 4
- Dried parsley - 1 tsp.
- Cream of tartar - ¼ tsp.
- Whole-wheat bread crumbs - 1 tbsp. + 1 ½ tsp.
- Minced garlic - 1 tsp.
- non-fat Milk - 2/3 c.
- Parmesan cheese - 2 oz.
- Baby spinach - 6 oz.
- All-purpose flour - 2 tbsps.
- Black pepper - 1/8 tsp.
- egg yolks - 2

Procedure:

1. Let your oven preheat to attain 425 F.
2. Oil spray 4 ramekins of six oz. and sprinkle with crumbs on all sides.
3. Using a bowl, whisk together tartar and egg.
4. Oil spray a pan and sauté garlic and spinach for 4 minutes. Turn off heat and add parsley.
5. In a pan, add flour, milk and black pepper, whisk well and allow it to boil, simmer as you keep whisking for 5 minutes. Let it cool.
6. Whisk the egg white to medium peaks.
7. In the milk mixture, add spinach mixture, add yolks, parmesan and mix.
8. Fold in egg whites in batches. Pour in the prepared ramekins, tap to get the excess air out and set on a baking tray.
9. Let bake for 5 minutes, change temperature to 350 F, Bake for an extra 20 minutes. Enjoy.

Nutrition per serving:

Calories 144, Fat 6.0 g, Sugar 3 g, Protein 14 g, Sodium 354 mg, Carbs 9 g

12.4 Lentil Medley

Serves: 8 | Prep Time: 20 minutes | Cook Time: 25 min

Ingredients:

- water - 2 c.
- diced red onion - 1
- sliced mushrooms - 2 c.
- Lentils - 1 c.
- cubed zucchini - 1
- Soft sun-dried tomato (not in oil) - ½ c.
- Fresh mint - ¼ c.
- Olive oil - 3 tbsps.
- cubed cucumber - 1
- Dried oregano - 1 tsp.
- Honey - 2 tsps.
- Rice vinegar - ½ c.
- chopped Baby spinach - 4 c.

- Dried basil - 1 tsp.
- Feta cheese - 1 c.

Procedure:

1. Cook lentils in water after rinsing for 25 minutes. Use cold water for draining and rinsing once again.
2. Transfer to a mixing bowl, mix in the remaining ingredients, toss and serve.

Nutrition per serving:

Calories 225 | Fat 8 g | Sugar 11 g | Protein 6.4 g |Sodium 400 mg | Carbs 29 g

12.5 Huevos Rancheros

Serves: 4 | Preparation time: 15 minutes | Cooking time: 25 minutes

Ingredients:

- Diced onion - ½ c.
- Canned crushed tomatoes, fire-roasted - 15 oz.
- Water - 2 tbsps.
- deseeded and diced poblano pepper - ½ c.
- Canola oil - 1 tsp.
- fresh jalapeño pepper - 1
- Minced garlic - 1 ½ tsps.

For Huevos

- avocado cut in fours - 1
- canola oil - 1 tsp.
- corn tortillas (6") - 4
- eggs - 4
- rinsed black beans - 1 (15 oz.) can
- shredded & low-fat Mexican blend cheese - ¼ c.

Procedure:

1. In a sizable pan, add oil and heat on medium flame, sauté your onion for about 2 minutes.
2. Mix in peppers and cook for 2 more minutes. Add in garlic. Continue cooking for an extra 1 minute.
3. Add water, salt and tomatoes, let it boil, reduce heat to low and let simmer for about 5 minutes. Take from heat and keep warm.
4. Using a skillet, add oil and cook egg for 4 minutes.
5. For each tortilla, add eggs and beans, tomato salsa, and the rest of the ingredients.
6. Roll and enjoy.

Nutrition per serving:

Calories 334, Fat 13.5 g, Sugar 9 g, Protein 17 g, Sodium 265 mg, Carbs 37 g

12.6 Zucchini Black Bean Tacos

Serves: 4 | Preparation time: 20 minutes | Cooking time: 0 minutes

Ingredients:

- Salsa, as needed

For tacos

- Chili powder - ½ tsp.
- corn tortillas - 8
- Chipotle powder - ½ tsp.
- rinsed Black beans - 1 (15 oz.) can
- Paprika - ¼ tsp.
- Garlic powder - ¼ tsp.
- zucchini, grated - 1

Avocado Crema (blend all ingredients)

- Greek yogurt, low-fat - ½ c.
- avocado - 1
- Juice of 1 lime

Procedure:

1. Using a bowl, add all the taco ingredients, except for tortillas.
2. Warm the tortillas in the oven.
3. Add the taco mix, salsa and avocado crema on top.
4. Enjoy.

Nutrition per serving:

Calories 245, Fat 10 g, Sugar 5 g, Protein 6.4 g, Sodium 321 mg, Carbs 35 g

12.7 Zucchini with Corn

Serves: 6 | Preparation time: 20 minutes | Cooking time: 20 minutes

Ingredients:

- Olive oil - 1 tbsp.
- Diced onion - 1/4 c.
- zucchinis cut into ¼" thick slices - 3
- Fresh corn kernels - 4 c.
- Black pepper - ¼ tsp.
- minced garlic clove - 1
- fresh jalapeño, chopped without seeds - 1
- Crumbled cotija cheese - 1/4 c.
- Salt - 1/8 tsp.

Procedure:

1. Set corn in water and boil, cook for 10 mins on low, cover, then drain.
2. In hot oil, add onion and garlic. Sauté for 5 minutes before adding zucchini and cook for an extra 5 minutes.
3. Add jalapenos, pepper, corn and pepper, cook for ten minutes.
4. Turn the heat off, serve with a topping of cheese.

Nutrition per serving:

Calories 202, Fat 5 g, Sugar 8 g, Protein 7 g, Sodium 164 mg, Carbs 40 g

12.8 Couscous with Beans & Vegetables

Serves: 6 | Preparation time: 20 minutes | Cooking time: 20 minutes

Ingredients:

- diced onion - 1
- red bell pepper cut into thin strips - 1
- sliced carrot - 1
- Olive oil - 2 tsps.
- Vegetable broth, low-fat - 1 c.
- zucchini cut into half-moons - 1
- celery rib, sliced - 1
- tomato, diced - 1
- Minced garlic - 1 tsp.
- Red kidney beans, rinsed - 2 (16 oz.) cans
- cubed sweet potato - 1
- Dried thyme - 1 tsp.
- Salt - 1/8 tsp.
- Ground cumin - 1 tsp.
- Minced parsley - ¼ c.
- Paprika - ½ tsp.
- Cayenne - 1/8 tsp.
- Whole-wheat couscous - 1 c.

Procedure:

1. Using a skillet set on a medium source of heat, add oil and heat. Sauté all vegetables for 5 minutes before adding garlic and cooking for approximately 30 seconds.
2. Mix in the rest of the ingredients, except for couscous, let it come to a simple boil while on high heat setting, turn the heat to low intensity then allow for simmering to take place for 15 minutes.
3. Cook couscous as per pack's instruction.
4. Serve the vegetables with fluffed couscous.

Nutrition per serving:

Calories 330, Fat 2.5 g, Sugar 8 g, Protein 16 g, Sodium 241 mg, Carbs 65 g

12.9 Roasted Kabocha with Wild Rice

Serves: 4 | Preparation Time: 20 minutes | Cooking Time: 2 hours

Ingredients:

- Olive oil - ¼ c.
- Chili powder - 1 tsp.
- Black pepper - ¼ tsp.
- Wild rice - ½ c.
- Kabocha squash - 3 pounds
- Pumpkin seeds - ½ c.
- Pomegranate seeds - ½ c.

- chopped fresh parsley, - ¼ c.
- Lime juice - 1 tbsp.
- Honey - 1 tsp.
- Lime zest - 1 tsp.

Procedure:

1. Let the oven preheat to 375 F.
2. With a fork, pierce the squash all over and place it on a baking sheet with aluminum foil.
3. Allow to roast for about 80 minutes.
4. Cut the squash into 5-6 pieces lengthwise. Take the middle part out.
5. Season the squash with oil (1 tbsp.) and sprinkles of pepper; set on your baking sheet flesh side up.
6. Broil the squash for 5-7 minutes.
7. In a skillet, add pumpkin seeds and oil (1 tbsp.) and allow to cook for 3 minutes. Mix in honey and chili powder, and continue cooking for 30 seconds. Take them out on a plate and cool.
8. Using a pan, add in water (1 ½ cups), and let it boil. Add rice and let boil, turn heat to low and let simmer for 25 minutes while covered, drain.
9. Using a bowl, add rice, pumpkin seeds, zest, juice, parsley, oil (2 tbsp.), and toss well.
10. Serve with broiled squash on top.

Nutrition per serving:

Calories 250, Fat 17.2 g, Sugar 8 g, Protein 6.4 g, Sodium 155 mg, Carbs

12.10 Acorn Squash & Coconut Creamed Greens Casserole

Serves: 4 | Preparation Time: 20 minutes | Cooking Time: 2 hours

Ingredients:

- coconut milk - 1 (15 oz.) can
- minced jalapeno without seeds - ½
- Grapeseed oil - 2 tbsps.
- Cornstarch - 1 tbsp.
- Chopped ginger - 2 tbsps.
- minced garlic cloves - 4
- Black pepper - ¼ tsp.
- Lime juice - 1 tbsp.
- diced plum tomatoes - 2
- chopped sweet onion - 1
- Light agave syrup - 1 tsp.
- packed and chopped Tuscan kale - 10 c.
- Ground cumin - 2 tsps.
- Acorn squash sliced into 1/8" of thickness - 1 ¼ pounds
- packed Swiss chard, chopped - 7 c.

Procedure:

1. Let the oven preheat to 425 F. mix coconut milk with the cornstarch.
2. Using a skillet set on medium source of heat, add and heat oil. Sauté onion for about 4 minutes.
3. Mix in garlic, ginger, jalapenos and continue cooking for 2 more minutes; add black pepper.
4. Add tomato to the onion mixture. Cook until done for 2 minutes, mix in cumin and cook for an additional 1 minute.
5. Add kale and chard before cooking to wilt and the liquid evaporates.
6. Add agave syrup and coconut milk. Let it simmer and cook the mixture for 3 minutes.
7. Add lime juice.
8. Into a baking dish (8 by 10"), add the creamed greens, add squash on top.
9. Bake for 25-30 minutes. Enjoy.

Nutrition per serving:

Calories 248, Fat 17.2 g, Sugar 8 g, Protein 11 g, Sodium 164 mg, Carbs 33 g

12.11 Warm Spiced Cabbage Bake

Serves: 4 | Preparation Time: 20 minutes | Cooking Time: 60 minutes

Ingredients:

- chopped raisins - 2 tbsps.
- Black pepper - ¼ tsp.
- chopped fresh dill - ½ c.
- chopped and toasted pine nuts - 1/3 c.
- Olive oil - 5 tbsps.
- Savoy cabbage (6 wedges) - 1 ½ pounds
- chopped sweet onion - 1
- sliced garlic cloves - 4
- Whole tomatoes, peeled & crushed - 1 (15 oz.) can
- Allspice - A pinch
- Sweet paprika - 1 tsp.
- low-fat Sour cream - ½ c.
- Ground cinnamon - ¼ tsp.
- Red pepper flakes - ¼ tsp.
- Salt – a pinch

Procedure:

1. Let your oven preheat to attain 400 F.
2. Using a bowl, add dill, nuts and raisins and mix together.
3. Using a skillet set on a medium high source of heat, add 2 tbsp. of oil. Cook cabbage wedges for 5-6 minutes on both sides, take it out on a plate and sprinkle black pepper.
4. Add the remaining oil in the skillet, sauté garlic and onion on low flame for 4 minutes.
5. Mix in spices and continue cooking for 1 more minute.
6. Mix in water (1 cup) and tomatoes, add the nut mixture (half). Let it simmer and add salt to season.
7. Add your cabbage wedges to skillet and set in oven before baking for half an hour.
8. Serve with the rest of the nut mixture and sour cream topping.

Nutrition per serving:

Calories 131, Fat 3 g, Sugar 3 g, Protein 21 g, Sodium 145 mg, Carbs 6 g

12.12 Polenta Squares with Cheese & Pine Nuts

Serves: 30 | Preparation Time: 20 minutes + Cooling | Cooking Time: 40 minutes

Ingredients:

- Quick-cooking polenta - 1 c.
- Crumbled gorgonzola cheese, low-fat - 1/3 c.
- Unsalted butter - 1 tbsp.
- boiling water - ¼ c.
- water - 4 c.
- balsamic vinegar - ⅔ c.
- Toasted pine nuts - 3 tbsps.
- Flat-leaf chopped fresh parsley - 2 tbsps.
- Grated zest - 1 tsp.
- Currants - 3 tbsps.

Procedure:

1. In a pan, add water (4 cups) and boil; slowly add polenta while whisking.
2. Whisk on low flame for 4 minutes till it thickens.
3. Add butter and pour in an oil sprayed baking pan (square-9”).
4. Cover with plastic wrap on top; it should touch the polenta surface, keep in the fridge for 60 minutes. Slice in 30 squares.
5. In your bowl, mix currants with boiling water (1/4 cup). Let it rest for 10 minutes draining.
6. Using a bowl, add currants, zest, pine nuts, and cheese.
7. In a pan, add vinegar, cook on medium heat for ten minutes, until reduced by 2 tbsp. Let it cool.
8. Using a skillet set over a medium source of heat, add oil and heat. Mix in polenta squares and cook one side for 6 minutes.
9. Serve with cheese mixture and drizzle of vinegar.

Nutrition per serving:
Calories 130, Fat 1.1 g, Sugar 8 g, Protein 3.1 g, Sodium 201 mg, Carbs 18 g

12.13 Curried Cauliflower with Chickpeas

Serves: 4 | Preparation Time: 20 minutes | Cooking Time: 75 minutes

Ingredients:

- Dried chickpeas, rinsed - 3/4 c.
- Minced ginger - 2 tbsps.
- Canola oil - 2 tsps.
- chopped onion - 1
- water - 3 c.
- cauliflower broken into florets - 1 medium head
- diced red bell pepper- 1
- minced garlic cloves - 3
- Curry powder - 2 tbsps.
- Salt - 1/8 tsp.
- Vegetable broth, low-sodium - 1 ½ c.

Procedure:

1. Cook chickpeas in a pressure cooker with water for 45 minutes on high pressure.
2. Let the pressure release naturally for 15 minutes, drain.
3. Sauté onion in hot oil for 3 minutes, add bell pepper and cook for 3 more minutes.
4. Mix in ginger and garlic, cook for 30 seconds.
5. In the pressure cooker, add cauliflower, salt, broth and curry powder. Add chickpeas with sautéed vegetables, cook on high pressure setting for 3 minutes. Release pressure quickly. Serve.

Nutrition per serving:
Calories 224, Fat 5.5 g, Sugar 10 g, Protein 11 g, Sodium 201 mg, Carbs 37 g

13 SIDES AND SMALL PLATES

13.1 Soy Sauce Green Beans

Serves: 12 | Preparation Time: 10 minutes | Cooking Time: 2 hours

Ingredients:

- olive oil - 3 tbsps.
- green beans- 16 oz. (455g)
- garlic powder - 1/2 tsp.
- coconut sugar - 1/2 c.
- low-sodium soy sauce - 1 tsp.

Procedure:

1. Using a slow cooker, add in soy sauce, green beans, sugar, oil, and garlic powder. Mix well before covering and allowing to cook for 2 hours on "low".
2. Toss well before dividing in serving plates and enjoy your side dish.

Nutrition per serving:

46 calories, 0.8g proteins, 3.6g carbs (0.6g sugars), 3.6g fats, 29mg sodium, 80mgpotassium

13.2 Sour Cream Green Beans

Serves: 8 | Preparation Time: 10 minutes | Cooking Time: 4 hours

Ingredients:

- green beans - 15 oz.
- corn - 14 oz.
- sliced mushrooms - 4 oz.
- cream of mushroom soup, low-fat and sodium-free - 11 oz
- low-fat sour cream - 1/2 c.
- chopped almonds - 1/2 c.
- low-fat cheddar cheese, shredded - 1/2 c.

Procedure:

1. Using a slow cooker, add in all ingredients and mix. Toss well and cook for 4 hours on low setting while covered.
2. Stir again one extra time. Set in serving plates and enjoy.

Nutrition per serving:

360 calories, 14g proteins, 58.3g carbs (10.3g sugars), 12.7g fats, 220mg sodium, 967mg potassium, 10g fibers, 14mg cholesterol

13.3 Cumin Brussels Sprouts

Serves: 4 | Preparation Time: 10 minutes | Cooking Time: 3 hours

Ingredients:

- low-sodium veggie stock - 1 c.
- Brussels sprouts, trimmed and halved - 1 pound
- rosemary, dried - 1 tsp.
- cumin, ground - 1 tsp.
- mint, chopped - 1 tbsp.

Procedure:

1. Using a slow cooker, combine all the above ingredients. Set a lid in place and cook for 3 hours on "low".
2. Divide in serving plates and enjoy your side dish.

Nutrition per serving:

56 calories, 4g proteins, 11.4g carbs (2.7g sugars), 0.6g fats, 65mg sodium, 460mg potassium, 4.5g fibers

13.4 Peach And Carrots

Serves: 6 | Preparation Time: 10 minutes | Cooking Time: 6 hours

Ingredients:

- peeled small carrots - 2 pounds

- cinnamon powder - 1/2 tsp.
- melted low-fat butter - 1/2 c.
- canned peach, unsweetened - 1/2 c.
- cornstarch - 2 tbsps.
- stevia - 3 tbsps.
- water - 2 tbsps.
- vanilla extract - 1 tsp.
- ground nutmeg - A pinch

Procedure:

1. Using a slow cooker, mix in all the above ingredients. Toss well before you cover and cook for 6 hours on "low".
2. Toss again one more time before setting in serving plates and enjoy your side dish.

Nutrition per serving:
139 calories, 3.8g proteins, 35.4g carbs (6.9g sugars), 10.7g fats, 199mg sodium, 25mg potassium, 4.2g fibers

13.5 Chive & Garlic "Mash"

Serves: 2 | Preparation Time:8 minutes | Cooking Time: 20 minutes

Ingredients:

- vegetable stock - 2 c.
- peeled Yukon potatoes - 2 pound
- peeled cloves garlic - 4
- almond milk - ½ c.
- flavored vinegar - ½ tsp.
- chopped chives - ¼ c.

Procedure:

1. Using an instant pot, add in potatoes, garlic and broth.
2. Cook for 9 minutes on HIGH pressure setting while the lid is locked.
3. Naturally release pressure for about 10 minutes
4. Drain and keep the appropriate liquid that will maintain the required consistency.
5. You then mash your potatoes. Add in milk, chives and vinegar as you stir.
6. Enjoy!

Nutrition per serving:
292 Calories, 15g Fat, 34g Carbs, 7g Protein, 123mg Potassium, 82mg Sodium

13.6 Spiced Broccoli Florets

Serves: 10 | Preparation Time: 10 minutes | Cooking Time: 3 hours

Procedure:

- broccoli florets - 6 c.
- low-fat shredded cheddar cheese - 1 ½ c.
- cider vinegar - ½ tsp.
- chopped yellow onion - ¼ c.
- tomato sauce, sodium-free - 10 oz.
- olive oil - 2 tbsps.
- black pepper - A pinch

Procedure:

1. Apply oil to your slow cooker for greasing. Mix in vinegar, broccoli, black pepper, tomato sauce and onion. Cook on high setting for 2½ hours on "high" while covered.
2. Sprinkle cheese over your mixture, cover again and let cook for 30 more minutes on "high". Set in serving plates and enjoy your side dish.

Nutrition per serving:
119 calories, 6.2g proteins, 5.7g carbs (2.3g sugars), 8.7g fats, 272mg sodium, 288mg potassium, 18mg cholesterol, 1.9g fibers

13.7 Mashed Cauliflower with Garlic

Serves: 4 | Preparation Time: 5 minutes | Cooking Time: 25 minutes

Ingredients:

- non-hydrogenated soft-bowl margarine - 1 tbsp.
- cauliflower - 1 head
- leek split into 4 parts, white only - 1
- clove garlic - 1

- Pepper - ¼ tsp.

Procedure:

1. Break up little bits of cauliflower. Steam the garlic, leeks, and cauliflower in water in a saucepan until they become tender for 25 minutes.
2. Using a food processor, add the vegetables and puree well to get a mashed potato-like texture. You can process in small portions at a given time.
3. Using a mixer if you want a finer finish. With a dishtowel, make sure to tightly keep the blender cap on. If the vegetables tend to be dusty, add some more hot water.
4. As per your taste, stir in margarine and pepper. Just serve.

Nutrition per serving:

Calories: 217, Fat: 5g, Fiber: 8g, Sugars 12g, Protein: 4g, Sodium: 25mg, Potassium: 276mg

13.8 Chinese-Style Asparagus

Serves: 2 | Preparation Time: 15 minutes | Cooking Time: 4 minutes

Ingredients:

- water - ½ c.
- soy sauce, reduced-sodium - 1 tsp.
- sugar - ½ tsp.
- fresh asparagus, remove woody ends and slice into 1 ½ inch pieces - 1½ pounds

Procedure:

1. Using a saucepan set over a medium high source of heat, mix in soy sauce, sugar and water and heat. Allow to get to boiling point before adding asparagus. Lower the heat intensity and let boil on low for 4 minutes until the asparagus becomes crispy and tender.
2. Set in serving bowls to serve.

Nutrition per serving:

Calories: 260, Fat: 5g, Carbs: 20g, Protein: 22g, Sodium: 89mg, Potassium: 695mg

13.9 Fresh Fruit Kebabs

Serves: 8 | Preparation Time: 35 minutes | Cooking Time: 0 minutes

Ingredients:

- low-fat lemon yogurt, sugar-free - 6 oz.
- lime juice, fresh - 1 tsp.
- pineapple chunks each ½ inch in size - 4
- red grapes - 4
- lime zest - 1 tsp.
- strawberries - 4
- peeled and quartered kiwi - 1
- banana, sliced into 4 ½" chunks - ½
- wooden skewers - 4

Procedure:

1. Using a shallow dish, add in lime zest, lime juice, and yogurt and whisk. Set in your refrigerator while covered until when ready for use.
2. To each of the skewers, thread each fruit. Serve alongside your lemon-lime dip.

Nutrition per serving:

Calories: 27, Fat: 10g, Carbs: 20g, Protein: 10g, Sodium: 3mg, Potassium: 138mg

13.10 Pomegranate And Ricotta Bruschetta

Serves: 8 | Preparation Time: 12 minutes | Cooking Time: 12 minutes

Ingredients:

- Grated lemon zest - 1/2 tsp.
- sliced Nut Bread, Whole Grain - 6
- Ricotta Cheese Low Fat - 1 c.
- Pomegranate Arils - 1/2 c.
- Fresh thyme - 2 tsps.

Procedure:

1. Toast your bread to brown lightly.
2. In the meantime, use a bowl to whisk lemon zest and cheese.
3. Slice halfway the toasted bread. Spread cottage cheese to the top.

4. Add a topping of pomegranate and thyme.
5. Enjoy.

Nutrition per serving:
Calories per Serving 69, Protein: 4.1g, Carbs: 11.1g, Fat: 1.0g, Saturated Fat: 0.2g, Sodium: 123mg, Potassium: 427mg

13.11 Carrot Sticks with Onion and Sour Cream

Serves: 8 | Preparation Time: 10 minutes | Cooking Time: 0 minutes

Ingredients:

- carrot sticks - 2 c.
- peeled and minced sweet onion - 1
- mayonnaise low fat - 2 tbsps.
- sour cream - ½ c.
- stalks celery, chopped - 4

Procedure:

1. Using a bowl, add in mayonnaise and sour cream. Whisk well to combine.
2. Add in onion and stir.
3. Set in the refrigerator for 1 hour and enjoy with carrot sticks and celery.

Nutrition per serving:
Calories per Serving: 60, Protein: 1.6g, Carbs: 7.2g, Fat: 3.1g, Saturated Fat: 1.7g, Sodium: 38 mg, Potassium: 577mg

13.12 Parsley Fennel

Serves: 4 | Preparation Time: 10 minutes | Cooking Time: 2h 30 minutes

Ingredients:

- avocado oil - 2 tsps.
- fennel bulbs, sliced - 2
- turmeric powder - 1/2 tsp.
- chopped parsley - 1 tbsp.
- Juice and zest of 1 lime
- veggie stock, low-sodium - 1/4 c.

Procedure:

1. In your slow cooker, add in and mix all the above ingredients and let cook for 2 ½ hours on LOW setting while covered.
2. Enjoy your side dish.

Nutrition per serving:
Calories 47, Fat 0.6g, Cholesterol 0mg, Sodium 71mg, Carbs 10.8g, Fiber 4.3g| Sugars 0.4g, Protein 1.7g, Potassium 521mg

13.13 Parsley Red Potatoes

Serves: 8 | Preparation Time: 10 min | Cooking Time: 6 hours

Ingredients:

- halved baby red potatoes - 16
- olive oil - 2 tbsps.
- chicken stock, low-sodium - 2 c.
- sliced carrot - 1
- chopped yellow onion - 1/4 c.
- chopped celery rib - 1
- black pepper - A pinch
- chopped parsley - 1 tbsp.
- minced garlic clove - 1

Procedure:

1. Using a slow cooker, add in potatoes, carrot, onion, garlic, black pepper, oil, stock, celery, and parsley. Toss well and cook for 6 hours on low setting while covered.
2. Set in serving plates and enjoy your side dish.

Nutrition per serving:
Calories 256, Fat 9.6g, Cholesterol 0mg, Sodium 846mg, Carbs 43.5g, Fiber 4.5g, Sugars 4.7g, Protein 4.5g, Potassium 48mg

13.14 Italians Style Mushroom Mix

Serves: 6 | Preparation Time: 5 minutes | Cooking Time: 25 minutes

Ingredients:

- halved mushrooms - 1 pound
- Italian seasoning - 1 tsp.
- olive oil - 3 tbsps.
- tomato sauce with no-salt-added - 1 c.
- yellow onion, chopped - 1

Procedure:

1. Mix the mushrooms with the oil, onion, Italian seasoning and tomato sauce, toss well, and allow to cook for 25 minutes while covered
2. Set in serving plates and enjoy your side dish.

Nutrition per serving:

Calories 96, Fat 7.5g, Cholesterol 1mg, Sodium 219mg, Carbs 6.5g, Fiber 1.8g, Sugars 3.9g, Protein 3.1g, Potassium 403mg

13.15 Honey sage carrots

Serves: 4 | Preparation Time: 27 minutes | Cooking Time: 8 minutes

Ingredients:

- sliced carrots - 2 c.
- ground black pepper - 1/4 tsp.
- butter - 2 tsps.
- honey - 2 tbsps.
- chopped fresh sage - 1 tbsp.
- salt - 1/8 tsp.
- Sugar

Procedure:

1. Load a medium saucepan with water and allow to boil. Mix in carrots and cook for 5 minutes until tender. Drain excess water and place aside.
2. A medium sauté pan is preheated, and butter is added. Add the carrots, sugar, sage, pepper, and salt until the pan is heated and the butter is melting. Sauté for approximately 3 minutes, stirring regularly. Enjoy.

Nutrition per serving:

Calories: 217, Fat: 5g, Fiber: 8g, Sugars 12g, Protein: 4g, sodium: 94mg, potassium: 460 mg

14 POULTRY RECIPES

14.1 Turkey with Spring Onions

Serves: 4 | Preparation Time: 10 minutes | Cooking Time: 30 minutes

Ingredients:

- black peppercorns - ½ tbsp.
- cubed boneless & skinless turkey breast - 1 pound
- water - 1 c.
- chopped spring onions - 2 tbsps.
- cubed tomatoes - 2
- olive oil - 1 tbsp.

Procedure:

1. Using your pan set on a medium high intensity source of heat, pour in oil and heat. Mix in your garlic and cook for about 5 minutes until well browned.
2. Mix in the remaining ingredients and cook while covered for 25 additional minutes.

Nutrition per serving:

167 calories, 20.5g protein, 8.7g carbs, 5.7g fat, 1.8g fiber, 48mg cholesterol, 1188mg sodium, 517mg potassium

14.2 Chicken with Tomatoes and Celery Stalk

Serves: 4 | Preparation Time: 10 minutes | Cooking Time: 40 minutes

Ingredients:

- skinless & boneless chicken breasts, cubed - 2 pounds
- celery stalk, chopped - 1
- cubed tomato - 1
- sliced red onions - 2
- cubed zucchini - 1
- olive oil - 2 tbsps.
- Black pepper – ¼ tsp.
- Water - 1 c.

Procedure:

1. Using a pot, add in all ingredients and mix well.
2. Cook over medium heat for 40 minutes while covered.

Nutrition per serving:

530 calories, 67.2g protein, 8.7g carbs, 24.1g fat, 2.4g fiber, 202mg cholesterol, 234mg sodium, 857mg potassium

14.3 Chicken Bowl with Red Cabbage

Serves: 4 | Preparation Time: 10 minutes | Cooking Time: 25 minutes

Ingredients:

- sweet paprika - 1 tsp.
- skinless & boneless boiled chicken breast, cubed - 1 pound
- carrots, peeled and grated - 2
- low-fat yogurt - 1/3 c.
- red cabbage head, shredded - 1
- black pepper - ½ tsp.

Procedure:

1. Mix chicken and carrots. Place in a bowl.
2. Add sweet paprika, yogurt, cabbage, and ground black pepper.
3. Carefully mix the meal.

Nutrition per serving:

261 calories, 27.1g protein, 16.7g carbs, 10.1g fat, 6.1g fiber, 73mg cholesterol, 130mg sodium, 889mg potassium

14.4 Chicken Sandwich

Serves: 4 | Preparation Time: 10 minutes | Cooking Time: 25 minutes

Ingredients:

- skinless & boneless boiled chicken breast sliced into 4 pieces - 1
- oregano, chopped - 1 tbsp.
- low-fat yogurt - 1 tbsp.
- low-fat cheddar cheese, shredded - ½ c.
- whole-wheat bread slices - 4

Procedure:

1. Mix low-fat yogurt with oregano.
2. Then spread yogurt mixture to the bread slices. Add a topping of sliced chicken breast and Cheddar cheese.
3. Top the sandwich with the rest of your bread slices.

Nutrition per serving:

265 calories, 21.2g protein, 22.1g carbs, 10.6g fat, 6.3g fiber, 47mg cholesterol, 985mg sodium, 572mg potassium

14.5 Turkey and Zucchini Tortillas

Serves: 4 | Preparation Time: 10 minutes | Cooking Time: 20 minutes

Ingredients:

- whole-wheat tortillas - 4
- fat-free yogurt - ½ c.
- boneless & skinless turkey breast cut into strips - 1 pound
- olive oil - 1 tbsp.
- cubed zucchini - 1

Procedure:

1. Mix olive oil, turkey, and zucchini and set in your tray.
2. Bake the ingredients for 20 minutes at 360F.
3. Then place the cooked ingredients on the tortillas and sprinkle with yogurt.

Nutrition per serving:

380 calories, 40.4g protein, 31g carbs, 10.5g fat, 4.9g fiber, 86mg cholesterol, 242mg sodium, 730mg potassium

14.6 Chicken with Eggplants

Serves: 4 | Preparation Time: 10 minutes | Cooking Time: 35 minutes

Ingredients:

- skinless, boneless and cubed chicken breasts - 2
- red onion, chopped - 1
- olive oil - 2 tbsps.
- eggplant, cubed - 1
- smoked paprika - ½ tsp.

Procedure:

1. Mix chicken breast, smoked paprika and olive oil and place in the tray.
2. Add red onion and eggplant.
3. Bake the meal at 360F for 35 minutes.

Nutrition per serving:

524 calories, 25.6g protein, 18.2g carbs, 41.3g fat, 7.7g fiber, 65mg cholesterol, 85mg sodium, 851mg potassium

14.7 Garlic Turkey

Serves: 4 | Preparation Time: 10 minutes | Cooking Time: 40 minutes

Ingredients:

- olive oil - 1 tbsp.
- big boneless, skinless and sliced turkey breast - 1
- minced garlic cloves - 2
- balsamic vinegar - 2 tbsps.

Procedure:

1. Using a baking dish, mix turkey alongside all ingredients and cook at 360F for 40 minutes.

Nutrition per serving:

149 calories, 17.2g protein, 5.2g carbs, 6.2g fat, 0.5g fiber, 45mg cholesterol, 1017mg sodium, 317mg potassium

14.8 Cheddar Turkey

Serves: 4 | Preparation Time: 10 minutes | Cooking Time: 30 minutes

Ingredients:

- boneless, skinless, and sliced turkey breast - 1 pound
- dried basil - ½ tsp.
- ground cumin - ½ tsp.
- olive oil - 2 tbsps.
- fat-free shredded cheddar cheese - 1 c.
- lime juice - 1 tbsp.

Procedure:

1. Mix turkey breast with olive oil, dried basil, cumin, and lime juice.
2. Set on a tray and let bake for 25 minutes.
3. Then top the turkey with Cheddar cheese and continue cooking for additional 5 minutes.

Nutrition per serving:

301 calories, 26.9g protein, 7g carbs, 18.4g fat, 1.2g fiber, 78mg cholesterol, 1330mg sodium, 487mg potassium

14.9 Parsnip and Turkey Bites

Serves: 4 | Preparation Time: 10 minutes | Cooking Time: 40 minutes

Ingredients:

- boneless, skinless and cubed turkey breast - 1 pound
- peeled and cubed parsnips - 2
- avocado oil - 2 tbsps.
- ground cumin - 2 tsps.
- chopped parsley - 1 tbsp.
- water - 1 c.

Procedure:

1. Using a pan set over a medium high source of heat, add in oil and heat. Mix in turkey breast and allow to sauté for about 5 minutes.
2. Mix in the other ingredients and let cook over a medium heat intensity for 30 minutes.

Nutrition per serving:

166 calories, 20.6g protein, 13.5g carbs, 3.1g fat, 2.7g fiber, 49mg cholesterol, 1192mg sodium, 542mg potassium

14.10 Nutmeg Chicken with Tender Chickpeas

Serves: 4 | Preparation Time: 10 minutes | Cooking Time: 40 minutes

Ingredients:

- chopped green bell pepper - 1
- canned chickpeas, drained and no-salt-added - 1 c.
- water - 1 c.
- chopped yellow onion - 1
- boneless, skinless and cubed turkey breast - 1 pound
- ground nutmeg - 1 tsp.
- coconut oil - 1 tsp.

Procedure:

1. Using a pan set over a medium high source of heat, add in coconut oil and let heat. Mix in onion, bell pepper, and turkey, and allow to cook for about 10 minutes as you occasionally stir.
2. Mix in the rest of your ingredients. Allow to simmer to about 30 minutes.

Nutrition per serving:

387 calories, 30g protein, 40.6g carbs, 12.3g fat, 10.6g fiber, 49mg cholesterol, 1201mg sodium, 905mg potassium

14.11 Garam Masala Turkey

Serves: 4 | Preparation Time: 10 minutes | Cooking Time: 30 minutes

Ingredients:

- boneless, skinless, and cubed turkey breast - 2 pounds

- green curry paste - 1 tbsp.
- garam masala - 1 tsp.
- olive oil - 2 tbsps.

Procedure:

1. Mix turkey breast with green curry paste, and garam masala.
2. Then add olive oil and transfer it to the tray.
3. Bake at 365F for 30 minutes.

Nutrition per serving:

224 calories, 19.8g protein, 16.9g carbs, 8.9g fat, 5g fiber, 38mg cholesterol, 941mg sodium, 491mg potassium

14.12 Hot Chicken Mix

Serves: 4 | Preparation Time: 10 minutes | Cooking Time: 30 minutes

Ingredients:

- chopped scallions - 4
- olive oil - 1 tbsp.
- skinless, boneless, and sliced chicken breast - 1 pound
- grated ginger - 1 tbsp.
- dried oregano - 1 tsp.
- ground cumin - 1 tsp.
- chili powder - 1 tsp.

Procedure:

1. Mix chicken breast with all remaining ingredients and place in the tray. .Bake the meal at 360F for 30 minutes.

Nutrition per serving:

180 calories, 25.1g protein, 3.9g carbs, 6.9g fat, 1.6g fiber, 73mg cholesterol, 97mg sodium, 551mg potassium

14.13 Mustard and Garlic Chicken

Serves: 4 | Preparation Time: 10 minutes | Cooking Time: 35 minutes

Ingredients:

- boneless and skinless chicken thighs - 1 pound
- avocado oil - 1 tbsp.
- mustard - 2 tbsps.
- minced garlic cloves - 3
- dried basil - ½ tsp.

Procedure:

1. Mix avocado oil with mustard, garlic, and basil.
2. Then rub the chicken thighs with mustard mixture. Bake for 35 minutes at 365F.

Nutrition per serving:

253 calories, 34.7g protein, 3.3g carbs, 10.5g fat, 1g fiber, 101mg cholesterol, 132mg sodium, 343mg potassium

14.14 Paprika Chicken

Serves: 4 | Preparation Time: 10 minutes | Cooking Time: 25 minutes

Ingredients:

- avocado oil - 1 tbsp.
- boneless, skinless, and cubed chicken breast - 1 pound
- smoked paprika - 1 tbsp.
- onion powder - ¼ tsp.

Procedure:

1. Rub the chicken breast with avocado oil, smoked paprika, and onion powder.
2. Set it in a baking tray and bake at 365F for 25 minutes.

Nutrition per serving:

237 calories, 25.8g protein, 4.5g carbs, 12.9g fat, 1.5g fiber, 73mg cholesterol, 81mg sodium, 652mg potassium

14.15 Chicken with Tomatoes

Serves: 4 | Preparation Time: 10 minutes | Cooking Time: 25 minutes

Ingredients:

- avocado oil - 2 tbsps.

- ground black pepper - 1 tsp.
- skinless, boneless, and cubed chicken breasts - 2
- cherry tomatoes, halved - 1 c.

Procedure:

1. Mix avocado oil chicken breast, and ground black pepper.
2. Place them on the tray, add cherry tomatoes and bake the meal at 365F for 25 minutes.

Nutrition per serving:
38 calories, 2g protein, 6.2g carbs, 1.2g fat, 2.5g fiber, 0mg cholesterol, 8mg sodium, 353mg potassium

14.16 Basil Turkey

Serves: 4 | Preparation Time: 10 minutes | Cooking Time: 25 minutes

Ingredients:

- olive oil - 1 tbsp.
- big boneless, skinless, and cubed turkey breast - 1
- dried basil - 1 tbsp.
- lemon juice - ½ tsp.

Procedure:

1. Mix turkey breast, lemon juice, dried basil, and olive oil.
2. Place the turkey on your tray and set in the oven.
3. Bake at 365F for about 25 minutes.

Nutrition per serving:
121 calories, 2.3g protein, 6.1g carbs, 10.8g fat, 1.9g fiber, 0mg cholesterol, 23mg sodium, 250mg potassium

15 RED MEAT DISHES

15.1 Pork with Cherry Tomatoes

Serves: 4 | Preparation Time: 10 minutes | Cooking Time: 30 minutes

Ingredients:

- avocado oil - 1 tbsp.
- cherry tomatoes, halved - 1 c.
- apple cider vinegar - 2 tbsps.
- pork tenderloin, chopped - 4 oz.

Procedure:

1. Place all ingredients in the tray and gently mix.
2. Cook the meal at 365F for 30 minutes.

Nutrition per serving:
125 calories, 9.1g protein, 6.8g carbs, 6.4g fat, 0.6g fiber, 24mg cholesterol, 49mg sodium, 269mg potassium

15.2 Thyme Pork Skillet

Serves: 4 | Preparation Time: 10 minutes | Cooking Time: 25 minutes

Ingredients:

- pork top loin, boneless, chopped - 1 pound
- olive oil - 1 tbsp.
- chopped yellow onion - 1
- dried thyme - 1 tbsp.

- water - 1 c.
- low-sodium tomato paste - 1 tbsp.

Procedure:

1. Set a pan over a medium high source of heat. Add in oil and heat. Mix in onion and allow to cook for about 5 minutes.
2. Toss in your meat and continue cooking for an additional 5 minutes.
3. Mix in the other ingredients. Continue cooking for additional 15 minutes on medium heat.

Nutrition per serving:

274 calories, 36.6g protein, 5.3g carbs, 11.2g fat, 1.2g fiber, 104mg cholesterol, 104mg sodium, 484mg potassium

15.3 Meat and Zucchini Mix

Serves: 4 | Preparation Time: 10 minutes | Cooking Time: 30 minutes

Ingredients:

- pork top loin boneless, trimmed, and cubed - 2 pounds
- olive oil - 2 tbsps.
- water - ¾ c.
- chopped marjoram - 1 tbsp.
- roughly cubed zucchinis - 2
- sweet paprika - 1 tsp.

Procedure:

1. Place all ingredients in the tray.
2. Gently mix and flatten the ingredients.
3. Cook the meal at 365F for 30 minutes.

Nutrition per serving:

359 calories, 61.1g protein, 5.7g carbs, 9.1g fat, 2.1g fiber, 166mg cholesterol, 166mg sodium, 1289mg potassium

15.4 Garlic Pork

Servings: 4 | Preparation time: 10 minutes | Cooking time: 40 minutes

Ingredients:

- olive oil - 3 tbsps.
- pork rib chop - 2 pounds
- sweet paprika - 2 tsps.
- garlic powder - 1 tsp.

Procedure:

1. Mix garlic powder, sweet paprika and olive oil before rubbing them to the pork rib chops.
2. Place the pork rib chop in the tray and bake at 365F for 40 minutes.

Nutrition per serving:

689 calories, 38.8g protein, 3.2g carbs, 57.1g fat, 1g fiber, 161mg cholesterol, 187mg sodium, 77mg potassium

15.5 Beef with Cauliflower Rice

Serves: 4 | Preparation Time: 10 minutes | Cooking Time: 40 minutes

Ingredients:

- cauliflower rice - 2 c.
- chopped beef top loin - 1 pound
- olive oil - 1 tbsp.
- dried oregano - 1 tsp.
- chopped tomato - 1
- water - ½ c.

Procedure:

1. Mix meat with olive oil, dried oregano, and transfer to the pot.
2. After this, add tomato and cauliflower rice.
3. Then top the ingredients with water and close the pot.
4. Cook the meal at 365f for 40 minutes.

Nutrition per serving:

449calories, 37.3g protein, 38.8g carbs, 14.9g fat, 1.1g fiber, 98mg cholesterol, 137mg sodium, 512mg potassium

15.6 Cilantro Beef Meatballs

Serves: 4 | Preparation Time: 10 minutes | Cooking Time: 30 minutes

Ingredients:

- almond flour - 3 tbsps.
- olive oil - 2 tbsps.

- minced pork tenderloin - 2 pounds
- dried and chopped cilantro - 1 tbsp.

Procedure:

1. Using a mixing bowl, add in cilantro, minced meat and almond flour and mix well.
2. Make the meatballs.
3. Use olive oil to brush the tray.
4. Set the meatballs in your tray. Bake them at 365F for 30 minutes.

Nutrition per serving:

502 calories, 67.7g protein, 8.9g carbs, 21.7g fat, 3.6g fiber, 247mg cholesterol, 539mg sodium, 1242mg potassium

15.7 Spiced Meat with Endives

Serves: 4 | Preparation Time: 10 minutes | Cooking Time: 35 minutes

Ingredients:

- chopped pork tenderloin - 1 pound
- water - 1 c.
- trimmed endives (shredded) - 2
- chili powder - 1 tsp.
- ground white pepper - 1 tsp.
- dried oregano - ½ tsp.
- olive oil - 1 tbsp.

Procedure:

1. Mix meat with olive oil, chili powder, white pepper, and dried oregano.
2. Put the meat in the saucepan and roast each side on medium heat for 2 minutes.
3. After this, add water and endives.
4. Simmer for 30 minutes while covered.

Nutrition per serving:

288 calories, 34.2g protein, 3.4g carbs, 11.6g fat, 1.2g fiber, 98mg cholesterol, 112mg sodium, 517mg potassium

16 DESSERTS

16.1 Walnut Cake

Serves: 8 | Preparation Time: 10 minutes | Cooking Time: 25 minutes

Ingredients:

- almond flour - 3 c.
- liquid stevia - 5 tbsps.
- chopped walnuts - ½ c.
- baking soda - 2 tsps.
- almond milk - 2 c.
- melted coconut oil - ½ c.

Procedure:

1. Mix almond flour with liquid stevia, almond milk, baking soda, and coconut oil.
2. Stir the mixture to make it smooth before adding walnuts.
3. Stir the mixture well.
4. Then set the cake mixture into your baking mold. Bake until the surface of the cake is light brown for 25 minutes at a heat intensity of 365F.

Nutrition per serving:

464 calories, 5.5g protein, 30.6g carbs, 37.8g fat, 3g fiber, 0g cholesterol, 328mg sodium, 201mg potassium

16.2 Vanilla Apple Cake

Serves: 4 | Preparation Time: 10 minutes | Cooking Time: 30 minutes

Ingredients:

- almond milk - 1 c.
- baking powder - 1 tsp.
- vanilla extract - 1 tsp.
- coconut flour - 2 c.
- green apples, sweet, cored, peeled and chopped - 2
- Cooking spray

Procedure:

1. Using a mixing bowl, add in coconut flour, vanilla extract, baking powder, and almond milk and mix well. Stir the mixture until smooth.
2. After this, add apples and gently mix the mixture one more time.
3. Spray the baking mold with cooking spray from inside.
4. Transfer the apple mixture to the baking mold, flatten it gently, and cook at 365F for 30 minutes.

Nutrition per serving:

305 calories, 4.7g protein, 29.8g carbs, 21.5g fat, 5.6g fiber, 0g cholesterol, 347mg sodium, 403mg potassium

16.3 Coconut and Cinnamon Cream

Serves: 4 | Preparation Time: 2 minutes | Cooking Time: 0 minutes

Ingredients:

- coconut cream - 1 c.
- coconut sugar - 2 c.
- cinnamon powder - 2 tbsps.
- coconut shred - 1 tbsp.

Procedure:

5. Using a blender, add in all ingredients, mix well and process for about 30 seconds.

Nutrition per serving:

602 calories, 1.6g protein, 125.5g carbs, 14.9g fat, 1.3g fiber, 0g cholesterol, 308mg sodium, 159mg potassium

16.4 Strawberries and Coconut Bowls

Serves: 4 | Preparation Time: 10 minutes | Cooking Time: 0 minutes

Ingredients:

- chopped strawberries - 2 c.
- coconut cream - 1 c.
- coconut shred - ¼ c.

Procedure:

1. Mix coconut cream with coconut shred.
2. Put the coconut mixture in the serving plates. Add a topping of strawberries and enjoy.

Nutrition per serving:

67 calories, 2.2g protein, 13g carbs, 0.2g fat, 1.4g fiber, 2g cholesterol, 29mg sodium, 112mg potassium

16.5 Cinnamon Plums

Serves: 4 | Preparation Time: 10 minutes | Cooking Time: 10 minutes

Ingredients:

- halved plums, stones removed - 1 pound
- cinnamon powder - ½ tsp.

Procedure:

1. Use the cinnamon powder to sprinkle over the plums. Set them on your baking tray.
2. Bake for 10 minutes at 365F.

Nutrition per serving:

31 calories, 0.2g protein, 8.1g carbs, 0.2g fat, 0.3g fiber, 0g cholesterol, 3mg sodium, 26g potassium

16.6 Baked Apples with Nuts

Serves: 4 | Preparation Time: 10 minutes | Cooking Time: 15 minutes

Ingredients:

- cored and halved green apples - 4
- ground cinnamon - 1 tsp.

- coconut oil - 1 tsp.
- chopped nuts - 2 oz.

Procedure:

1. Put the apples in the tray and sprinkle with ground cinnamon and coconut oil.
2. Then sprinkle the apples with nuts and bake at 365F for 15 minutes.

Nutrition per serving:

156 calories, 1.6g protein, 33.4g carbs, 2.3g fat, 5.1g fiber, 0g cholesterol, 15mg sodium, 240g potassium

16.7 Green Tea and Banana Sweetening Mix

Serves: 3-4 | Preparation Time: 10 minutes | Cooking Time: 5 minutes

Ingredients:

- coconut cream - 1 c.
- pitted avocados, chopped - 2 c.
- peeled and chopped bananas - 2
- green tea powder - 2 tbsps.
- palm sugar - 1 tbsp.
- grated lime zest - 2 tbsps.

Procedure:

1. Using an instant pot, add in all the ingredients.
2. Toss this, cover, and then cook for 5 minutes on Low. Perform a manual, natural pressure release, divide and serve it cold.

Nutrition per serving:

Calories: 207, Fat: 2.1g, Carbs: 11.2g, Net Carbs: 8.1g, Protein: 3.1g, Fiber: 8g, Sodium: 154mg, Potassium: 187mg.

16.8 Grapefruit Compote

Serves: 4 | Preparation Time: 5 minutes | Cooking Time: 8 minutes

Ingredients:

- palm sugar - 1 c.
- Sugar-free red grapefruit juice - 64 oz.
- chopped mint - ½ c.
- peeled and cubed grapefruits - 2

Procedure:

1. Take all ingredients and combine them into Instant Pot.
2. Cook for 8 minutes on Low setting, then divide into serving bowls and enjoy!

Nutrition per serving:

Calories: 131, Fat: 1g, Carbs: 12g, Net Carbs: 11g, Protein: 2g, Fiber: 2g, Sodium: 175mg, Potassium: 198mg.

16.9 Pot Applesauce

Serves: 8 | Preparation Time: 10 minutes | Cooking Time: 10 minutes

Ingredients:

- apples - 3 pounds
- water - ½ c.

Procedure:

1. Core and peel the apples and then put them at the bottom of the Instant Pot and then secure the lid. Ensure the vent is sealed before cooking for 10 minutes. Perform a natural pressure release.
2. From there, when it's safe to remove the lid, take the apples and juices and blend this till smooth.
3. Store it in jars or enjoy immediately.

Nutrition per serving:

Calories: 88, Fat: 0g, Carbs: 23g, Net Carbs: 19g, Protein: 0g, Fiber: 4g, Sodium: 186mg, Potassium: 321mg.

16.10 Rice and Fruits Pudding

Serves: 4 | Preparation Time: 10 minutes | Cooking Time: 25 minutes

Ingredients:

- cooked black rice - 1 c.
- cored and cubed pears - 2
- cinnamon powder - 2 tsps.
- coconut milk - ½ c.

Procedure:

1. Using a mixing bowl, add in all ingredients and mix well. Set to your baking ramekins.
2. Bake the pudding for 25 minutes at 350F.

Nutrition per serving:

341 calories, 2.3g protein, 85.2g carbs, 0.9g fat, 3.8g fiber, 0g cholesterol, 13mg sodium, 192g potassium

16.11 Rhubarb and Pear Compote

Serves: 4 | Preparation Time: 10 minutes| Cooking Time: 15 minutes

Ingredients:

- roughly chopped rhubarb - 2 c.
- chopped pears - 2
- water - 2 c.

Procedure:

1. Using a pot, add in all ingredients. Heat until the mixture boils.
2. Simmer the compote for 15 minutes.
3. Cool the compote well before serving.

Nutrition per serving:

53 calories, 0.7g protein, 11.8g carbs, 0.2g fat, 1.1g fiber, 0g cholesterol, 6mg sodium, 178g potassium

16.12 Lime Cake

Serves: 6 | Preparation Time: 10 minutes | Cooking Time: 35 minutes

Ingredients:

- whole wheat flour - 2 c.
- melted coconut oil - 2 tbsps.
- whisked egg - 1
- baking powder - 1 tsp.
- coconut milk - 1 c.
- sliced lemon - ½

Procedure:

1. Mix flour with baking powder, coconut oil, egg, and coconut milk.
2. When the mixture is homogenous, transfer it to the baking pan.
3. Top the cake with lemon slices and bake at 360F for 35 minutes.

Nutrition per serving:

324 calories, 6.2g protein, 42.3g carbs, 15.3g fat, 2.1g fiber, 27g cholesterol, 35mg sodium, 252g potassium

16.13 Coconut Shred Bars

Serves: 6 | Preparation Time: 10 minutes | Cooking Time: 25 minutes

Ingredients:

- coconut flour - 2 c.
- baking powder - 1 tsp.
- nutmeg (ground) - ½ tsp.
- melted coconut oil - 1 c.
- coconut shred - 1 c.
- whisked egg - 1

Procedure:

1. Add all the above ingredients into your bowl and mix until smooth.
2. Set the mixture in your baking tray, gently flatten and bake at a heat intensity of 380 F for 25 minutes. Slice the bars and enjoy cold.

Nutrition per serving:

579 calories, 3.7g protein, 53.7g carbs, 41.9g fat, 2g fiber, 27g cholesterol, 17mg sodium, 275g potassium

16.14 Cocoa Squares

Serves: 4 | Preparation Time: 10 minutes | Cooking Time: 20 minutes

Ingredients:

- chopped peaches - 3
- baking soda - ½ tsp.
- coconut flour - 1 c.
- melted coconut oil - 4 tbsps.
- cocoa powder - 2 tbsps.

Procedure:

1. Blend the peaches with all remaining ingredients to obtain a smooth mixture.
2. Using a lined square pan, pour in the mixture, spread well before baking in your oven for 20 minutes at 375 F.
3. When the dessert is cool, cut it into squares.

Nutrition per serving:

221 calories, 3.1g protein, 17.2g carbs, 17.8g fat, 3.4g fiber, 0g cholesterol, 162mg sodium, 282g potassium

17 SMOOTHIES RECIPES

17.1 Blueberry-Vanilla Yogurt Smoothie

Serves: 2 | Preparation Time: 5 minutes | Cooking Tim: 0 minutes

Ingredients:

- blueberries (frozen) - 1½ c.
- nonfat vanilla Greek yogurt - 1 c.
- nonfat or low-fat milk - 1 c.
- frozen and peeled banana, sliced - 1
- ice - 1 c.

Procedure:

1. Using a mixer, add in all ingredients. Blend well until you have a creamy and smooth consistency.
2. Enjoy immediately.

Nutrition per serving:

Calories: 228, Fat: 1g, Sodium: 63mg, Potassium: 470mg, Carbs: 45g, Fiber: 5g, Sugars: 34g, Protein: 12g

17.2 Peaches And Greens Smoothie

Serves : 2 | Preparation Time: 5 minutes | Cooking Time: 0

Ingredients:

- fresh spinach - 2 c.
- frozen peaches (or fresh, pitted) - 1 c.
- ice - 1 c.
- low-fat or nonfat milk - ½ c.
- plain nonfat or low-fat Greek yogurt - ½ c.
- vanilla extract - ½ tsp.
- Optional: no-calorie sweetener of choice

Procedure:

1. Add all of the components to a mixer and process until smooth.
2. Enjoy immediately.

Nutrition per serving:

Calories: 191; Total Fat: 0g; Saturated Fat: 0g; Cholesterol: 7mg; Sodium: 157mg; Potassium: 984mg; Total Carbs: 30g; Fiber: 3g; Sugars: 23g; Protein: 18g

17.3 Banana Smoothie

Serves: 1 | Preparation Time: 10 minutes | Cooking Time: 5 minutes

Ingredients:

- frozen banana - 1
- 1% low-fat milk - ½ c.
- Honey - 1 tbsp.

- vanilla yogurt, fat-free - 1 (6 oz.) carton
- crushed ice - ½ c.

Procedure:

1. Add all the above ingredients into your blender.
2. Pulse it until smooth and creamy on high setting.
3. Set in a glass to serve.

Nutrition per serving:

Calories 82, Carbs: 3.1 g, Protein: 4 g, Fat: 0.2 g, Saturated fat: 0g, Cholesterol: 0 mg, Sodium: 11 mg, Fiber: 2.4 g, Sugar: 4.3 g, Calcium: 111 mg,| Potassium: 659mg

17.4 Chocolate Berry Smoothie

Serves: 1 | Preparation Time: 10 minutes| Cooking Time: 5 minutes

Ingredients:

- cold water - 1 ½c.
- Frozen blueberries - ¼ c.
- avocado - ½
- Cashews - 2 tbsps.
- Organic cocoa powder - 2 tbsps.
- Vanilla extract - ½ tsp.

Procedure:

1. Add all the above ingredients into your blender.
2. Pulse on high setting until the mixture becomes smooth and creamy.
3. Pour in a glass and enjoy it.

Nutrition per serving:

Calories 251, Total Fat 17.1 g, Fiber 7.8 g , Protein 6.5 g, Sugar 8.1 g, Sodium 56 mg , Potassium: 1412mg

17.5 Tropical Turmeric Smoothie

Serves: 1 | Preparation Time: 10 minutes | Cooking Time: 5 minutes

Ingredients:

- turmeric - ½ tsp.
- Almond milk - 1 c.
- ginger - ½ tsp.
- banana - 1
- Olive oil - 1 tbsp.
- frozen mango - ½ c.
- cinnamon - ½ tsp.

Procedure:

1. Using your blender, mix in the above ingredients.
2. Pulse it using high speed setting until the mixture becomes smooth and creamy.
3. Set in a glass and serve.

Nutrition per serving:

Calories 143, Total Fat 4.5 g, Fiber 3.4 g, Protein 3.3 g, Sugar 11 g, Sodium 21 mg, Potassium: 962mg

17.6 Carrot Juice Smoothie

Serves: 1| Preparation Time: 10 minutes | Cooking Time: 5 minutes

Ingredients:

- almond milk (unsweetened) - 1 c.
- ripe banana - 1
- cinnamon - ½ tsp.
- fresh ginger - ½ tbsp.
- carrot juice - ½ c.
- frozen pineapple - 1 c.
- Ground turmeric - ¼ tsp.
- Lime juice - 1 tbsp.

Procedure:

1. Using your blender, add in and mix the above ingredients.
2. Pulse using high speed until the mixture becomes smooth and creamy.
3. Serve in a glass.

Nutrition per serving:

Calories: 143, Fat: 2.4g, Carbs: 31g, Sugar: 17.4g, Sodium: 113mg, Fiber: 4g, Protein: 2.3g, Potassium: 697mg

17.7 Mixed Berries Smoothie

Serves: 2 | Preparation Time: 4 minutes | Cooking Time: 0 minutes

Ingredients:

- frozen blueberries - ¼ c.
- frozen blackberries - ¼ c.
- almond milk (unsweetened) - 1 c.
- vanilla bean extract - 1 tsp.
- flaxseeds - 3 tsps.
- chilled Greek yogurt - 1 scoop
- Stevia as needed

Procedure:

1. Mix everything in a blender and emulsify.
2. Pulse the mixture four time until you have your desired thickness.
3. Serve in a glass.

Nutrition per serving:

Calories: 221, Fat: 9g, Protein: 21g, Carbs: 10g, Sodium: 78 mg

17.8 Satisfying Berry and Almond Smoothie

Serves: 4 | Preparation Time: 10 minutes | Cooking Time: 0 minutes

Ingredients:

- whole banana - 1
- blueberries (frozen) - 1 c.
- almond butter - 1 tbsp.
- almond milk - ½ c.
- Water, enough as required

Procedure:

1. Add the listed ingredients to your blender and blend well until you have a smoothie-like texture.
2. Chill and serve.
3. Enjoy!

Nutrition per serving:

Calories: 321, Fat: 11g, Carbs: 55g, Protein: 5g, Sodium: 46 mg

17.9 Refreshing Mango and Pear Smoothie

Serves: 1 | Preparation Time: 10 minutes | Cooking Time: 0 minutes

Ingredients:

- Chopped ripe mango, cored - 1
- mango, peeled, pitted and chopped - ½
- chopped kale - 1 c.
- plain Greek yogurt - ½ c.
- ice cubes - 2

Procedure:

1. Add pear, mango, yogurt, kale, and mango to a blender and puree.
2. Add ice and blend well to obtain a mixture with a smooth texture.
3. Enjoy!

Nutrition per serving:

Calories: 293, Fat: 8g, Carbs: 53g, Protein: 8g, Sodium: 36 mg

17.10 Blackberry and Apple Smoothie

Serves: 2 | Preparation Time: 5 minutes | Cooking Time: 20 minutes

Ingredients:

- frozen blackberries - 2 c.
- apple cider - ½ c.
- cubed apple, - 1
- non-fat lemon yogurt - 2/3 c.

Procedure:

1. In a blender, add the above ingredients. Thoroughly blend well to obtain a smooth consistency.
2. Chill before serving.

Nutrition per serving:

Calories: 200, Fat: 10g, Carbs: 14g, Protein 2g, Sodium: 42mg

17.11 Raspberry Green Smoothie

Serves: 1 | Preparation Time: 10 minutes |
Cooking Time: 10 minutes

Ingredients:

- Raspberries – 1 c.
- Water – 1 c.
- spinach - ¼ c.
- Chia seeds - 1 tbsp.
- Lemon juice - 2 tbsps.
- banana - 1
- Almond butter - 1 tbsp.

Procedure:

1. Using a blender, add in all ingredients. Pulse well to get a creamy and smooth consistency.
2. Set in a glass and enjoy.

Nutrition per serving:

Calories: 176, Fat: 2.1 g, Carbs: 6.7 g, Sugar: 11.5 g, Sodium: 45 mg, Fiber: 7.6 g, Protein: 3.4 g, Potassium: 534mg

17.12 Blueberry Smoothie

Serves: 2 | Preparation Time: 10 minutes |
Cooking Time: 5 minutes

Ingredients:

- spinach - 1 c.
- pineapple - 2 c.
- coconut water - 4 c.
- blueberries - 1 c.
- apple - 1
- watermelon - 2 c.

Procedure:

1. Using your blender, add in ingredients.
2. Pulse on high setting until you obtain a creamy and smooth consistency.
3. Set in a glass to enjoy.

Nutrition per serving:

Calories: 213, Fat: 4.3 g, Carbs: 10.4 g, Sugar: 17 g, Sodium: 48 mg, Fiber: 7.9 g, Protein: 5 g, Potassium: 1817mg

17.13 Avocado Smoothie

Serves: 1 | Preparation Time: 10 minutes |
Cooking Time: 5 minutes

Ingredients:

- Cacao powder - 2 tbsps.
- Avocado - ½
- frozen banana - ½
- Chia seeds - ½ tsp.
- Plain almond milk - ¼ c.
- Lime juice (optional) - 2 tbsps.

Procedure:

1. With the use of your blender, add the above ingredients. Process on high speed to get a creamy and smooth consistency.
2. Enjoy.

Nutrition per serving:

Calories: 234, Fat: 4.4 g, Carbs: 12.3 g, Sugar: 16.4 g, Sodium: 53 mg, Fiber: 8.4 g, Protein: 5.6 g, Potassium: 1618mg

17.14 Chocolate and Peanut Butter Smoothie

Serves: 4 | Preparation Time: 5 minutes |
Cooking Time: 0 minutes

Ingredients:

- unsweetened cocoa powder - 1 tbsp.
- peanut butter - 1 tbsp.
- banana - 1
- maca powder - 1 tsp.
- unsweetened soy milk - ½ c.
- rolled oats - ¼ c.
- flaxseeds - 1 tbsp.
- maple syrup - 1 tbsp.
- water - 1 c.
- Soy Milk – as needed

Procedure:

1. Add in the above ingredients to your blender, then process until creamy and smooth consistency is achieved. Add water or soy milk if necessary.

2. Serve.

Nutrition per serving:
Calories: 474, Fat: 16.0g, Carbs: 27.0g, Fiber: 18.0g, Protein: 13.0g, Sodium: 53mg, Potassium: 89mg.

17.15 Ultimate Fruit Smoothie

Serves: 1 | Preparation Time: 10 minutes | Cooking Time: 10 minutes

Ingredients:

- strawberries - 2
- 2% milk - ½ c.
- mango, cut into chunks - ½
- fresh peach sliced - ½
- orange juice - ½ c.
- pineapple - ¼ c.

Procedure:

1. Using a blender, mix in strawberries, milk, mango chunks, peach slices, orange juice and pineapple.
2. Blend well until smooth.
3. Add more milk if required.
4. Serve

Nutrition per serving:
225 calories, protein 5.8g, carbs 46.4g,fat 3.1g, cholesterol 9.8mg, sodium 35.9mg, Potassium: 1329mg

17.16 Oat Cocoa Smoothie

Serves: 1 | Preparation Time: 10 minutes | Cooking Time: 5 minutes

Ingredients:

- vanilla extract - 1 tsp.
- Skim milk - ¾ c.
- plain low-fat yogurt - ½ c.
- Ground flaxseed - 1 tbsp.
- banana - 1
- Unsweetened cocoa powder - 1 tbsp.
- Quick-cook oats - ¼ c.
- ground cinnamon - a dash

Procedure:

1. Place all ingredients in your blender. Process well to obtain a smooth consistency. Add more milk if required.
2. Enjoy.

Nutrition per serving:
350 calories, 19 g protein, 5 g fat, 1 g saturated fat, 60 g carbs, 7 g fiber, 6 mg cholesterol, 177 mg sodium, 1381mg potassium

17.17 Tropical Green Breakfast Smoothie

Serves: 2 | Preparation Time: 10 minutes | Cooking Time: 5 minutes

Ingredients:

- banana cut in chunks - 1
- baby spinach - 1 c.
- plain Greek yogurt - 1/4 c.
- Pineapple chunks - 1 c.
- Pineapple juice or water - ¼ c.
- oats - 1/3 c.
- mango cut in chunks1

Procedure:

1. Place all ingredients in your blender. Process well to obtain a smooth consistency.
2. Enjoy.

Nutrition per serving:
265 calories, protein 6 g, carbs 32.3 g, fat 3.4 g, cholesterol 7.5 mg, sodium 21.4 mg, potassium: 532mg

17.18 Green Apple Smoothie

Serves: 2 | Preparation Time: 10 minutes | Cooking Time: 5 minutes

Ingredients:

- Apple cider - 1 c.
- banana - 1
- Kale, stems removed - 2 c.
- cinnamon – a pinch

- Green apple cut into chunks - 1 c.
- Water or ice - 1 c.

Procedure:

1. Place all ingredients in your blender. Process well to obtain a smooth consistency.
2. Enjoy.

Nutrition per serving:

Calories 233, Total Fat 0.5g, Sodium 31.7mg, Total Carbs 56.4g, Dietary Fiber 3.6g, sugars 30.8g, Protein 2g, Potassium: 479mg

18 SNACKS RECIPES

18.1 Corn and Cayenne Pepper Spread

Serves: 4 | Preparation Time: 30 minutes | Cooking Time: 0 minutes

Ingredients:

- cayenne pepper - ½ tsp.
- boiled corn - 2 c.
- non-fat cream cheese - 1 c.

Procedure:

1. In the bowl, put all ingredients from the list above.
2. Carefully mix the spread.

Nutrition per serving:

215 calories, 4g protein, 18.4g carbs, 16.2g fat, 3.8g fiber, 0mg cholesterol, 22mg sodium, 397mg potassium

18.2 Black Beans Bars

Serves: 12 | Preparation Time: 2 hours | Cooking Time: 0 minutes

Ingredients:

- no-salt-added canned and drained black beans - 1 c.
- chia seeds - ½ c.
- coconut cream - 1 tbsp.

Procedure:

1. 1.Blend the black beans until smooth.
2. After this, mix them with chia seeds and coconut cream.
3. Make the bars from the mixture and store them in the fridge.

Nutrition per serving:

Calories 600, 6.4g protein, 16.9g carbs, 8g fat, 6.5g fiber, 1mg cholesterol, 19mg sodium, 328mg potassium

18.3 Pepper and Chickpeas Hummus

Serves: 4 | Preparation Time: 10 minutes | Cooking Time: 0 minutes

Ingredients:

- no-salt-added canned chickpeas, drained and rinsed - 14 oz.
- sesame paste - 1 tbsp.
- roasted chopped red peppers - 2
- Juice of ½ lemon
- chopped walnuts - 4

Procedure:

1. In your blender, combine the chickpeas with the sesame paste, red peppers, lemon juice and walnuts, pulse properly, divide in serving bowls. Enjoy your snack.

2. Enjoy!

Nutrition per serving:
Calories 231, fat 12, fiber 6, carbs 15, protein 14, sodium 300mg, potassium 714mg

18.4 Lemony Chickpeas Dip

Serves: 4 | Preparation Time: 10 minutes | Cooking Time: 0 minutes

Ingredients:

- no-salt-added canned chickpeas, drained, rinsed - 14 oz.
- grated zest of 1 lemon
- Juice of 1 lemon
- olive oil - 1 tbsp.
- pine nuts - 4 tbsps.
- chopped coriander - ½ c.

Procedure:

1. Using a blender, pulse lemon juice, oil, lemon zest, coriander and chickpeas.
2. Set in serving bowls and top with sprinkles of pine nuts before enjoying.

Nutrition per serving:
Calories 200, fat 12g, fiber 4g, carbs 9g, protein 7g, sodium 212mg, potassium 544mg

18.5 Red Pepper Muffins with Mozzarella

Serves: 12 | Preparation Time: 10 minutes | Cooking Time: 30 minutes

Ingredients:

- flour (whole wheat) - 1 ¾ c.
- coconut sugar - 2 tbsps.
- baking powder - 2 tsps.
- black pepper - A pinch
- egg - 1
- almond milk - ¾ c.
- roasted and chopped red pepper - 2/3 c.
- low-fat shredded mozzarella - ½ c.

Procedure:

1. Using a bowl, combine coconut sugar, flour, baking powder, black pepper, egg, milk, red pepper and mozzarella, stir well, divide into a lined muffin tray, place in your oven. Set to bake for 30 minutes at a heat intensity of 400°F.
2. Enjoy!

Nutrition per serving:
Calories 149, fat 4, fiber 2, carbs 14, protein 5 sodium 64mg, potassium 474mg

18.6 Nuts And Seeds Mix

Serves: 6 | Preparation Time: 10 minutes | Cooking Time: 0 minutes

Ingredients:

- pecans - 1 c.
- hazelnuts - 1 c.
- almonds - 1 c.
- shredded coconut - ¼ c.
- walnuts - 1 c.
- dried papaya pieces - ½ c.
- dates, dried, pitted and chopped - ½ c.
- sunflower seeds - ½ c.
- pumpkin seeds - ½ c.
- raisins - 1 c.

Procedure:

1. Using a bowl, mix the coconut, pecans, hazelnuts, almonds, walnuts, papaya, dates, sunflower seeds, pumpkin seeds and raisins, toss and enjoy as a snack.
2. Enjoy!

Nutrition per serving:
Calories 188, fat 4, fiber 6, carbs 8, protein 6, sodium 39mg, potassium 575mg

18.7 Tortilla Chips with Chili

Serves: 6 | Preparation Time: 10 minutes | Cooking Time: 20 minutes

Ingredients:

- whole wheat tortillas, each cut into 6 wedges - 12

- olive oil - 2 tbsps.
- chili powder - 1 tbsp.
- cayenne pepper - A pinch

Procedure:

1. Line your baking sheet using an aluminum foil. Spread over the tortillas, add cayenne, oil, and chili powder. Toss well and set in your oven to ensure you bake for 20 minutes at 350 degrees F.
2. Enjoy as a dish.

Nutrition per serving:

Calories 199, fat 3, fiber 4, carbs 12, protein 5, sodium 266mg, potassium 549mg

18.8 Kale Chips

Serves: 8 | Preparation Time: 10 minutes | Cooking Time: 15 minutes

Ingredients:

- kale leaves - 1 bunch
- olive oil - 1 tbsp.
- smoked paprika - 1 tsp.
- black pepper - A pinch

Procedure:

1. On a baking sheet, spread kale leaves. Add oil, paprika, and black pepper. Toss well before setting in your oven to bake for 15 minutes at 350 degrees F.
2. Set into bowls and enjoy your snack.

Nutrition per serving:

Calories 177, fat 2, fiber 4, carbs 13, protein 6, sodium 15mg, potassium 436mg

18.9 Hearty Buttery Walnuts

Serves: 4 | Preparation Time: 10 minutes | Cooking Time: 0 minutes

Ingredients:

- walnut halves - 4
- almond butter - ½ tbsp.

Procedure:

1. Spread butter over two walnut halves. Top with other halves.
2. Enjoy!

Nutrition per serving:

Calories: 90, Fat: 10g, Carbs: 0g, Protein: 1g, Sodium: 1 mg, Potassium: 440mg

18.10 Spiced Walnuts

Serves: 4 | Preparation Time: 10 minutes | Cooking Time: 15 minutes

Ingredients:

- walnuts - 2 c.
- red vinegar - 3 tbsps.
- olive oil - A drizzle
- cayenne pepper - A pinch

Procedure:

1. Using a mixing bowl, mix walnuts, red vinegar, olive oil, and cayenne pepper.
2. Set the walnuts to a baking tray. Allow to bake for about 15 minutes at 365°F. Stir occasionally to ensure no burning.

Nutrition per serving:

388 calories, 15g protein, 6.2g carbs, 36.9g fat, 4.3g fiber, 0mg cholesterol, 2mg sodium, 331mg potassium

18.11 Radish Chips

Serves: 4 | Preparation Time: 10 minutes | Cooking Time: 20 minutes

Ingredients:

- thinly sliced radishes - 1 pound
- olive oil - 2 tbsps.

Procedure:

1. Mix radish slices with olive oil and transfer them to a baking tray.
2. You then bake the chips for approx. 20 minutes at 365F. Toss the radish from time to time to avoid burning.

Nutrition per serving:

78 calories, 0.8g protein, 3.9g carbs, 7.1g fat, 1.8g fiber, 0mg cholesterol, 44mg sodium, 266mg potassium

18.12 Aromatic Avocado Fries

Serves: 4 | Preparation Time: 5 minutes | Cooking Time: 10 minutes

Ingredients:

- peeled and pitted avocados cut into wedges - 2
- avocado oil - 1 tbsp.
- ground cardamom - 1 tsp.

Procedure:

1. Sprinkle the avocado wedges with avocado oil and cardamom.
2. After this, line a baking paper to a baking tray and arrange avocado wedges inside your tray one by one.
3. Bake the fried for 10 minutes at 375F. Flip to cook the other side after 5 minutes.

Nutrition per serving:

236 calories, 1.9g protein, 6.3g carbs, 8.6g fat, 23.1g fiber, 0mg cholesterol, 6mg sodium, 488mg potassium

18.13 Carrot Chips

Serves: 4 | Preparation Time: 10 minutes | Cooking Time: 30 minutes

Ingredients:

- thinly sliced carrots - 4
- avocado oil - 2 tbsps.
- chili flakes - 1 tsp.
- turmeric powder - ½ tsp.

Procedure:

1. Mix carrot with avocado oil, chili flakes, and turmeric powder.
2. Set the chips on your lined baking sheet. You should bake at 400F for approximately 25 minutes, and flip after 10 minutes to cook the other side.

Nutrition per serving:

88 calories, 0.6g protein, 6.5g carbs, 7.1g fat, 1.8g fiber, 0mg cholesterol, 42mg sodium, 214mg potassium

18.14 Minty Tapenade

Serves: 4 | Preparation Time: 4 minutes | Cooking Time: 0 minutes

Ingredients:

- pitted black olives, chopped - 2 c.
- chopped mint - 1 c.
- avocado oil - 2 tbsps.
- coconut cream - ½ c.

Procedure:

1. Using your blender, add in the above ingredients and carefully blend.

Nutrition per serving:

166 calories, 2.1g protein, 8.2g carbs, 15.4g fat, 4.7g fiber, 0mg cholesterol, 598mg sodium, 211mg potassium

18.15 Nutritious Snack Bowls

Serves: 4 | Preparation Time: 10 minutes | Cooking Time: 20 minutes

Ingredients:

- sunflower seeds - 1 c.
- chia seeds - 1 c.
- water - 1 c.
- cored apples cut into wedges - 2
- ground cardamom - ¼ tsp.

Procedure:

1. Mix water, chia seeds and ground nutmeg and stir gently.
2. Leave the mixture for 20 minutes.
3. After this, mix cooked chia seeds with sunflower seeds, and apples, and gently mix.

Nutrition per serving:

291 calories, 6.3g protein, 27.1g carbs, 19.8g fat, 11.2g fiber, 0mg cholesterol, 6mg sodium, 297mg potassium

18.16 Potato Chips

Serves: 4 | Preparation Time: 10 minutes | Cooking Time: 20 minutes

Ingredients:

- peeled gold potatoes, thinly sliced - 4
- garlic powder - ¼ tsp.
- olive oil - 2 tbsps.
- sweet paprika - 1 tsp.

Procedure:

1. Line a baking paper to a baking sheet. Spread over with sliced potato, add the other ingredients. Gently mix and flatten.
2. Bake the chips for 20 minutes at 390F. Flip after 10 minutes to cook the other side.

Nutrition per serving:

118 calories, 1.3g protein, 13.4g carbs, 7.4g fat, 2.9g fiber, 0mg cholesterol, 19mg sodium, 361mg potassium

18.17 Hot Walnuts

Serves: 8 | Preparation Time: 5 minutes | Cooking Time: 15 minutes

Ingredients:

- smoked paprika - ½ tsp.
- chili powder - ½ tsp.
- garlic powder - ½ tsp.
- avocado oil - 1 tbsp.
- walnuts - 14 oz.

Procedure:

1. Mix walnuts with smoked paprika, and all other ingredients.
2. After this, place the walnuts in your baking tray before flattening well.
3. Allow to bake at 355°F for 15 minutes. Stir them from time to time.

Nutrition per serving:

310 calories, 12g protein, 5.3g carbs, 29.5g fat, 3.6g fiber, 0mg cholesterol, 3mg sodium, 273mg potassium

18.18 Cranberry Crackers

Serves: 4 | Preparation Time: 3 hours 5 minutes | Cooking Time: 0 minutes

Ingredients:

- vanilla extract - ¼ tsp.
- rolled oats - 2 tbsps.
- shredded coconut - 2 tbsps.
- cranberries - 1 c.

Procedure:

1. Put the cranberries in the blender.
2. Add rolled oats, vanilla extract, and shredded coconut.
3. Blend the mixture well.
4. Pour into the baking dish. Bake for 25 minutes or until a skewer inserted in the center comes out clean.
5. Cool on a rack before wrapping in cling film and freezing for at least 2 hours and up to 3 months.
6. Allow the loaf to defrost slightly for 15 minutes so that the exterior is not rock hard frozen.
7. Preheat your oven to 250°F. Put one shelf in the center and another beneath it.
8. Slice the biscuits thinly with a serrated bread knife and place them on two big baking pans; you can cram them in since they won't expand or stick.
9. Bake for 50 minutes, or until light golden, switching pans halfway.
10. Allow the biscuits to cool on the tray; they will stiffen and shatter when broken.

Nutrition per serving:

66 calories, 0.8g protein, 5.4g carbs, 4.4g fat, 1.8g fiber, 0mg cholesterol, 3mg sodium, 102mg potassium

19 SAUCES AND DRESSING RECIPES

19.1 Salsa Verde

Serves: 5 | Preparation Time: 10 minutes | Cooking Time: 5 minutes

Ingredients:

- fresh finely chopped cilantro - 4 tbsps.
- fresh finely chopped parsley - 1/4 c.
- grated garlic cloves - 2
- lemon juice - 2 tsps.
- olive oil - 3/4 c.
- capers - 2 tbsps.
- black pepper - 1/2 tsp.

Procedure:

1. Add the above ingredients to a bowl. It can be mixed by hand or with an immersion blender. Mix until desired consistency is achieved.
2. You can serve over burgers, sandwiches, salads and more. One is allowed to refrigerate for a maximum of 5 days or for longer once you place in a freezer.

Nutrition per serving:

Total Fat: 25.3g, Cholesterol: 0mg, Sodium: 475mg, Protein: 0.2g, Potassium 151mg.

19.2 Caramel Sauce

Serves: 8 | Preparation Time: 10 minutes | Cooking Time: 35 minutes

Ingredients:

- raw cashews - 1/2 c.
- melted coconut cream - 1/2 c.
- liquid stevia - 10 drops
- vegan butter - 2 tbsps.
- vanilla extract - 3 tsps.

Procedure:

1. Preheat your oven to attain 325 degrees F.
2. Place nuts on a greased baking tray and toast until crunchy and lightly golden for 20 minutes.
3. Let the nuts cool slightly and add them to your food processor. Blend to obtain a slightly lumpy consistency.
4. Mix in the rest of your ingredients and blend well until you achieve a smooth and creamy consistency. Do not over blend or the coconut cream will become separated from the rest of the ingredients
5. If not using immediately, refrigerate in an airtight container. To reheat the caramel to make it more flowable, add to a saucepan and gently warm on low heat. It can be served with your favorite keto vegan treats, such as ice cream.

Nutrition per serving:

Total Fat: 9.8g, Cholesterol: 0mg, Sodium: 29mg, Total carbs: 4.6g, Sodium: 103mg, Potassium: 161mg.

19.3 Authentic Greek Tzatziki Sauce

Serves: makes 1½ cups | Preparation Time: 10 minutes | Cooking Time: 0

Ingredients:

- plain Greek yogurt - 1 c.
- Persian cucumbers - 2
- extra-virgin olive oil - 1 tbsp.
- chopped fresh dill - 2 tbsps.
- freshly chopped mint - 2 tbsps.
- minced garlic clove - 1

- lemon juice - 2 tbsps.
- kosher salt - ½ tsp.

Procedure:

1. Using a box grater to grate the cucumbers.
2. In a medium bowl, mix the lemon juice, grated cucumbers, yogurt, dill, mint, olive oil, garlic, and salt.

Nutrition per serving:

Calories: 45, Total fat: 0g, Saturated fat: 0g, Cholesterol: 0mg, Sodium: 105mg, Potassium: 125mg, Total Carbs: 3g, Fiber: 0g, Sugars: 2g, Protein: 3g, Magnesium: 10mg, Calcium: 45mg

19.4 Beef Taco Filling

Serves: 4 | Preparation Time: 10 minutes | Cooking Time: 20 minutes

Ingredients:

- ground extra lean sirloin, 95% lean - 1 pound (454 g)
- medium taco sauce - ½ bottle
- diced green peppers (fresh or frozen) - 1 c.
- diced onions (fresh or frozen) - 1 c.

Procedure:

1. Using a nonstick skillet, add in beef and heat over a medium-high source of heat. Cook for about 3 minutes before reducing heat to medium intensity. Put in onions and peppers. Proceed to cook for 5 or more minutes, or until thoroughly browned.
2. Add taco sauce, reduce your heat intensity and let simmer for 10 minutes.

Nutrition per serving:

Calories: 140, Protein: 17 g, Carbs: 7 g, Fat: 4 g, Cholesterol: 48 mg, Fiber: 1 g, Sodium: 164 mg, Potassium: 344 mg

19.5 Creamy Avocado Alfredo Sauce

Serves: 4 | Preparation Time: 10 minutes | Cooking Time: 2 minutes

Ingredient:

- peeled and pitted ripe avocado - 1
- olive oil - 1 tbsp.
- dried basil - 1 tbsp.
- clove garlic - 1
- lemon juice - 1 tbsp.
- salt - ⅛ tsp.

Procedure:

1. Add in above ingredients in your food processor. Blend well to get a smooth and creamy sauce.
2. Pour over vegetable noodles and enjoy.

Nutrition per serving:

Calories: 104, Total Fat: 10g, Saturated Fat: 1g, Cholesterol: 0mg, Sodium: 43mg, Potassium: 229mg, Total Carbs: 4g, Fiber: 3g, Sugars: 0g, Protein: 1g

19.6 Vegan Ranch Dressing

Serves: 3 | Preparation Time: 5 minutes | Cooking Time: 10 minutes

Ingredients:

- vegan mayo - 1 c.
- coconut milk - 1 1/2 c.
- scallions - 2
- peeled garlic cloves - 2
- fresh dill - 1 c.
- garlic powder - 1 tsp.
- pepper - ¼ tsp.

Procedure:

1. Add scallion, fresh dill and garlic cloves to your food processor. Pulse well to ensure finely chopped.
2. Mix in the remaining ingredients and continue blending to obtain a smooth and creamy consistency. Makes a great

creamy salad dressing. Store in the refrigerator.

Nutrition per serving:

Total Fat: 11.9g, Cholesterol: 0mg, Sodium: 50mg, Fiber: 4g, Potassium 187mg.

19.7 Easy Quick Tangy Barbecue Sauce

Serves: 1½ cups | Preparation Time: 6 minutes | Cooking Time: 1 min

Ingredients:

- no-salt tomato paste - 1 (8 oz.) can
- apple cider vinegar - 1½ tbsps.
- Dijon mustard - 2 tbsps.
- onion powder - 1 tsp.
- molasses - 2 tsps.
- soy sauce (low-sodium) - 1 tbsp.
- garlic powder - 1 tsp.

Procedure:

1. Add the garlic powder, tomato paste, soy sauce, vinegar, Dijon mustard, molasses, and onion powder in a medium bowl and mix well.
2. Pour it in an airtight container and refrigerate for a maximum week.

Nutrition per serving:

Calories: 32, Total Fat: 0g, Saturated Fat: 0g, Protein: 2g, Total Carbs: 7g, Fiber: 1g, Sugars: 4g, Cholesterol: 0mg, Sodium: 240mg, Potassium: 340mg

19.8 Fresh Tomato Basil Sauce

Serves: 6 | Preparation Time: 5 minutes | Cooking Time: 10 minutes

Ingredients:

- olive oil - 2 tbsps.
- no-salt, crushed, or chopped tomatoes - 4 (15 oz.) cans
- finely chopped garlic cloves - 3
- dried basil - 1 tbsp.
- Salt - ¼ tsp.
- Freshly ground black pepper - ¼ tsp.

Procedure:

1. Using a large saucepan, add in oil and heat. Mix in garlic and sauté until browned lightly for about 1 minute, ensure it doesn't burn. Mix in the basil and tomatoes. Add in pepper and salt for seasoning. Cook for 10 minutes over medium heat while uncovered.
2. Serve over pasta, grains, beans, or vegetables.

Nutrition per serving:

Calories: 103, Total Fat: 5g, Saturated Fat: 1g, Cholesterol: 0mg, Sodium: 32mg, Potassium: 735mg, Total Carbs: 15g, Fiber: 3g, Sugars: 0g, Protein: 3g

19.9 Greek Yogurt Dressing with Basil

Serves: 2 cups | Preparation Time: 5 minutes | Cooking Time: 10 minutes

Ingredients:

- chopped fresh basil - ¼ c.
- chopped sage - ¼ c.
- nonfat (0%) plain Greek yogurt - 1 c. (240mL)
- chopped fresh coriander - ½ c.
- minced onion - 1
- minced cloves garlic - 2
- extra-virgin olive oil - 2 tbsps.
- juice from 1 orange - 2 tbsps.
- maple syrup - ½ tsp.
- salt - ⅛ tsp.
- ground black pepper - ⅛ tsp.

Procedure:

1. Mix together the basil, coriander, and sage in your food processor and puree a few times until they have been ground up slightly. Scrape down the sides.
2. Pour in the onion, garlic, Greek yogurt, olive oil, salt, orange juice, ¼ cup water, maple syrup, and pepper and puree until

smooth and ingredients have been fully incorporated.

3. Enjoy or refrigerate for a maximum of 1 week.

Nutrition per serving:
Calories: 26, Total fat: 2 g, Saturated fat: <1 g, Total carbs: 1 g, Protein: 2 g, Cholesterol: <1 mg, Sodium: 27 mg, Potassium: 53 mg, Fiber: <1 g, Sugars: 1 g

19.10 Meaty Spaghetti Sauce

Serves: 6 | Preparation Time: 15 minutes | Cooking Time: 30 minutes

Ingredients:

- ground 95% lean beef, extra-lean - 1 pound
- no salt added tomato sauce - 1 (15 oz.) can
- no salt added diced tomatoes - 1 (14½ oz.) can
- garlic cloves, minced or squeezed through garlic press - 2
- chopped onions (fresh or frozen) - ½ c.
- Italian seasoning - 1 tsp.
- dried basil - 1 tsp.

Procedure:

1. In a nonstick skillet set over a medium high source of heat, mix in ground beef and cook for 3 minutes. Turn down heat to medium intensity. Add in garlic and onions. Proceed with the cooking for 5 additional minutes, or until browned well.
2. Add diced tomatoes and tomato sauce and simmer 10 - 15 minutes. Sprinkle seasonings in last few minutes of cooking.

Nutrition per serving:
Calories: 184, Protein: 23 g, Carbs: 8 g, Fat: 7 g, Cholesterol: 67 mg, Fiber: 2 g, Sodium: 105 mg, Potassium: 733 mg

19.11 Creamy Avocado Cilantro Lime Dressing

Serves: 2 | Preparation Time: 5 minutes | Cooking Time: 0 minutes

Ingredients:

- Diced avocado - 1
- water - ½ c.
- cilantro leaves - ¼ c.
- fresh lime or lemon juice (about 2 limes or lemons) - ¼ c.
- ground cumin - ½ tsp.

Procedure:

1. Using a blender, add all the ingredients (high-speed blenders work best for this), and pulse until well combined. Add more seasoning if need be. It is best served within 1 day.

Nutrition per serving:
Calories: 94, Fat: 7.4g, Carbs: 5.7g, Protein: 1.1g, Fiber: 3.5g, Sodium: 67mg, Potassium 176mg.

19.12 Maple Dijon Dressing

Serves: 1 | Preparation Time: 5 minutes | Cooking Time: 0 minutes

Ingredients:

- apple cider vinegar - ¼ c.
- Dijon mustard - 2 tsps.
- maple syrup - 2 tbsps.
- low-sodium vegetable broth - 2 tbsps.
- black pepper - ¼ tsp.

Procedure:

1. Using a resealable container, mix the apple cider vinegar, maple syrup, vegetable broth, Dijon mustard, and black pepper until well incorporated.
2. The dressing can be refrigerated for a maximum of 5 days.

Nutrition per serving:

Calories: 82, Fat: 0.3g, Carbs: 19.3g, Protein: 0.6g, Fiber: 0.7g, Sodium: 53mg, Potassium: 67mg.

19.13 Tahini Lemon Dressing

Serves: makes ½ cup | Preparation Time: 5 minutes | Cooking Time: 0

Ingredients:

- pure maple syrup - ¼ tsp.
- tahini - ¼ c.
- warm water - 3 tbsps.
- cumin (ground) - ¼ tsp.
- kosher salt - ¼ tsp.
- lemon juice - 3 tbsps.
- cayenne pepper - ⅛ tsp.

Procedure:

1. Using a bowl, add in water, cumin, salt, cayenne pepper, tahini, lemon juice, and maple syrup. Mix well to make the mixture smooth.
2. Place in the refrigerator until ready to serve.
3. Store any leftovers in an airtight container and place in your refrigerator for a maximum of 5 days.

Nutrition per serving:

Calories: 91, Total fat: 7.3g, Saturated fat: 1.1g, Cholesterol: 0mg, Sodium: 80mg, Potassium: 77mg, Total Carbs: 5g, Fiber: 1g, Sugars: 1g, Protein: 3g, Magnesium: 15mg, Calcium: 66mg

19.14 Tahini Yogurt Dressing

Serves: makes 1 cup | Preparation Time: 5 minutes | Cooking Time: 0

Ingredients:

- plain Greek yogurt - ½ c.
- tahini - ⅓ c.
- freshly squeezed orange juice - ¼ c.
- kosher salt - ½ tsp.

Procedure:

1. Using a mixing bowl, add in tahini, Greek yogurt, orange juice and salt. Mix well until the tahini becomes smooth. Add more juice if needed to help smooth it out.
2. Refrigerate until when ready to serve.
3. Store any leftovers in an airtight container and place in the refrigerator for a maximum of 5 days.

Nutrition per serving:

Calories: 70, Total fat: 2.1g, Saturated fat: 1.1g, Cholesterol: 0mg, Sodium: 80mg, Potassium: 85mg, Total Carbs: 4g, Fiber: 1.1g, Sugars: 1g, Protein: 4.2g, Magnesium: 12mg, Calcium: 66mg

20 10 WEEKS MEAL PLAN

I prepared a meal plan for 10 weeks which is about 2 1/2 months. Repeating this meal plan 5-6 times throughout the year, starting from the first week after the tenth, you will have concluded your annual nutrition plan. To ensure the habit of this diet and the results, we recommend applying it for 3 years, consequently for a total of 1000 days.

Week 1

Day	Breakfast/Smoothie	Lunch	Dinner	Dessert/ Snack/ Side
Monday	Millet Cream	Cilantro Halibut	Black-Bean and Vegetable Burrito	Walnut Cake
Tuesday	Blueberry-Vanilla Yogurt Smoothie	Roasted Brussels Sprouts	Turkey with Spring Onions	Strawberries and Coconut Bowls
Wednesday	Refreshing Mango and Pear Smoothie	Pasta with Peas & Tomatoes	Pork with Cherry Tomatoes	Corn and Cayenne Pepper Spread
Thursday	Sausage Casserole	Parsnip and Turkey Bites	Ginger Sea Bass	Hot Walnuts
Friday	Bean Casserole	White Beans with Spinach and Pan-Roasted Tomatoes	Garam Masala Turkey	Coconut and Cinnamon Cream
Saturday	Tropical Green Breakfast Smoothie	Cod and Asparagus	Basil Turkey	Nuts And Seeds Mix
Sunday	Cheese Hash Browns	Spiced Meat with Endives	Veggies Stuffed Bell Peppers	Grapefruit Compote

Week 2

Day	Breakfast/Smoothie	Lunch	Dinner	Dessert/ Snack/ Side
Monday	Tropical Turmeric Smoothie	Roasted Kabocha with Wild Rice	Five-Spices Sole	Cocoa Squares
Tuesday	The Amazing Feta Hash	Veggie Pita Rolls	Cilantro Beef Meatballs	Radish Chips
Wednesday	Artichoke Eggs	Chicken with Tomatoes and Celery Stalk	Butternut-Squash Macaroni and Cheese	Soy Sauce Green Beans
Thursday	Banana Breakfast Smoothie	Shallot and Salmon Mix	Cheddar Turkey	Rice and Fruits Pudding
Friday	Apples and Raisins Bowls	Nutmeg Chicken with Tender Chickpeas	Vegetarian Black Bean Pasta	Black Beans Bars
Saturday	Raspberry Green Smoothie	Couscous with Beans & Vegetables	Greek Flatbread with Spinach, Tomatoes & Feta	Kale Chips
Sunday	Scallions and Sesame Seeds Omelet	Cilantro Beef Meatballs	Zucchini Black Bean Tacos	Coconut Shred Bars

Week 3

Day	Breakfast/Smoothie	Lunch	Dinner	Dessert/ Snack/ Side
Monday	Tomato and Spinach Eggs	Chicken with Tomatoes	Easy Beet and Goat Cheese Risotto	Nutritious Snack Bowls
Tuesday	Chocolate and Peanut Butter Smoothie	Limes and Shrimp Skewers	Spiced Meat with Endives	Cinnamon Plums
Wednesday	Dill Omelet	Meat and Zucchini Mix	Lentil Medley	Spiced Walnuts
Thursday	Carrot Juice Smoothie	Veggies Stuffed Bell Peppers	Chicken Bowl with Red Cabbage	Carrot Chips
Friday	Omelet with Peppers	Huevos Rancheros	Beef with Cauliflower Rice	Lime Cake
Saturday	Ultimate Fruit Smoothie	Curried Cauliflower with Chickpeas	Tender Salmon with Chives	Sour Cream Green Beans
Sunday	Sausage Casserole	Zucchini Black Bean Tacos	Spiced Meat with Endives	Pepper and Chickpeas Hummus

Week 4

Day	Breakfast/Smoothie	Lunch	Dinner	Dessert/ Snack/ Side
Monday	Peaches And Greens Smoothie	Minty Avocado Soup	Spinach Soufflés	Rhubarb and Pear Compote
Tuesday	Artichoke Eggs	Black-Bean and Vegetable Burrito	Garlic Turkey	Vanilla Apple Cake
Wednesday	Millet Cream	Warm Spiced Cabbage Bake	Baked Sweet Potatoes with Cumin	Minty Tapenade
Thursday	Blueberry Smoothie	Butternut-Squash Macaroni and Cheese	Roasted Kabocha with Wild Rice	Cumin Brussels Sprouts
Friday	Oat Cocoa Smoothie	Tuna and Pineapple Kebob	Chicken Sandwich	Baked Apples with Nuts
Saturday	Cheese Hash Browns	Mushroom and Eggplant Casserole	Garlic Pork	Hearty Buttery Walnuts
Sunday	Raspberry Green Smoothie	Zucchini with Corn	Parsley Shrimp	Lemony Chickpeas Dip

Week 5

Day	Breakfast/Smoothie	Lunch	Dinner	Dessert/ Snack/ Side
Monday	Strawberry Sandwich	Coconut Avocado Soup	Fennel and Salmon	Instant Pot Applesauce
Tuesday	Chocolate Berry Smoothie	Turkey and Zucchini Tortillas	Black-Eyed Peas and Greens Power Salad	Red Pepper Muffins with Mozzarella
Wednesday	The Amazing Feta Hash	Coconut Cod	Chicken with Tomatoes	Tortilla Chips with Chili
Thursday	Satisfying Berry and Almond Smoothie	Garam Masala Turkey	Roasted Brussels Sprouts	Hot Walnuts
Friday	Blackberry and Apple Smoothie	Cast Iron Roots and Grain	Curried Cauliflower with Chickpeas	Green Tea and Banana Sweetening Mix
Saturday	Tomato and Spinach Eggs	Lentil Medley	Baked Cod	Minty Tapenade
Sunday	Green Apple Smoothie	Basil Turkey	Rosemary Endives	Nutritious Snack Bowls

Week 6

Day	Breakfast/Smoothie	Lunch	Dinner	Dessert/ Snack/ Side
Monday	Mixed Berries Smoothie	Chunky Black-Bean Dip	Paprika Chicken	Nuts And Seeds Mix
Tuesday	Avocado Smoothie	Easy Chickpea Veggie Burgers	Chicken with Eggplants	Cranberry Crackers
Wednesday	Scallions and Sesame Seeds Omelet	Mushroom Barley Soup	Limes and Shrimps Skewers	Grapefruit Compote
Thursday	Blueberry-Vanilla Yogurt Smoothie	Vegetarian Black Bean Pasta	Hot Chicken Mix	Carrot Chips
Friday	Apples and Raisins Bowls	Cheddar Turkey	Healthy Vegetable Fried Rice	Pepper and Chickpeas Hummus
Saturday	Tropical Green Breakfast Smoothie	Ginger Sea Bass	Cilantro Beef Meatballs	Potato Chips
Sunday	Bean Casserole	Pork with Cherry Tomatoes	Red Beans and Rice	Cinnamon Plums

Week 7

Day	Breakfast/Smoothie	Lunch	Dinner	Dessert/ Snack/ Side
Monday	Dill Omelet	Acorn Squash & Coconut Creamed Greens Casserole	White Beans with Spinach and Pan-Roasted Tomatoes	Walnut Cake
Tuesday	Blackberry and Apple Smoothie	Chicken Bowl with Red Cabbage	Zucchini with Corn	Corn and Cayenne Pepper Spread
Wednesday	Omelet with Peppers	Paprika Chicken	Pasta with Peas & Tomatoes	Instant Pot Applesauce
Thursday	Oat Cocoa Smoothie	Baked Cod	Polenta Squares with Cheese & Pine Nuts	Peach And Carrots
Friday	Tropical Turmeric Smoothie	Eggplant Parmesan	Couscous with Beans & Vegetables	Cocoa Squares
Saturday	Refreshing Mango and Pear Smoothie	Spiced Meat with Endives	Cilantro Halibut	Tortilla Chips with Chili
Sunday	Scallions and Sesame Seeds Omelet	Baked Sweet Potatoes with Cumin	Thyme Pork Skillet	Coconut and Cinnamon Cream

Week 8

Day	Breakfast/Smoothie	Lunch	Dinner	Dessert/ Snack/ Side
Monday	Banana Breakfast Smoothie	Mustard and Garlic Chicken	Huevos Rancheros	Green Tea and Banana Sweetening Mix
Tuesday	Green Apple Smoothie	Fennel and Salmon	Warm Spiced Cabbage Bake	Aromatic Avocado Fries
Wednesday	Sausage Casserole	Celery, Cucumber and Zucchini Soup	Veggie Pita Rolls	Kale Chips
Thursday	Mixed Berries Smoothie	Turkey with Spring Onions	Easy Chickpea Veggie Burgers	Spiced Broccoli Florets
Friday	Artichoke Eggs	Easy Beet and Goat Cheese Risotto	Parsnip and Turkey Bites	Red Pepper Muffins with Mozzarella
Saturday	Blueberry Smoothie	Hot Chicken Mix	Coconut Cod	Radish Chips
Sunday	Cheese Hash Browns	Five-Spices Sole	Turkey and Zucchini Tortillas	Rice and Fruits Pudding

Week 9

Day	Breakfast/Smoothie	Lunch	Dinner	Dessert/ Snack/ Side
Monday	Chocolate Berry Smoothie	Garlic Pork	Tuna and Pineapple Kebob	Carrot Sticks with Onion and Sour Cream
Tuesday	Ultimate Fruit Smoothie	Spinach Soufflés	Cilantro Beef Meatballs	Baked Apples with Nuts
Wednesday	Dill Omelet	Parsley Shrimp	Cast Iron Roots and Grain	Coconut Shred Bars
Thursday	Avocado Smoothie	Chicken with Eggplants	Eggplant Parmesan	Lemony Chickpeas Dip
Friday	Omelet with Peppers	Red Beans and Rice	Nutmeg Chicken with Tender Chickpeas	Potato Chips
Saturday	Satisfying Berry and Almond Smoothie	Thyme Pork Skillet	Cod and Asparagus	Rhubarb and Pear Compote
Sunday	Millet Cream	Rosemary Endives	Chicken Sandwich	Hearty Buttery Walnuts

Week 10

Day	Breakfast/Smoothie	Lunch	Dinner	Dessert/ Snack/ Side
Monday	The Amazing Feta Hash	Tender Salmon with Chives	Acorn Squash & Coconut Creamed Greens Casserole	Vanilla Apple Cake
Tuesday	Peaches And Greens Smoothie	Polenta Squares with Cheese & Pine Nuts	Shallot and Salmon Mix	Cranberry Crackers
Wednesday	Chocolate and Peanut Butter Smoothie	Beef with Cauliflower Rice	Mushroom and Eggplant Casserole	Strawberries and Coconut Bowls
Thursday	Tomato and Spinach Eggs	Black-Eyed Peas and Greens Power Salad	Mustard and Garlic Chicken	Aromatic Avocado Fries
Friday	Strawberry Sandwich	Garlic Turkey	Chunky Black-Bean Dip	Spiced Walnuts
Saturday	Carrot Juice Smoothie	Healthy Vegetable Fried Rice	Meat and Zucchini Mix	Black Beans Bars
Sunday	Apples and Raisins Bowls	Greek Flatbread with Spinach, Tomatoes & Feta	Chicken with Tomatoes and Celery Stalk	Lime Cake

21 MEDITERRANEAN DIET COOKBOOK FOR BEGINNERS

22 INTRODUCTION

Before going forward, I would like to convey my heartiest gratitude to you for choosing and downloading my book amongst the hundreds of other books. I truly believe that you will find something of value within the information provided on these pages. The Mediterranean Diet is a dietary pattern widely considered healthy and beneficial for overall health. The diet is typically high in fruits, vegetables, and whole grains and low in saturated fat and cholesterol. It emphasizes eating mostly plant-based foods, with moderate amounts of meat and dairy. According to the Centers for Disease Control and Prevention (CDC), the Mediterranean Diet is associated with a lower risk of heart disease, stroke, chronic diseases such as obesity and type 2 diabetes, certain cancers, and premature death. The Mediterranean Diet is centered around consuming plenty of fruits, vegetables, whole grains, nuts, legumes, olive oil, fish, and seafood, moderate amounts of red wine (if consumed), and limited amounts of processed foods. These foods provide ample amounts of vitamins and minerals essential for good health. In addition to being rich in antioxidants and other nutrients, these foods are also low in calories and contain few unhealthy fats or sugars. The Mediterranean diet is beneficial because it incorporates many fruits, vegetables, and whole grains. These foods are sources of antioxidants, which protect cells from damage and can help to prevent chronic diseases. Additionally, the Mediterranean diet is low in fat and saturated, which has been linked to heart disease and other health problems. In addition to being healthy, the Mediterranean diet is also affordable. A study published in The Lancet found that people who followed a Mediterranean diet were more likely to be able to afford high-quality and nutritious food. This means the diet is accessible to more people than other dietary patterns. What further sets the Mediterranean diet apart from most other dietary regimes is that it doesn't come with a huge list of restrictions. Rather, it focuses on healthy eating and promotes physical and social activities to keep the heart and mind healthy for years to come. There is a reason why the people of the Mediterranean have such long life spans, and this book will let you know exactly why. Throughout the book, you will find a plethora of information covering the fundamentals of the diet, followed by a plethora of inspiring and amazing recipes to choose from. So, without any more delays, let's jump right in, shall we?

22.1 What is a Mediterranean Diet?

The Mediterranean diet is a healthy, balanced diet that is derived from the traditional diets of countries in the Mediterranean region. These countries have long histories of healthy living and include countries like Greece, Italy, Spain, and Cyprus. The Mediterranean diet has been shown to be effective in reducing the risk of heart disease, stroke, and other chronic diseases.This is a dietary pattern that is traditionally consumed in the regions of the Mediterranean Sea. The diet consists of fruits, vegetables, nuts, beans, and whole grains, with moderate amounts of meat and dairy products. It has been linked with a reduced risk of heart disease, stroke, and some types of cancer. There are many reasons why the Mediterranean diet is beneficial for your health. First, the antioxidants in fruits and vegetables help to protect your body against diseases. Second, the high intake of fiber and low intake of sugar in this diet helps you to maintain a healthy weight. Third, the variety of nutrients in the Mediterranean diet provides you with all the essential vitamins and minerals your body needs. Finally, adding more plants to your diet can help you feel full longer and reduce your appetite overall. So if you're looking for a healthier way to eat that is also environmentally friendly and delicious.

22.2 The History of the Mediterranean Diet

In the case of the Mediterranean diet, the diet is even more talked about and has long been a source of pride for the people living around the Mediterranean. For as long as history can remember, this area has played host to many enduring tails that have helped define human civilizations. From the rise of the Greeks to the conquest by the Romans, the rise of the Persians traveling westward to annex the Greeks, the great Crusades in the 10th century, and the subsequent dominance of the European nations in colonizing the rest of the New World, the Mediterranean Diet has been in the center of it all. Efforts to promote the diet are not recent. As far back as the 160ss, there are already historical indications that the Mediterranean diet was being promoted as a way to embrace a healthier lifestyle. Giacomo Castelvetro, in 1614, published a book in England detailing fruits, vegetables, and herbs in Italian cooking that are a perfect mix for English cuisines. In the late 19th century, there were also documented efforts of how the locals tried to teach immigrants into the area the importance of the Mediterranean diet for health and well-being. And then, during that time period, the increase in European immigration into the Ameri can colonies led to the subsequent migration of the Mediterranean diet into the west. The establishment of the New England Kitchen, for example, was originally intended to reinforce the Yankee cooking culture. The idea behind this was to quickly Americanize poor immigrants by introducing them to the local diet in the 19th century United States. However, the opposite of it became true. Instead of being assimilated into Yankee cooking and culinary practices, the Mediterranean diet grew stronger and influenced the locals. The New England kitchen effectively acted as a quick way to hasten food distribution from California farms into the major urban and immigration centers, allowing mainly Mediterranean groups to eat their customary diets. In the end, historians surmised that the satisfying flavors of the Mediterranean diet provide the best chance of influencing people to abandon unhealthy foods in favor of fresh vegetables, fruit, grains, and olive oil. This precipitated the growth in popularity and following of the Mediterranean diet, which continues to this day. But that growth would again see a boost when our continued quest to improve our understanding of nutrition gave rise to multiple studies that only reinforced the value of the Mediterranean diet.

22.3 Who Is This Diet Suitable For?

One of the best aspects of the Mediterranean diet is that it is appropriate for everyone. Children, young adults, and the elderly can all benefit from the nutrient-dense foods that are essential to the Mediterranean diet. The Mediterranean diet is excellent since it is neither restricted nor rigid. It is a way of life rather than a diet. As a result, it allows everyone to join and enjoy the colorful and diverse array of Mediterranean-style cuisine that comprise it. So you may involve your entire family in this new way of eating. In reality, mealtimes are an experience where complete multigenerational families traditionally spend time together and bond in Mediterranean towns and villages. Transitioning from high-fat and

sugary ready meals in front of the television to healthy meals served at the dinner table can transform your family life while also providing considerable health benefits to all members of your family.
Even better, you can follow the Mediterranean diet at home, work, or school. Pack the kids a great Greek salad for lunch, or make some falafel flatbreads to take to a park picnic. Your family and friends will be grateful to you for exposing them to this great way of eating.

22.4 The Food Pyramid of the Mediterranean Diet

Fruits, veggies, whole grains, and fish are the cornerstones of the Mediterranean diet, which is a healthy eating plan. It is based on the theory that a diet high in fruits and vegetables, moderate in proteins, and low in saturated fats leads to health benefits. The food pyramid of the Mediterranean diet is a visual representation of this eating plan. The pyramid consists of six sections: fruits, vegetables, grains, oils, salt, and dairy. There are five tiers in the food pyramid of the Mediterranean Diet. It is important to remember this food pyramid as it will be your guide in choosing what to put on your plate. Here it is:
Tier 1: Regular Social and Physical Activities
That's right, the biggest tier in the pyramid is dedicated not to food but to relationships with others and with yourself.
Tier 2: Vegetables, Fruit, Whole Grains, Beans, Legumes, Seeds, Nuts, Herbs, Spices, and Olive oil
The bulk on your plate should consist mostly of vegetables, with the rest sprinkled on top. In layman's terms, go green with a rainbow of colors on top. This is a stark contrast to the typical Western diet, which consists mostly of red meat and starchy sides.
Tier 3: Fish and Seafood
If you feel the need to eat meat, then always choose seafood first, especially wild-caught fish. In the diet, fish should be served at least twice a week.
Tier 4: Eggs, Yogurt, Cheese, and Poultry
Eggs and dairy products can be enjoyed regularly in the Mediterranean diet, but it is emphasized that they should only be served in small portions.
Tier 5: Meat and Sweets
People in the Mediterranean diet are not in the habit of slaughtering their farm animals unless it is a special occasion, so meats do not play a central role in their diet. If they do serve meat, they make sure to have plenty of vegetables with it. Sweets are also enjoyed on special occasions, such as once a week.
At first, it might seem difficult to constantly have to buy fresh whole foods, but when you plan ahead, everything will be so much easier. It also would not hurt to grow some of your own. Many people have learned to grow herbs and spices, for instance.

22.5 Specific Guidelines for Mediterranean Diet

The Mediterranean diet also has set the following key guidelines in choosing foods to serve and eat in order to achieve the optimum benefits of this diet:
Go for Wholesome Fats
A Mediterranean diet is high in healthy fats, such as olive oil, nuts, and seeds, and low in saturated fats. These types of fats are important for a healthy diet because they help to reduce inflammation and protect the heart.

- Use olive oil or other healthy fats when frying food. These oils will help to preserve the vitamins and minerals that are lost when foods are cooked in oil that is not of Mediterranean origin.
- Use butter or ghee when roasting vegetables or meats. These fats will give the food a delicious flavor and help to keep it moist.
- Use nuts, seeds, or legumes as ingredients in Mediterranean dishes. These foods are high in fiber, essential fatty acids, and other nutrients that can enhance the health of your diet.

Nuts of various types, as well as canola oil, may include healthy lipids and linolenic acid. Linolenic acid is an omega-3 fatty acid. Omega-3 fatty acids are beneficial to one's health because they can minimize blood clotting, lessen the risk of a heart attack, lower triglyceride levels, keep blood pressure stable, and boost blood vessel strength.

Various forms of fatty fish, which are widely used in Mediterranean dishes, are also high in omega-3 fatty acids. Lake sardines, trout, herring, mackerel, albacore tuna, and salmon are examples of fatty fish. The Mediterranean Sea is overflowing with these fatty fish.

Go for Greens and Grains

If you're looking to follow a Mediterranean diet, make sure to add more greens and grains to your meals. Experts recommend at least six servings of colorful vegetables and two servings of whole grains each day. Here are some tips for incorporating these foods into your diet:

4. Add a salad as a main course or side dish: A salad is a great way to get loads of nutrients and fiber while switching up your routine. Choose fruits, vegetables, and lean protein sources like grilled chicken or fish instead of processed foods.
5. The best way to kick off the day is with a bowl of high-fiber oatmeal topped with your favorite nuts, seeds, and fruits. Add in some yogurt or milk for added benefits.
6. Snack on fresh fruits and vegetables: Keep your snacks healthy by opting for fresh fruits and vegetables instead of processed snacks. Grab some grapes, figs, carrots, or apples instead of chips or candy bars.

Drink Red Wine in Moderation

The Mediterranean diet is a heart-healthy method of eating that has been connected with lower risks of heart disease, stroke, and several forms of cancer. One key component of the Mediterranean diet is the consumption of red wine, which has been shown to have health benefits. However, like any other alcoholic drink, red wine should be consumed in moderation. Here are guidelines for how much red wine to enjoy on a Mediterranean diet:

If you are enjoying a glass or two of red wine each day as part of your Mediterranean diet, aim to drink no more than one glass per day. For people who don't drink alcohol, limit yourself to one cup per day.

If you are trying to cut back on your alcohol intake, start by swapping out one glass of red wine for one cup of herbal tea or water. If you find that you are still craving a glass of red wine, then consider going for a lower-calorie option like an iced tea or unsweetened cranberry juice instead.

If you are pregnant or breastfeeding, it is best to avoid drinking alcohol altogether. In addition, pregnant women should limit their intake to only two glasses per week, and breastfeeding mothers should drink only breast milk or unsweetened iced tea.

Sharing Meals Together

One of the most important components of this diet plan is that it emphasizes the social parts of your life. It recognizes that humans are social animals who need to spend time with others. Even if you are an introvert who prefers not to spend all of your time in loud, noisy, and busy places, it is still necessary for you to engage in some social interaction on a regular basis. This diet plan requires you to learn how to eat at least one meal a day with your family. And this should be made a huge deal. Rather than sitting down and preparing dinner in five minutes, make at least one of your meals a great occasion that everyone can enjoy. Even if you only start with one meal each week, this will make a difference. If you can set aside an hour or more each week to prepare this meal, you will be able to work on strengthening your bonds with others in your family. Enjoy your dinner, talk to others, share tales and knowledge, and tell them about your day. This is a terrific way to calm down in this fast-paced world, reconnect, and may do incredible things for your stress levels and happiness. Begin with one or two slow and leisurely meals with your family, and then go to adding more social activities to your life. This does not have to be stressful, and it should not be. Consider meeting a buddy for coffee, having a play date at the park, or doing something else that gets you out of the house while still allowing you to connect with others and have a pleasant time.

The Importance of Physical Exercise

When following a Mediterranean diet, it is important to get enough physical activity. The recommended amount of exercise for a person of any age is 150 minutes per week. However, people following a Mediterranean diet should aim for at least 225 minutes per week of moderate-intensity aerobic activity or 75 minutes per week of vigorous-intensity aerobic activity. This amount of exercise can be achieved by participating in a variety of activities, such as walking, cycling, swimming, and playing tennis. In addition to getting the recommended amount of exercise, it is also important to make sure that the physical activity is done in a healthy way. This means that the exercise should be moderate-intensity and include a mix of aerobic and anaerobic activity. Aerobic activity includes activities such as walking, running, and swimming; anaerobic activity includes activities such as biking, weightlifting, and football.

Learning How to Manage Your Stress

One of the most significant factors preventing people from sticking to their diets is stress. The Mediterranean diet is recognized to aid with stress management, so it's vital to follow some recommendations if you wish to keep to it while under stress. For starters, try to relax before meals by taking a few minutes for yourself. Eating carefully and paying attention to the flavor and texture of the meal may help you manage the rush that would otherwise cause you to overeat. Alternatively, aromatherapy - many people find that scents like lavender or lemon help to calm them down before eating. Secondly, make sure you have enough of water and non-caffeinated liquids with you when you're on the road. When you're anxious, your body releases cortisol - a hormone that can boost your appetite and make it difficult to keep to your diet. Avoid caffeine close to meals if possible, as it will only make things worse. Finally, stay positive and remind yourself why you're doing this. If you find yourself getting frustrated or tempted by unhealthy foods, remember why you decided to start following the Mediterranean diet in the first place. This way, you'll be more likely to stick to your plan no matter what happens. As you can see, the Mediterranean diet is not just about you working on the foods that you consume. Instead, it is all about changing the way that you live your lifestyle. Many times, Americans are going to feel stressed out and tired because they have too much going on. They don't slow down and spend time with those who matter. They don't even slow down to enjoy their meal. They are moving fast, doing too much work, and they are just not happy with their quality of life.

The Mediterranean diet is a great way to improve your health. Not only does it promote a healthy weight, but it also contains antioxidants, fiber, and other nutrients that can help prevent disease. If you're looking for a healthy eating plan that's also easy to follow, the Mediterranean diet may be the perfect fit for you.

22.6 Tips for Eating Out On a Mediterranean Diet

When dining out on a Mediterranean diet, it is important to keep in mind some tips and tricks. Here are four simple tips to follow:

7. Order fresh fruits and vegetables as your main course instead of meat. This will help you stay on track with your dietary goals and fill up on healthy nutrients.
8. Try to avoid eating high-calorie items like dessert or bread. Stick to low-fat versions or choose a dish with grilled or roasted chicken as the main protein source.
9. Whenever possible, order wine or water instead of sugary drinks. These drinks can spike your blood sugar levels and make it harder to stick to your diet overall.
10. Take advantage of the Mediterranean diet's emphasis on whole grains, legumes, and nuts. These foods provide fiber, protein, and other nutrients that can boost your health overall.

23 UNDERSTANDING THE SCIENCE BEHIND THE MEDITERRANEAN DIET

Since Dr. Ancel Keys, the Minnesota-based physiologist who extolled the virtues of the Mediterranean diet about fifty years ago, more evidence has emerged demonstrating that there are beneficial effects to be obtained by consuming a diet based on a high intake of fresh fruits and vegetables, whole grains, fish, and moderate amounts of liquor on a regular basis. The Mediterranean diet, when combined with regular physical activity and quitting smoking, can reduce 80 percent of coronary heart disease, 70 percent of strokes, and 90 percent of Type 2 diabetes. One of the key reasons science supports this diet is that it has a greater fat intake. And the fact that it comes in the form of monounsaturated and polyunsaturated fats found in olive oil, which lower triglyceride levels while increasing HDL or "good cholesterol," makes it even better. There is scientific evidence that the Mediterranean diet not only reduces the risk of heart disease but also of other ailments and diseases such as Alzheimer's and cancer. The evidence is not only empirical but also the result of several rounds of research and numerous studies on the efficacy of consuming a diet patterned after the Southern Mediterranean lifestyle, the results of which have unequivocally confirmed what was already known - that the Mediterranean diet is the real thing. It works, and it is far superior to any drug developed with the goal of improving your health and extending your life. The benefit of this diet is that it may be followed and benefited from at any stage of life. It is not only a fantastic strategy to prevent disease, but it is also a good approach to lower the risk factors associated with heart disease. A study conducted by the University of Barcelona on patients with risk factors such as obesity, smoking, and diabetes established this unambiguously. They were divided into three groups, one of which was given a low-fat diet and the other two types of Mediterranean diet plans. The disparity in results gained from the two types of Mediterranean diets and the low-fat diet was so remarkable that the latter study had to be halted after five years! The incidence of heart attacks and strokes fell by 30% among those who followed Mediterranean diets. The low-fat diet was so bland and tasteless that scientists were forced to allow individuals to switch to their regular diet, which was significantly tastier due to its preponderance of red meat and commercially prepared food products. In the end, without reproducing the technical specifics of the several studies that unequivocally indicate that the Mediterranean diet is beneficial, one could make do by attributing it to a variety of obvious reasons. The most important reason is that it enhances longevity. Not just that, it comprehensively enhances your quality of life. Just look at the number of benefits that accrue to you by following this wonder diet:

11. Makes your brain sharper and healthier
12. Protects you against chronic diseases and helps fight cancer
13. Lowers risk of heart disease by reducing blood pressure and "bad" cholesterol
14. Defends you against diabetes
15. Keeps depression at bay
16. Helps you lose weight
17. Protects you against Parkinson's disease
18. Protects you against Alzheimer's disease
19. It is good for arthritis
20. Good for your dental health
21. Good for your eyesight

24 THE POTENTIAL BENEFITS OF THE DIET

The Mediterranean diet is renowned for being full of healthy foods, such as fruits, vegetables, fish, lean meats, and nuts which makes it an excellent choice if you want to improve your physical and mental wellbeing.

24.1 Improves Hearth Health

The Mediterranean diet is a nutrient-rich, low-calorie diet that is associated with a lower incidence of heart disease. Some of the key nutrients found in the Mediterranean diet include:

22. Omega-3 fatty acids: A rich source of omega-3 fatty acids can improve heart health by reducing the risk of arrhythmia and heart disease.
23. Fiber: A source of soluble fiber can help to decrease bad cholesterol levels and improve blood sugar control.
24. Vitamins and minerals: The Mediterranean diet is rich in vitamins and minerals, including potassium, magnesium, folate, and vitamin C, which are all important for heart health.

24.2 Aids In Weight Loss

When you want to lose weight, the Mediterranean diet is often recommended as one of the best ways to go. It's a diet that is high in fruits, vegetables, and whole grains, low in saturated fats and cholesterol, and moderate in protein. There is also a very large emphasis on leading a healthy and productive lifestyle while completely avoiding any kind of processed foods. All of these together combined helps to lose weight in the long run and stay healthier.

24.3 Improves Your Outlook

The Mediterranean diet has been shown to improve your appearance in a number of ways. The rich nutrients and antioxidants in the foods help to reduce the look of wrinkles, age spots, and other signs of aging. In addition, the low levels of saturated fat and cholesterol in the diet help to improve your heart health. Finally, healthy portion sizes and frequent meals help to keep your calorie intake lower, which can help to reduce your weight.

24.4 Protects You Against Diseases

The Mediterranean diet, which is derived from the traditional food habits of people in the Mediterranean region, has been linked with a decreased risk of diseases such as heart disease, stroke, cancer, and Alzheimer's disease. The main components of the Mediterranean diet are fruits, vegetables, whole grains, legumes, and nuts, in addition to moderate amounts of fish and dairy products. The Mediterranean diet is believed to be beneficial because it is high in antioxidants and contains healthy fats.

24.5 Keeps Your Energy Levels Up

Logically, when you put higher-quality fuels into your body, then you will enjoy better performance from your body. The Mediterranean diet works on exactly this principle. By fueling your body with fruits and vegetables, whole grains, and moderate quantities of fish, lean meats, and other protein sources, you can enjoy a boost in your energy levels. Your fatigue and sensations of sluggishness should be reduced, and you may also enjoy better quality sleep which will allow you to wake up each morning feeling completely rejuvenated.

25 MANY DISEASES THE DIET CAN FIGHT

While many people may start to look at the Mediterranean diet as a way to lose weight, it won't take long researching the diet or long being on a diet before you realize that it can help you in so many other ways as well. Countless different health benefits come from eating the way that the Mediterranean diet asks you to. You just need to decide that it is time to get started.

There are so many different health benefits that are going to show themselves when it comes to this diet plan that once you get started, you will wonder why you didn't decide to do it earlier. Some of the best health benefits, though certainly not the only ones, include:

25.1 Can Help Prevent Heart Disease

Heart disease is a leading cause of death in the United States, and it's responsible for more deaths than any other type of cancer. A healthy diet is one of the best ways to reduce your risk of heart disease, but it's not always easy to follow a healthy diet. One way to help make eating a healthy diet easier is to follow a Mediterranean diet. The Mediterranean diet, which is heavy in fruits, vegetables, legumes, and nuts, has been shown to protect against heart diseases. The diet is low in saturated fats and cholesterol, and it emphasizes whole grains and low-fat dairy products.

There is mounting evidence that eating a Mediterranean-style diet can help protect against heart disease. The Mediterranean diet is rich in fruits, vegetables, and whole grains and low in saturated fat and cholesterol. These foods have been shown to reduce the risk of heart attack and stroke. In addition, the Mediterranean diet has been linked with a decreased risk of obesity, which also contributes to heart disease.

25.2 Can Help Cognition and Memory in Older Adults

Although the ability to remember things tends to deteriorate as we get older, the Mediterranean diet has been shown to reverse this trend in the elderly. Fruits, vegetables, whole grains, and moderate amounts of wine make up the bulk of the diet. In addition, it is rich in omega-3 fatty acids and antioxidants. The advantages of the Mediterranean diet for memory are likely attributable to the diversity of foods it comprises as well as the antioxidants and other nutrients it contains. The cognitive decline and Alzheimer's disease could be warded off by these nutrients.

The high levels of antioxidants in the Mediterranean diet may help prevent neurodegenerative diseases by neutralizing dangerous free radicals. Free radicals are molecules that can damage cells and cause inflammation. The antioxidants found in the Mediterranean Diet can help scavenge free radicals before they cause too much damage. Additionally, the Mediterranean Diet is high in monounsaturated fatty acids (MUFA), which have been shown to improve cognitive function in both young and old adults. In addition to reducing oxidative stress, MUFA has been linked with improved memory and cognitive function due to its role in improving blood flow to the brain. A study published in The Journals of Gerontology, Series B, found that those following a Mediterranean diet had better scores on tests of memory and cognitive function than those who followed a traditional American diet. The study assessed 116 older adults who were divided into two groups: one group followed a Mediterranean diet, and the other followed a typical American diet. The participants were assessed for their memory and cognitive function at baseline and again six months later. The Mediterranean group had significantly better scores on tests of memory and cognitive function than the American group at both time points. The researchers believe that the beneficial effects of the Mediterranean diet on memory may be due to its high levels of antioxidants, which have been shown to protect against brain damage and age-related cognitive decline. In addition, the lower levels of inflammation found in those following a Mediterranean diet may also contribute to improved memory function.

25.3 Can Lower Your Risk of Depression

You will also discover that this type of food plan is capable of improving more than just your memory. According to a recent study published in Molecular Psychiatry, there is a strong correlation between the Mediterranean diet and a lower prevalence of depression. This was a massive study, but it was because it was an amalgamation of information from 41 distinct studies, four of which would look at the relationship between the Mediterranean diet and depression over time in over 37,000 adults. When these four studies were examined, it was discovered that those who followed this diet had a substantially lower risk of depression, up to 33% lower than those who followed alternative diets that did not compare to the Mediterranean diet at all. What this means for your health is that if you are suffering from depression or want to avoid it because you have a family history of the disease, following a Mediterranean diet may

be the best option for you. The Mediterranean diet is a popular way of eating that has been linked with a lower incidence of cancer. Research has found that people who eat a Mediterranean diet are less likely to develop prostate, ovarian, and other cancers. Scientists aren't sure why the diet is protective, but they believe that it may be because of the high levels of antioxidants and fiber in foods on a diet.
However, This program is rich in fruits, vegetables, whole grains, and seafood and has been associated with a lower risk of cancer. The diet is thought to reduce the risk by promoting a healthy lifestyle that includes regular exercise and a healthy diet. Studies have also shown that the Mediterranean diet can help to reduce the growth of cancer cells.

25.4 Can Help You Fight Some Types of Cancer

The Mediterranean diet is a popular way of eating that has been linked with a lower incidence of cancer. Research has found that people who eat a Mediterranean diet are less likely to develop prostate, ovarian, and other cancers. Scientists aren't sure why the diet is protective, but they believe that it may be because of the high levels of antioxidants and fiber in foods on a diet. However, This program is rich in fruits, vegetables, whole grains, and seafood and has been associated with a lower risk of cancer. The diet is thought to reduce the risk by promoting a healthy lifestyle that includes regular exercise and a healthy diet. Studies have also shown that the Mediterranean diet can help to reduce the growth of cancer cells.

25.5 Can Help You to Fight Off Type 2 Diabetes

The Mediterranean diet is a diet that is high in healthy fats, low in processed foods, and rich in fruits and vegetables. Studies have shown that people who follow a Mediterranean diet are less likely to develop type 2 diabetes. This is because the Mediterranean diet is rich in healthy fats, which helps to prevent obesity and insulin resistance. Furthermore, the Mediterranean diet is also high in fruits and vegetables, which are antioxidants and contain nutrients that help to regulate blood sugar levels. The Mediterranean diet is a healthy way to eat that can help to prevent type 2 diabetes.

25.6 Can Help Reduce Inflammation

Inflammation is increasingly the silent cause of many chronic diseases. Arthritis is an inflammation of the joints caused by a multitude of factors, including purine-rich diets. Other inflammatory disorders cause discomfort to the soft tissues of the digestive tract. Endometriosis, a disorder characterized by inflammation of the uterine walls, is a particular source of concern among women. A study led by Dr. Tamer Seckin of the Endometriosis Foundation of America discovered that a Mediterranean-style diet could truly help cure or lessen the inflammation associated with endometriosis. This is primarily due to the inclusion of anti-inflammatory items in the diet. Overall, studies have demonstrated that a diet high in anti-inflammatory substances can reduce internal inflammation. This diet is also virtually fully gluten-free and free of processed foods, both of which are known inflammatory triggers.

25.7 Can Help You Fight Alzheimer's

Alzheimer's disease is a serious concern in many countries throughout the world since it is a disease that is rapidly spreading, yet we still don't know what causes it or how to cure it. Recent studies on the effects of the Mediterranean diet, on the other hand, may contribute to scientific advancements in this area.

Patients who were advised to follow the Mediterranean diet showed "significant improvement in executive functioning in male participants vs. females who consumed a Mediterranean diet," according to Samantha Gardener, a Ph.D. candidate at Edith Cowan University in Western Australia. Gardener's study also claimed that the Mediterranean diet causes a "slowing of metabolic syndrome, kidney protection, and a lower risk of various chronic diseases." The study concludes, "our findings underline the importance of consuming a balanced diet in terms of reducing risk for cognitive decline and Alzheimer's disease." Of course, many more studies and studies will be needed to completely understand the process underlying Alzheimer's disease, but one thing is certain: a good diet is critical to overall health and even more so to brain health and the prevention of degenerative disorders. Perhaps it is no surprise that the elderly in Sicily continue to operate normally despite their senior age and can enjoy the benefits of a quiet and peaceful existence far into their golden years. If that's all in the diet, then there's a lot to be said about embracing healthy eating habits like those promoted by the Mediterranean diet.

26 MEDITERRANEAN DIET VS. OTHER PROGRAMS

The Mediterranean Diet, as would be evident by now, is not really a diet that has been thought up to address certain lifestyle or health-related issues. It is a name given to the lifestyle and dietary habits of villagers living in the Southern Mediterranean region over centuries. But now that it has been identified by premier nutritionists and medical authorities as being the panacea for all the ills that result from following the modern Western hedonistic lifestyle, it might not be remiss to stack it up with other well-heralded diets and see how it fares.

26.1 The DASH Diet vs. the Mediterranean Diet

The Mediterranean diet is a popular way of eating that emphasizes fruits, vegetables, whole grains, and nuts; it's also low in saturated fat and cholesterol. The DASH diet, on the other hand, is rich in fruits, vegetables, whole grains, and low-fat dairy products; it's also low in saturated fat and cholesterol. The two diets have many similarities. They both emphasize fresh foods and limit processed foods. Both diets are high in fiber and low in sugar. And both diets have been shown to be effective for weight loss. However, there are some differences between the two diets. The Mediterranean diet is more balanced than the DASH diet. The DASH diet is high in protein and low in carbs, which can lead to weight gain if not balanced with other nutrients. The Mediterranean diet is also higher in monounsaturated fats and lowers in polyunsaturated fats than the DASH diet. These differences may account for some of the different effects these diets have on health. Overall, the DASH diet is a good way to eat for people who are looking to improve their health. It is low in sugar and high in fruits, vegetables, whole grains, and low-fat dairy products. The Mediterranean diet is also a good way to eat, but it may be more balanced for people who are looking to maintain their weight.

26.2 The Paleo Diet vs. the Mediterranean Diet

The Mediterranean diet is one of the most popular diets in the world, and for a good reason. It is packed with nutrients and antioxidants, and it has been shown to protect against diseases like heart disease, stroke, and cancer. Here is a look at the main difference and similarities between the Paleo diet and the Mediterranean diet.

The Paleo diet is based on the theory that humans were originally hunter-gatherers who ate a diet consisting mainly of meat, nuts, and vegetables. The Paleo diet is not recommended for people who are pregnant or breastfeeding, as it can be harmful to their health.

The Mediterranean diet is based on the theory that humans were originally farmers who ate a diet consisting of grains, fruits, and vegetables. The Mediterranean diet is generally recommended for people who are pregnant or breastfeeding, as it can be beneficial to their health. However, some variations of the Mediterranean diet include moderate amounts of meat.

Both the Paleo diet and the Mediterranean diet are considered healthy diets. They both contain nutrients and antioxidants that can protect against diseases. The key difference between the two diets is that the Paleo diet is not recommended for pregnant or breastfeeding women, while the Mediterranean diet is generally safe for these groups of people.

26.3 The Average American Diet vs. the Mediterranean Diet

The ordinary American diet (or the diet of the average individual like you and me) is plainly a Mediterranean lifestyle. It does not involve a deliberate attempt to achieve specific results. That said, it is the polar opposite of the Mediterranean diet.

It is primarily characterized by the use of processed foods, refined carbs, fried foods, red meat, refined sugar, and high-fat dairy products. This type of diet is high in heart-harming trans fats and salt. Not only that, but To round out the bleak image, this diet is devoid of whole grains, fruits, and vegetables. This diet may be beneficial to the multibillion-dollar food and beverage business, but it is detrimental to the health and longevity of the hundreds of millions of Americans who consume it.

Those who consume what is plainly the dangerous typical American diet have a considerably more sedentary lifestyle, thanks to the love affair most Americans have with their cars, in contrast to the Southern Mediterranean people who supplement their healthy food with an active lifestyle. Though comparisons are always distasteful, comparing the Mediterranean Diet to the disease-inducing average American diet is hardly worth the work.

26.4 The Atkins Diet vs. the Mediterranean Diet

One popular variation of the Mediterranean diet is the Atkins diet. The Atkins diet is a low-carbohydrate, high-fat diet. It is similar to the Mediterranean diet in that it is low in saturated fat, cholesterol, and sugar. However, the Atkins diet includes more processed foods than the Mediterranean diet. The two diets also have different amounts of protein. The Atkins diet recommends that 20 to 30 percent of your daily caloric intake come from protein, while the Mediterranean diet recommends about 10 to 15 percent of your daily caloric intake come from protein. The two diets also have different amounts of carbohydrates. The Atkins diet allows up to 50 grams of carbohydrates per day, while the Mediterranean diet allows up to 60 grams of carbohydrates per day. The two diets have several other differences. The Atkins diet is more restrictive in terms of what types of foods you can eat, while the Mediterranean diet allows for more variety. The Atkins diet also recommends avoiding saturated fats, while the Mediterranean diet allows for a moderate amount of saturated fat. The two diets also have different recommendations for how often you should exercise. The Atkins diet recommends doing moderate amounts of exercise every day, while the Mediterranean diet does not recommend any specific amount of exercise.

27 FOOD CONSUMPTION GUIDELINES

The first thing that you will want to look at when it comes to starting on a new diet plan is the foods that you are allowed to consume on this diet plan. With this diet plan, it is important that you spend your time eating foods that are wholesome and full of nutrients. If you are able to find foods that only have one ingredient in them, then you are well on your way to getting all of the good health benefits that you are looking for.

There are a lot of great meals that you will be able to eat on this diet plan. You are going to love all of the great flavor and more that you can get, especially considering there will be no added sugars or preservatives in this meal plan. It is all-natural and wholesome, and you are going to feel so much better in a short amount of time.

Some of the foods that you are able to eat when you choose to go on this kind of diet plan include:

27.1 Foods To Consume Plenty

Fish and Seafood

The Mediterranean diet is known for its high intake of fish and seafood. These foods are considered to be healthy because they are high in unsaturated fats and antioxidants. Some fish to consider include:

25. Salmon: This fish is high in omega-3 fatty acids and is a great source of protein. It can be cooked in many ways, including grilled or baked.
26. Shrimp: These small shrimps are packed with protein and vitamins, and minerals. They can be cooked in many ways, including stir-fry or grilled.
27. Mussels: Mussels are a popular seafood choice in the Mediterranean diet. They are high in zinc and have low levels of cholesterol. They can be steamed or boiled.
28. Tilapia: Tilapia is a healthy fish that is low in fat and cholesterol. It can be grilled, baked, or broiled.
29. Sardines: Sardines are another good fish choice for the Mediterranean diet. They are high in EPA and DHA fatty acids, which are beneficial for your health. Sardines can be grilled, boiled, or fried.

Vegetables and Fruits

A Mediterranean diet is healthy because it emphasizes the consumption of fruits and vegetables. These foods are packed with vitamins, minerals, antioxidants, and fiber. They are also low in saturated fat and cholesterol.

One of the best ways to enjoy a Mediterranean diet is to fill up on fruits and vegetables every day. Here are some of the most common vegetables and fruits that are featured in this type of diet:

Vegetables:

- Artichokes
- Asparagus
- Beans
- Bell Peppers
- Broccoli
- Celery
- Cucumbers
- Eggplant
- Fennel bulb
- Garlic
- Green beans
- Lettuce (e.g. romaine, garden, Boston)
- Mushrooms (e.g. shiitake, portobello)
- Okra
- Onion
- Parsley

- Peppers (e.g. bell, jalapeño, anaheim)
- Potatoes
- Rutabaga
- Spinach
- Tomatoes

Fruits:

- Avocados
- Bananas
- Cherries
- Dates
- Figs
- Grapefruit
- Kiwifruit
- Lemons
- Mandarin oranges
- Mango
- Melons (e.g. honeydew, watermelon)
- Orange juice
- Papaya
- Pineapple
- Plums
- Pomegranate juice
- Raspberries
- Strawberries
- Tangerines

Nuts and Seeds

If you're following a Mediterranean diet, you might want to add some nuts to your daily routine. Nuts are a great source of healthy fats and antioxidants, which can protect you against diseases. In fact, a study published in the journal "Nutrition Research" found that people who ate more nuts had a lower risk of developing heart disease, cancer, and Alzheimer's disease. Here are six nuts that are especially beneficial to a Mediterranean diet:

1. Walnuts

Walnuts are an excellent source of omega-3 fatty acids, which can help protect your heart health. They also contain vitamin E, magnesium, and zinc.

2. Pecans

Pecans are another great option for those following a Mediterranean diet. They're high in fiber and contain antioxidants like beta-carotene and selenium. Additionally, they're loaded with monounsaturated fats and minerals like copper and iron.

3. Cashews

Cashews are a good source of both Omega-6 and Omega-3 fatty acids. They also contain vitamins B6 and E, which can support cognitive function and reduce the risk of heart disease.

4. Almonds

Almonds area good source of both Omega-6 and Omega-3 fatty acids. They also contain fiber, magnesium, and copper.

5. Brazil Nuts

Brazil nuts are a great source of selenium, a mineral that is important for thyroid health and the prevention of cancer.

6. Macadamia Nuts

Macadamia nuts are high in antioxidants and monounsaturated fats, which can help reduce the risk of heart disease and promote healthy skin.

Legumes

Legumes are another food group that you can focus on as well. You can choose from some different options to add to your meals, including chickpeas, peanuts, lentils, peas, and beans.

Whole Grains And Potatoes

You can eat some fantastic whole grains, but make sure you choose whole grain pasta and bread rather than white pasta and bread loaded with sugars and other processed ingredients. When you're trying to load up your plate, these can assist quite a deal.

There are numerous whole grain options to include in your meals, and the recipes in this manual will help you incorporate as many as you need. Whole oats, buckwheat, couscous, barley, rye, brown rice, whole wheat pasta, whole wheat bread, sweet potatoes, turnips, and white potatoes are some of the alternatives.

Keep in mind that you can eat as much whole grain bread and pasta as you like with this group. However, you should avoid any white kinds of pasta and bread that are deemed processed. These will not give you the same vitamins and nutrients as whole grains will, and they should be avoided as much as possible.

Herbs and Spices

In a Mediterranean diet, herbs and spices are a big part of the cuisine. There are many different types of herbs and spices that can be used in cooking, and each has its own unique flavor and aroma. Here are some of the most common herbs and spices used in Mediterranean cuisine:

- Basil: Basil is a popular herb in Mediterranean cuisine. It has a strong minty flavor and is often used in Greek salads or as a garnish on dishes.
- Cinnamon: Cinnamon is another common herb used in Mediterranean cuisine. It has a warm, spicy flavor that can add depth to dishes.
- Cilantro: Cilantro is a popular herb found in Mexican, South American, and some Mediterranean dishes. It has a delicate, lemony flavor that pairs well with other spices.
- Garlic: Garlic is one of the key ingredients in many Mediterranean recipes. Its strong garlic flavor makes it an essential component of many dishes.
- Oregano: Oregano is another common herb found in Mediterranean cuisine. Its strong herbal flavor can be seen in dishes like Greek hummus or Italian pesto sauce.
- Sage: Sage is a common herb used in Mediterranean cuisine. Its flavor is reminiscent of woodsy notes, and it can be used in dishes like lamb or chicken dishes.
- Tarragon: Tarragon is another common herb used in Mediterranean cuisine. Its flavor is reminiscent of licorice, and it can be used in dishes like chicken or fish dishes.
- Thyme: Thyme is another common herb used in Mediterranean cuisine. Its flavor is reminiscent of a bouquet of flowers, and it can be used in dishes like vegetable or fish dishes.
- Za'atar: Za'atar is a common herb found in Mediterranean cuisine. Its flavor is reminiscent of French lavender, and it can be used in dishes like lamb or chicken dishes.

Other common ingredients in Mediterranean cuisine include olives, lemon, feta cheese, and balsamic vinegar.

Healthy Fats

One of the most important aspects of adopting the Mediterranean diet is eating plenty of healthy fats. These will help you stay full and fed for extended periods of time, allowing you to consume fewer calories overall.

When it comes to finding the good fats that will benefit you on this diet plan, you have a few different possibilities. When it comes to healthy fats, extra virgin olive oil reigns supreme on this diet. However, there are additional healthy fats to consider, such as coconut oil, avocado oil, avocados, and olives.

27.2 Foods That You Can Have in Moderation

With the list of foods above, you can eat as many of those as you would like. As long as you learn how to listen to your body and only eat until you are hungry, you will find that you can enjoy as many of those foods as you want. But there are some other foods that you need to enjoy more in moderation on this diet plan. They aren't taken out of the diet, but you shouldn't consume them as much as you do some of the other foods above. Some of the foods that you should eat in moderation include:

Read Meat

Too much red meat can increase your risk of heart disease and other health problems, so it's important to choose the right types of red meat when following this diet.

Ideally, you should limit yourself to no more than two servings per week of red meat, which includes lamb, beef, pork, and veal. If you do choose to include red meat in your diet, make sure to select leaner cuts that have less fat and cholesterol. Try to avoid high-fat meats like bacon and sausage, which are packed with calories and harmful fats.

Dairy

Some dairy products that are generally consumed on the Mediterranean diet are cheese, yogurt, milk, and eggs. These foods can provide a good amount of calcium and other nutrients that are essential for healthy bones and teeth. However, if you are following the Mediterranean diet in moderation, you should avoid dairy products that contain high levels of saturated fat or cholesterol.

Eggs

As long as you eat them in moderation, eggs are just fine on this diet plan. They are going to provide you with a good amount of protein and can be a great way to start out the morning. And you can cook them in any manner that you would like, such as hard-boiled, fried, poached, or scrambled.

Poultry

Poultry can be another great way for you to get in the protein that you are looking for to keep your body healthy. But you do need to eat it in moderation, rather than all of the time. One option would be turkey, which can help you to get lots of good protein and other nutrients as well.

27.3 Foods To Avoid While Following A Mediterranean Diet

When following the Mediterranean diet, it's important to keep your diet balanced and include a variety of foods. While there are many healthy options to choose from, you should avoid certain types of food when following this diet.

Below are a few foods to avoid when following the Mediterranean diet:

- Processed foods: These foods typically contain high levels of sugar, salt, and unhealthy fats. Instead of eating these types of foods on a regular basis, make sure to eat them in moderation whenever possible.
- Chips and other unhealthy snacks: Snacks such as chips and candy are typically high in calories and unhealthy fats. Instead of eating these types of snacks, try enjoying a small piece of fruit or yogurt instead.
- Deep-fried items: Many items at fast food restaurants or convenience stores are deep-fried. These foods are not only unhealthy but also often contain high amounts of saturated fat. Instead of eating these types of foods, try opting for healthier snacks such as salad or fruit.

- Alcohol: While alcoholic beverages are not typically considered part of the Mediterranean diet, they can still be unhealthy if consumed in large amounts. Limit yourself to one or two drinks per day, and make sure to avoid sugary drinks as well.

By following these guidelines, you can maintain a healthy Mediterranean diet while still enjoying delicious food.

27.4 Oils to know about

One of the best ways to implement a Mediterranean-style diet is to use oils. Many of these oils are beneficial for your health and can be used in many different ways. Here are a few of the best oils to use on a Mediterranean diet:

- Extra-virgin olive oil is a great option for cooking and can be used in salad dressing, dips, pasta sauces, and even as a main dish. It's packed with antioxidants and has been linked with lower rates of heart disease, obesity, and cancer.
- Canola oil is another good option for cooking. It's low in saturated fat and has been shown to be helpful in reducing inflammation and controlling blood sugar levels.
- Sesame oil is known for its anti-inflammatory properties and can be used in many different ways, including as a dipping sauce or as part of a stir-fry.
- Flaxseed oil is high in omega-3 fatty acids, which have been linked with a number of health benefits, such as reducing the risk of heart disease, lowering cholesterol levels, boosting brain function, and improving joint health.
- Cold-pressed sesame oil is a great option for those who are looking for a healthier version of soy sauce. It's low in calories and has a mild flavor that can be used in many different dishes.
- Coconut oil is a great option for baking and can be used in place of vegetable oil or butter. It's high in saturated fat but has a low-calorie count, making it a great choice for those looking to cut down on their overall caloric intake.
- Ghee is a type of clarified butter that is made from milk and has a high-fat content. It's been shown to be beneficial for cholesterol levels and can be used in place of other types of fats in recipes.

28 HOW THE DIET CAN HELP WITH WEIGHT LOSS

Mediterranean diets are known for being high in fiber, healthy fats, and antioxidants. These diets have been shown to be effective for weight loss because they help control cravings and provide a variety of nutrients that help maintain energy levels. They also promote a healthy weight distribution and can help prevent heart disease, cancer, and other chronic illnesses.

That is the beauty of working with this diet plan. It isn't just something that you lose weight on quickly and then gains it all back. Instead, it is a series of healthy lifestyle choices that will all come together to help you to lose weight. And it all happens by eating foods that are delicious and have a lot of flavors while enjoying life. It is so much better than wasting your time and stressing out about counting calories all the time.

28.1 Focusing On The Mediterranean Dietary Style

The main thing that is different about this diet plan compared to some of the others that you may have heard about in the past is that it is not just about the foods you eat; it is about making healthy changes to every part of your life. You need to take some time to pay attention to lifestyle changes, including exercising more often, changing your portion sizes, socializing, and drinking more water, in order to see the long-term results. There are a lot of diets for weight loss out there, but many of them are going to come and go. They may help you lose weight, but the weight loss may be short-term, or the diet plan is too difficult to stick with.

This isn't what you will see with the Mediterranean diet. With this choice, you will start to pay more attention to your individual lifestyle, including your stress levels, your socialization, the types of foods that you decide to eat, how much physical activity you add to your life, your portion sizes, and more. You can start to change these things each day, and then this forces you into some great long-term habits that will help you to lose weight and keep it off.

- Eat More Fruits and Vegetables: The mainstay of the Mediterranean diet is fruits and vegetables, both of which are high in antioxidants and other nutrients that help promote weight loss. Aim to eat at least five servings of fruits and vegetables per day.
- Choose Leaner Meat Options: Just because the Mediterranean diet is high in healthy foods doesn't mean you have to give up your favorite meat dishes. In fact, choosing leaner meats can help you lose weight while eating in accordance with the Mediterranean diet guidelines. Try opting for chicken instead of beef or lamb or using skinless poultry instead of fatty poultry like chicken thighs or drumsticks.
- Avoid Processed Foods: Many processed foods are loaded with sugar, sodium, and unhealthy fats. Limit your intake of processed foods to a few times per week.
- Drink Plenty of Water: A lack of water can lead to weight gain because it causes the body to retain water weight. Aim to drink at least 8 cups of water per day.
- Exercise Regularly: According to the National Institutes of Health, regular exercise can help you lose weight and improve your overall health. Workout for 30 minutes on most days of the week.

28.2 How to Pay Attention to Calories Without Counting Them

Even on the Mediterranean diet, you need to be careful with the number of calories that you consume. But you don't need to spend your time counting those calories. These calories are going to be a big concept when it comes to losing weight. Basically, the calories are going to be the amount of energy that is found in the foods you eat, as well as the amount of energy that your body is going to use as you move through the day.

Your body is always in need of fuel or energy, not only for daily activities like exercising, cleaning, cooking, and more, but also for the basic biological functions that you do, such as thinking and breathing. Everyone is going to have a different metabolism. And your own personal metabolic rate is going to determine how fast you are able to burn calories. This can depend on your physical fitness level, genetics, gender, and age.

No matter what, though, you will not be able to lose weight if you take in more calories than you are able to burn through daily activity and exercise. If you want to be able to lose weight, you need to be able to create a calorie deficit, but you can do this without having to actually count out all of the calories that you eat and all that you burn. Making some small changes to your lifestyle, like exercising more and reducing how big your portions are, can help you to reduce the number of calories that you take in.

28.3 How to Suppress Your Appetite

One of the biggest issues that a lot of people face when they go on a diet plan is that they feel hungry. Their bodies are used to eating a ton of food, and not being able to eat as much can make them feel off. The good news is that when you follow the Mediterranean diet the proper way, you will be able to eat lots of healthy foods that will keep your appetite to a minimum, even if you are eating fewer calories than before. If you're looking to lose weight on the Mediterranean diet, you need to be mindful of how much food you're eating. The Mediterranean diet is known for its high-quality, plant-based foods and moderate amounts of dairy. However, if you're looking to lose weight on the Mediterranean diet, you might be tempted to overeat. Here are some tips on how to suppress your appetite in a healthy way:

- Eat slowly and chew your food well.
- Drink plenty of water and avoid sugary beverages.
- Enjoy your food but don't overeat.
- Avoid eating late at night or in front of the TV.
- Practice portion control and eat smaller meals throughout the day

28.4 Lead A Stress-Free Life

Stress can cause a lot of hormones to go everywhere. And when we are in the fight or flight response of our stress hormones, it is really hard to make good nutritional decisions that are going to help us lose weight, as well as improve other aspects of our health. Because of this, it is so important that you learn how to reduce your stress. You need to be the one in control over your diet and the things that you do in life, not your hormones. And reducing stress can make that so much easier.

There are a lot of things that you can do to reduce stress, and as long as they aren't something unhealthy like drinking heavily or smoking, then you can choose the one that is right for you. Pick something that allows you to take care of yourself. Choose something that is easy to stick with. Do something that is just for yourself and has nothing to do with all of your obligations. Whether it is reading a book for a few minutes, devotionals, spending time with some friends, taking a bath, or something else, try to carve out a few minutes a day when you can put things aside and just focus on what you want to.

As you can see, there are a lot of reasons why you would want to use the Mediterranean diet to help you to lose weight. If you are like many Americans, or even many people throughout the world, trying to stay healthy and lose weight can be hard. But when you are following this kind of diet plan, you will be able to keep your hormones in check, reduce stress, and eat lots of healthy foods while being more active. When all of this comes together, weight loss will be a breeze.

28.5 Reasons Why You May "Not" Be Losing Weight

Are you not seeing the results you want with your diet? One big reason why people may not be losing weight on a Mediterranean diet is that they are not properly digesting the food. The Mediterranean diet is rich in fiber, which can help to keep you full and prevent overeating. If you are not digesting your food properly, your body will not be able to extract all of the nutrients that it needs. This can lead to weight gain and other health problems. Make sure that you are eating enough fiber each day by including plenty of fruits, vegetables, and whole grains in your diet. Are you not meeting your daily calorie goals? If you are not consuming enough calories, your body will start to burn muscle instead of fat. This can lead to weight loss stalls and even weight gain in some cases. Make sure that you are keeping track of how many calories you are eating each day, and make sure that you are adding in enough protein and healthy fats to balance out your caloric intake. Are you lacking in essential vitamins and minerals? One of the benefits of a Mediterranean diet is that it is rich in antioxidants and other nutrients that help to support weight loss. Make sure that you include plenty of fruits, vegetables, nuts, and whole grains in your diet to get the nutrients that you need to lose weight. Do you have any food allergies or intolerances? If you have any allergies or intolerances, it can be difficult to tolerate specific foods in a Mediterranean diet. This can lead to difficulty losing weight and other health problems. If you think that you may have a food allergy or intolerance, talk to your doctor about testing for these conditions.

29 COMMON MISTAKES TO AVOID

When starting anything new, mistakes are unavoidable. In this chapter, I am going to give you a quick rundown of some of the mistakes I made when I first started eating the Mediterranean way, as well as share some slipups friends and family members had.

29.1 Keeping Your Portions In Check

I know I've been going on and on about moderation. I will, unfortunately, have to talk about it some more under the guise of portion control. Managing how much you eat is particularly important if you're trying to lose weight, but it is also a factor if you want to maintain your weight and, with it, your health. Portion control is important for staying healthy because it can help you maintain a healthy weight, control your calorie intake, and avoid overeating. It's also important to remember that not all calories are created equal. Some calories are more filling than others, so it's important to eat enough of the right kinds of foods to stay on track.

29.2 Overloading On Carbs

The Mediterranean diet is high in fiber and low in processed foods, which can make it a great choice for people who are looking to drop weight. However, if you're not careful with how much carbohydrates you eat, you could end up overloading on carbs and putting your health at risk. The key to avoiding this problem is to divide your carbohydrates into smaller servings throughout the day rather than eating large amounts all at once. This way, you'll stay satisfied and won't be tempted to overeat later on.

29.3 Not Eating Enough Fish

You won't reap the heart- and brain-boosting health benefits of fish and seafood if you don't eat enough of it. Aim for three times a week, and you'll get all the omega-3 fatty acids your brain and body need. If you're a vegetarian or you dislike seafood, don't worry, just supplement with fish and seaweed oil.

29.4 Eating the Wrong Dairy

Dairy is a mainstay of many Mediterranean diets, but it's important to be aware of the types of dairy that are best suited for this diet. Some popular dairy products that are typically not recommended for the Mediterranean diet include full-fat dairy products and processed foods with added sugar. Instead, opt for low-fat or non-dairy versions of these products when possible. Additionally, limit your intake of milk and other dairy products during the day to two cups per day. This will help to keep your blood sugar levels stable and give you the nutrients you need to maintain a healthy weight.

29.5 Not Having Enough Beans

Beans should be part of the healthy foundation of the Mediterranean meal plan. Some people prefer to leave this superfood off their plates because it takes longer to prepare than other food, and beans give some people gas. Beans are a great source of protein, fiber, and B vitamins, which are all important for a healthy diet. They also contain anti-inflammatory properties, which can help reduce the risk of diseases such as cancer.

29.6 Thinking Wine is Water

One of the most common mistakes people make when following a Mediterranean diet is drinking too much wine. While wine is a welcome part of many Mediterranean-style dishes, overindulging can lead to weight gain and other health problems. Moderation is key when it comes to wine consumption, so aim for no more than two glasses per day.

29.7 Using Extra-Virgin Olive Oil at a High Heat

It can be tempting to use extra virgin olive oil at high heat when cooking Mediterranean-style dishes, but this can lead to problems. Extra virgin olive oil is a delicate oil and can easily break down or scorch if used too quickly or at high heat. In fact, the FDA recommends using it only at low or medium heat.

29.8 Not Following The 10 Commandments

It's not as serious as it sounds, I promise. The 10 commandments perfectly sum up what the Mediterranean Diet and lifestyle are all about. And, if you follow them diligently, you're set to gain a healthy body and a longer life.

Don't worry if you wander off the path now and again. You won't be condemned to a sickly life spent in an out-of-shape body. Just get back to following the Mediterranean Diet and living the lifestyle, and you'll be a-okay.

The ten commandments of the Mediterranean Diet and lifestyle are:

- Fill your plate with an abundance of fresh, non-processed food.
- Do not let any saturated fat, trans fat, sodium, or refined sugar cross your lips.
- Don't use margarine or butter; in its place, use olive oil or trans- fat-free vegetable spread.
- Eat your fill of vegetables but limit the portions of other foods.
- Drink enough water.

- Don't drink too much red wine.
- Get your heart rate up for at least 30 minutes a day.
- Don't smoke.
- Unwind and relax, specifically after eating.
- Laugh a lot, smile, and enjoy life.

30 WEEK-ROUND SHOPPING LIST

Shopping list items vary from country to country, and also items change according to seasons. Your first choice should be seasonal and local ingredients. No need to buy fancy and expensive imported ingredients. Here is a basic list mentioned below:

Vegetables:

- Zucchini
- Tomatoes
- Spinach
- Potatoes
- Peppers
- Peas
- Onion
- Okra
- Mushrooms
- Green beans
- Garlic
- Eggplant
- Cucumber
- Celery
- Cauliflower
- Carrots
- Cabbage
- Broccoli
- Beets

Greens:

- Chicory
- Dandelions
- Beet greens
- Amaranth

Fruits:

- Orange
- Lemons
- Apples
- Pears
- Cherries
- Watermelon
- Cantaloupe
- Peaches
- Pears
- Figs
- Apricots

Dairy Products:

- Plain Greek yogurt
- Sheep's milk yogurt
- Feta cheese
- Fresh cheese like ricotta
- Parmesan
- Mozzarella
- Graviera
- Mizithra

Meat And Poultry:

They should be eaten rarely, like once a week.

- Chicken
- Beef
- Veal
- Pork

Fish and Seafood:

Preferably eat small fatty fish. You can eat canned fish as well.

- Anchovies
- Sardines
- Shrimp
- Calamari
- Herbs Snd Spices:
- Oregano
- Parsley
- Dill

Grains and Bread:

- Mint
- Basil
- Whole grain bread
- Whole grain breadsticks
- Pita bread
- Cumin
- Allspice
- Cinnamon
- Phyllo
- Pasta
- Rice
- Bulgur
- Pepper
- Sea salt
- Sage
- Couscous

Fats and Nuts:

- Extra virgin olive oil
- Tahini
- Almonds
- Walnuts
- Pine nuts
- Pistachios
- Sesame seeds
- Beans:
- Lentils
- Chickpeas
- White Beans
- Fava Beans
- Pantry Items:
- Canned tomatoes
- Olives
- Sun-dried tomatoes
- Capers
- Honey
- Thyme
- Herbal Tea

31 A NOTE ON MEAL PREP

Meal prep is the process of preparing meals ahead of time so that you can have them on hand when you need them. It can be a great way to save time and money, and it can also be a healthy way to eat. There are many different types of meal prep, and it can be done with or without food storage.

31.1 Exploring The Concept Of Meal Prepping

Prepping meals can be a lot of work, but it's worth it to have healthy, well-balanced meals that are easy to grab and go. There are a lot of different ways to prep meals, but one popular way is to meal prep in bulk. This means cooking a bunch of different meals and storing them in containers so you can easily grab one and go. Keeping that in mind, let us dissect Meal Prepping a bit more.
"Meal Prepping is the process of planning what you are going to eat (and how you are going to make it) ahead of time."
The core objective of prepping your meal ahead of time is to:

- Help you save a lot in the money-saving department by allowing you to set up a rough estimate of your food budget early on ahead.
- Enforce you to stick to the plan and eat as much healthy food as possible.
- Minimize food wastage.
- Clear your head off the burden of "What to cook next" and ease your mind by minimizing any food-related stress.
- Prevent the wasting of time by letting you know exactly "What" you are going to eat and "When."
- Help you avoid monotony in your daily meal by spicing up the routine from time to time.

31.2 Amazing Advantages Of Meal Prep

- It helps you to save a lot of money by allowing you to set up a rough estimate of your food budget ahead of time
- It allows you to stick to a healthy plan and eat as much healthy food as possible
- It minimizes food wastage
- It clears off the burden of "What you should cook next" and eases your mind, clearing it up of any food-related stress.
- Prevent the wasting of time by letting you know exactly "What" you are going to eat and "When."
- Help you avoid monotony in your daily meal by spicing up the routine from time to time.
- Meal Prepping helps you to control your portions by adjusting a set amount of food per meal. This gives you greater control over what you eat, helping in weight loss as well
- Greater control of your food routine will help you create a more balanced and nutritious diet plan in the long run
- Since everything is pre-planned, it will help you to avoid the rush of "Last minute preparations" and make the cooking process more comfortable for you
- Meal Prepping will help you to seamlessly multitask with other famous works, as opposed to sitting in the kitchen all day to cook. Since you will keep everything prepared, it will save a lot of time from your daily routine and allow you to focus on other activities.

31.3 The Ideas to Know About

Keep in mind that the following are just some of the hundreds of Meal Prep ideas that are designed to inspire you to explore and come up with your own ideas as well!

Use the following as references as to how you can prepare the ingredients and store them prior to cooking.

Make A Plan Ahead Of Time: If you are reading this book, then you have probably decided to go on a Clean Eating diet journey. An excellent way to start this off is to start with a small number of recipes, for perhaps 7 days. Choose which recipes you are going to use and make a rough idea inside your head. Make a list and buy the ingredients accordingly ahead of time.

Keep A Good Supply Of Mason Jars: Mason jars are terrific, not only for storing memories! But also for storing healthy salads! Assuming that you are a good buff, it might be a good idea to prepare your salads ahead of time and store them in mason jars. Make sure to keep the salad dressing at the bottom of the jar to ensure that nothing greens don't get soggy!

Three-Way Seasoning In One Pan: If your diet requires you to stick with lean meats such as chicken, then seasoning them from time to time might become somewhat of a chore. A simple solution to that is to prepare a pan with aluminum foil dividers. Using these will allow you to season three or more (depending on how many dividers you are using) types of chicken seasoning to be done using the same pan!

Boil Eggs In An Oven Instead Of A Pot: Now, this might sound a little bit weird at first, but it is highly effective! The problem here comes with the number of eggs that can be boiled in one go. If you are using a standard-sized pot, then you would probably be able to squeeze in 5 or 6 eggs max in one batch. However, if you try to bake your eggs in muffin tins using an oven, then you will be able to get a dozen or perfectly hard-boiled eggs in no time!

Keep Your Prepared Smoothies Frozen In Muffin Tins: Plopping out some different ingredients early in the morning might be a chore for some people. A simple solution to that is to go ahead and freeze up your blended smoothies in muffin tins. This will not only save up time but will also give you a good dose of satisfaction as you wake up in the morning and toss a few "smoothie cups" into the blender for a simple yet healthy breakfast.

Roast Vegetables That Require The Same Time In One Batch: When you are preparing large batches of vegetables for roasting, it is smart to go ahead and create batches of vegetables depending on how long they take to roast. For example, you can create a batch of rapid-cooking vegetables such as mushrooms, asparagus, or cherry tomatoes and a batch of slow-roasting veggies such as potatoes, cauliflowers, and carrots to minimize time loss and maximize output.

Learn To Effectively Use A Skewer: When you think of skewers, you automatically think of kabobs! But Skewers aren't necessarily designed to be used only with street meats. Wooden skewers can help you to measure how much meat you are going to consume in one go. So, you can punch in your meat in multiple skewers and divide them evenly and store them for the rest of the week. When the time comes, take out one skewer and cook it up!

Keep A Good Supply Of Sectioned Plastic Containers: Sectioned containers like the one shown above are an absolute necessity for serious meal-prepping savants! These will effortlessly give you enough space to separate every single component of your meal while making sure that you don't mix everything up and create a mess. The separate ingredients would also be straightforward to find and use!

Keep A Tab Of Your Accomplishments: This is perhaps the essential aspect of a meal prepping routine. Always make sure to measure your progress somehow and set small milestones for you to accomplish. Achieving these milestones will encourage you and inspire you further to keep pushing yourself until you reach your final goal. Alternatively, looking at your positive progress will significantly motivate you to push forward as well. Now that you have a basic understanding of the concepts of diet and meal prepping let me give you a breakdown of just some of the fantastic benefits of meal prep!

Different Types Of I hope that meal prep will become a regular routine in your home like it is in ours. In order to make that happen, it is essential that you invest in and choose the right storage containers. When I was ready to invest in a set of containers, I bought a few different options—glass, metal, and plastic (BPA-free, of course). This way, I could do a trial run to figure out what I liked best before I made a big purchase. Trying a few to see what you like and what works best in your kitchen will save you time and money in the long run.
Good-quality containers are essential for keeping your food fresh as long as possible. Here are some things to look for when buying containers for meal prepping:

BPA-free.
If you're looking for a safe and environmentally friendly way to store your belongings, you may want to consider using storage containers made of plastic that are free of bisphenol A (BPA). BPA is a chemical that is often used in the manufacturing of plastics, and it has been linked to health concerns such as hormone disruption and developmental issues in children.
There are a variety of storage containers made without BPA, and some of the most popular options include glass and stainless steel containers. While there are some benefits to using these types of containers, they may not be ideal for all situations. For example, glass containers are heavier than plastic ones, which can make them more difficult to move around. Additionally, stainless steel containers can be difficult to clean if they get dirty.
If you're undecided about which type of storage container is best for you, it's worth considering your needs and preferences before making a decision. There are plenty of options available that will meet your needs without exposing you or your belongings to dangerous chemicals.

31.4 Different Types Of Storage

I hope meal prep will become a regular routine in your home like ours. To make that happen, you must invest in and choose the right storage containers. When I was ready to invest in a set of containers, I bought a few different options—glass, metal, and plastic (BPA-free, of course). This way, I could do a trial run to determine what I liked best before making a big purchase. Trying a few to see what you like and what works best in your kitchen will save you time and money in the long run.
Good-quality containers are essential for keeping your food fresh as long as possible. Here are some things to look for when buying containers for meal prepping:

BPA-free.
Suppose you're looking for a safe and environmentally friendly way to store your belongings. In that case, you may consider using storage containers made of plastic free of bisphenol A (BPA). BPA is a chemical often used in manufacturing plastics, and it has been linked to health concerns such as hormone disruption and developmental issues in children.
There are a variety of storage containers made without BPA, and some of the most popular options include glass and stainless steel containers. While there are some benefits to using these containers, they may not be ideal for all situations. For example, glass containers are heavier than plastic ones, making them more difficult to move around. Additionally, stainless steel containers can be difficult to clean if they get dirty.

Suppose you're undecided about which type of storage container is best for you. In that case, it's worth considering your needs and preferences before deciding. Plenty of options will meet your needs without exposing you or your belongings to dangerous chemicals.

Stackable.

I know we all have a cupboard or a drawer packed full of containers and lids. If you begin to make meal prep a part of your regular routine, a lot of containers will start to accumulate. Stackable containers will keep your cupboards functional and organized, making life easier.

Freezer-safe.

A freezer-safe container is a great option for long-term storage because it's temperature and humidity resistant. This container is also ideal for storing perishable items, like food. These containers are heavy-duty materials, like steel, and can hold much weight. They're also easy to clean.

Microwave-safe.

Another type of microwave-safe food storage container is the Pyrex container. Pyrex is a popular brand name for glassware that is heat resistant up to 480 degrees Fahrenheit. Pyrex containers are often used to store foods like soups, stews, and chili in the oven or microwave.

In addition to storing food in traditional containers, there are special holders designed specifically for microwave use. These holders are often called "microwave mugs" or "microwave pouches," They come in different sizes and shapes to fit any type of food.

Dishwasher-safe.

Dishwasher-safe containers are designed to be washed in a dishwasher. This means they will not corrode or warp over time, making them ideal for storing food. Non-dishwasher-safe containers, on the other hand, may not be able to be washed in a dishwasher, but they are still generally safe to use. They may have a coating that makes them resistant to moisture and corrosion, or they may simply be made from thicker materials that are more durable.

Suppose you need to store food in a container that will not be washed in a dishwasher. In that case, choosing a container made from a non-corroding material is important. Some examples of non-corroding materials include glass or stainless steel. If you need to store food in a container that will be washed in a dishwasher, it is best to choose a container that is made from plastic or silicone.

Glass Containers

Glass containers are one type of storage container that is becoming increasingly popular. Here are some reasons why glass containers are a good choice for storage:

- They are lightweight and easy to move around.
- They are shatterproof and unbreakable.
- They can be recycled.

If you're looking for a storage container that is environmentally friendly and will last for years, glass is a great option.

Plastic Containers

Plastic containers are very popular for meal prep— they're lightweight, stack easily, and many are now micro- waivable and freezable. But as I mentioned, my go-to is glass. Plastic containers may leach harmful substances into the food stored in them. Plastic is not biodegradable, which means it isn't possible for our earth to naturally absorb the material back into the soil; instead, plastic actually contaminates it. Unlike glass and metal, plastic absorbs odors and tastes like whatever you stored in it previously. If you have ever stored fish in a plastic container, I'm guessing it still smells like fish to this day. While it's a fact that plastic is cheaper than other options, it's also true that it will not last as long. If you choose to go with plastic containers, always look for an indicator that they are BPA-free.

Mason Jars

Mason (canning) jars are also great for storing food. Made of glass, Mason jars are inexpensive and perfect for storing salads and salad dressings. A combination of wide-mouth quart and pint jars and some smaller four-ounce jars for dressings will go a long way when preparing meals. I incorporate them a few times throughout the preps for quick storage.

Stainless Steel

Stainless steel food containers are ideal for storing and transporting food. They are durable, leak-proof, and easy to clean. They come in various sizes and shapes, so you can find the perfect one for your needs. Here are some of the most common types of stainless steel food containers:

- Food storage container sets. These sets come with various-sized containers, so you can easily store your food in one place.
- Glass storage jars. These jars are perfect for storing small amounts of food. They are also easy to clean and sterilize.
- Plastic storage containers. These containers are perfect for storing large quantities of food. They are durable, and they don't corrode or rust over time.
- Stainless steel pots and pans. Stainless steel pots and pans are ideal for cooking and baking foods. They are resistant to heat and won't damage your food or cookware.
- Stainless steel bowls and plates. These bowls and plates are perfect for serving food to customers or guests. They are dishwasher safe, so you can easily clean them afterward.

31.5 Safe Reheating Guidelines

You can safely reheat your prepped meals by following simple guidelines in the microwave, in the oven, or on the stovetop.

Safely Reheating Meals In The Microwave

While a microwave won't always produce the same results as an oven, using a microwave for reheating prepped meals is often much faster and more convenient. Here are a few general tips for getting the best results when reheating your prepped meals in a microwave oven.

Always Remove The Lids

There are many myths surrounding microwaving food. Some people believe you should never remove the lid of a microwave-safe food container because this will cause the heat from the microwaves to cook the food from the inside out. Others think it's necessary to keep the lid on to create a hot and moist environment for cooking your food. The truth is that neither of these practices is necessary - they can both be harmful.

The main problem with keeping the lid on is that it prevents steam from escaping. This steam heat cooks your food more quickly than if you left the oven door open. It also causes condensation inside the container, leading to bacteria growth. By removing the lid, you allow steam and moisture to escape, which reduces the chances of bacteria growth and gives your food a better chance of becoming nutrient-rich and delicious.

So what should you do? Always remove the lids when microwaving foods unless you have a reason not to (like adding ingredients). This will help reduce bacteria and make your food tastier and more nutritious!

Be Sure To Thaw Frozen Meals Before Reheating

Thawed foods should be placed in a single layer on a paper towel-lined plate and microwaved on high for 2 minutes or until heated through. Frozen food will heat up quickly and could reach dangerous temperatures. Instead, defrost your food before heating it in the oven.

Three Minutes On High Usually Does The Trick

As a general rule, microwaving refrigerated prepped meals for about 3 minutes on high should be sufficient for most of the recipes in this book. If possible, larger ingredients such as proteins should be removed from containers and reheated in the microwave first to ensure other foods don't become overcooked in the process. Also, ensure the food's surface is as smooth as possible to ensure even reheating.

Only Reheat Glass Containers Or Microwave Safe Ones

Microwave reheating guidelines can be tricky, but using glass containers can make the process safer. According to the Food and Drug Administration, microwaves are not meant to heat food above 455 degrees Fahrenheit. Additionally, heating food in a plastic container can release harmful chemicals into the food. By heating food in a glass container, you reduce the risk of harmful chemicals leaching into your food. Furthermore, using a glass container will also keep your microwaves clean. Alternatively, you may also opt for containers marked "Microwave Safe."

Safely Reheating Meals In An Oven Or On The Stovetop

Are you tired of cleaning up your microwave after using it to reheat food? There is a simple solution that you can use to help minimize the amount of mess that you make. Instead of using a dish, use a baking sheet. This will help to reduce the amount of grease and food particles that are created when microwaving food. Additionally, using a baking sheet will help to prevent the food from sticking to the bottom of the microwave oven. By following these simple guidelines, you can avoid cleaning your microwave often and create less of a mess in the process.

Reheat To The Same Temperature The Meal Was Prepared To

When reheating your meals, the meals should be reheated to the same temperatures they were originally cooked to, and for most recipes in this book, reheating your meals on the middle oven rack for 20 minutes in a preheated oven setto350°F(180°C) should be sufficient. Use a thermometer to check the meals every 5 minutes, after 10 minutes.

Use A Baking Sheet To Minimize The Mess

Whenever reheating a meal in the oven, place it on a baking tray lined with parchment paper. This will prevent any liquids that bubble over from the container from dripping onto the surface of your oven, which can create a mess.

Stick To The Stovetop For Certain Recipes

While a conventional oven or microwave oven will work for reheating the majority of the recipes in this book, some recipes that were originally prepared in a frying pan or in a pot, such as soups, are best reheated in a large frying pan or pot placed over medium heat on the stovetop.

Use A Thermometer To Check The Temperature

Whichever method you follow to reheat your meals, it's best to check the internal temperature of the food to ensure it's been reheated to the proper cooking temperature. A simple oven or kitchen thermometer is all you'll need to do this.

How to Thaw Safely

There are various methods for thawing raw proteins, such as meat, poultry, and fish. To begin, put it in the refrigerator the night before. A full turkey or chicken will require 2 to 3 days in the refrigerator to properly defrost. Smaller products, like frozen shrimp, can be placed in a chilly water bath for 1 to 2 hours. When thawing food this way, ensure no dishes are in the sink. You can also microwave frozen raw proteins to defrost them. However, some meats or fish may begin to cook because the heat is distributed unevenly. If you use the microwave to thaw food, it is recommended that you cook it right soon. You can use the same methods mentioned above to prepare cooked meals. Thawing in the refrigerator is preferable because the food remains at a safe temperature throughout. After completely thawed, the meal can be stored in the refrigerator for 3 to 4 days. Any reheated food should have an internal temperature of 165eF, which should be tested using a thermometer inserted in the thickest section of the dish.

32 BREAKFAST RECIPES

32.1 Bacon And Brie Omelet Wedges

Preparation Time: 10 minutes
Cooking Time: 10 minutes
Servings: 4

Ingredients:

- Dijon Mustard – 1 Tsp.
- Olive Oil – 2 Tbsp.
- Smoked Bacon – 7 Oz.
- Eggs – 6 Whole (Lightly Beaten)
- Chives, Snipped Up – Small Bunch
- Ounce Of Sliced Brie – 3 And ½ Oz. (Sliced)
- Red Wine Vinegar – 1 Tsp.
- Cucumber Sliced Up Diagonally – 1 Whole (Deseeded And Sliced)
- Radish – 7 Oz. (Sectioned)

Procedure:

1. Turn on your grill
2. Take a small-sized pan and add 1 tsp. of oil
3. Allow it to heat up over the grill
4. Add bacon and fry them until nice and crisp
5. Drain the bacon on kitchen paper
6. Take another non-sticky frying pan and place it over the grill
7. Heat up 2 tsp. of oil
8. Add bacon, eggs, and chives to the frying pan and sprinkle ground pepper
9. Cook over low heat until it is semi set
10. Carefully lay the Brie on top
11. Grill until the Brie has set and shows a golden texture
12. Remove the pan and cut the omelet up into wedges
13. Take a small bowl and create a salad by mixing olive oil, mustard, vinegar, and seasoning
14. Add cucumber and radish to the bowl
15. Mix well and serve it alongside the Omelet wedges
16. Enjoy!

Storage: It can be stored in the refrigerator for 2-3 days. Alternatively, you may store it in your freezer for 2 months at most.

Nutrition value per serving: Calories: 35 kcal, Fat: 31 g, Carbs: 3 g, Protein: 25 g, Sodium: 245 mg

32.2 Black Olive Breakfast Loaf

Preparation Time: 10 minutes
Cooking Time: 60 minutes
Servings: 4

Ingredients:

- Bread Flour – 3 Cups
- Active Dry Yeast – 2 Tsp.
- White Sugar – 2 Tbsp.
- Salt – 1 Tsp.
- Black Olives – ½ Cup (Chopped)
- Olive Oil – 3 Tbsp.
- Warm Water (110 Degree Fahrenheit) – 1 And ¼ Cups
- Cornmeal – 1 Tbsp.

Procedure:

1. Take a large-sized bowl and add flour, sugar, yeast, salt, black olives, water, and olive oil
2. Mix well to prepare the dough
3. Turn the dough onto a floured surface and knead it well for about 5-10 minutes until elastic

4. Keep it on the side and allow it to rise for about 45 minutes until it has doubled in size
5. Punch the dough down and knead again for 10 minutes
6. Allow it to rise for 30 minutes more
7. Round up the dough on the kneading board
8. Place upside down in a bowl and line it up with a lint-free, well flour towel
9. Allow it to rise until it has doubled in size
10. While the bread is rising up for the third and final time, take a pan and fill it up with water
11. Place it at the bottom of your oven
12. Pre-heat your oven to a temperature of 500°F
13. Turn the loaf out onto a sheet pan and lightly oil it
14. Dust with some cornmeal
15. Bake for about 15 minutes
16. Lower the heat to 375°F
17. Bake for another 30 minutes
18. Enjoy!

Storage: It can be stored in the refrigerator for 2-3 days. Alternatively, you may store it in your freezer for 2 months at most.

Nutrition value per serving: Calories: 138 kcal, Fat: 3 g, Carbs: 22 g, Protein: 3 g, Sodium: 245 mg

32.3 Mediterranean Bread With Melted Cheese

Preparation Time: 10 minutes
Cooking Time: 5 minutes
Servings: 4

Ingredients:

- Fresh parsley – ¼ cup (chopped)
- Black pepper – ¼ tsp.
- Salt- 1 tsp.
- Garlic clove – 1 (minced)
- Olive oil – 1 tbsp.
- Feta cheese – ¼ cup (crumbled)
- Mozzarella cheese – ½ cup (shredded)
- Bread – 1 loaf

Procedure:

1. Preheat the oven to 350 degrees.
2. Place loaf bread on a baking sheet and brush with olive oil. Sprinkle with garlic, salt, and pepper. Bake for 10 minutes or until the bread is golden brown.
3. Add mozzarella cheese, feta cheese, and parsley to the top of the bread, spreading them nicely, and bake for an additional 5 minutes or until the cheese is melted.
4. Serve warm.

Storage: It can be stored in the refrigerator for 2-3 days. Alternatively, you may store it in your freezer for 2 months at most.

Nutrition value per serving: Calories: 477 kcal, Fat: 25 g, Carbs: 45 g, Protein: 16 g, Sodium: 245 mg

32.4 Vegetarian Shepherd's Pie

Preparation Time: 20 minutes
Cooking Time: 30 minutes
Servings: 4

Ingredients:

- Olive oil – 1 tbsp.
- Onion – 1 whole (chopped)
- Green bell pepper 1 whole (chopped)
- Carrots – 1 whole (peeled and chopped)
- Celery Rib – ½ cup (chopped)
- Garlic cloves -4 (minced)
- Dried thyme – 1 tsp.
- Dried basil- ½ tsp.
- Black pepper – ¼ tsp.
- Tomatoes 14 oz. (diced)
- Red kidney beans – 10 oz. (rinsed and drained)
- Corn – 6 oz. (drained)
- Vegetable broth – 2 cups

Procedure:

1. Preheat the oven to 350 degrees F (175 degrees C).
2. Heat oil in a large skillet over medium heat. Add onion, bell pepper, carrots, celery rib, and garlic; cook until vegetables are tender.
3. Stir in thyme, basil, and black pepper.
4. Add tomatoes with their juice, kidney beans, corn, and flour. Bring to a boil; cook until thickened.
5. Pour mixture into a greased 9x13 inch baking dish. Bake for 30 minutes or until heated through.
6. Once the surface has a golden texture, serve and enjoy.

Storage: It can be stored in the refrigerator for 2-3 days. Alternatively, you may store it in your freezer for 2 months at most.
Nutrition value per serving: Calories: 552 kcal, Fat: 24 g, Carbs: 64 g, Protein: 20 g, Sodium: 245 mg

32.5 Fresh Watermelon And Arugula Meal

Preparation Time: 10 minutes
Cooking Time: 15 minutes
Servings: 4
Ingredients:
Salad

- Feta Cheese – 1/3 Cup (Crumbled)
- Arugula – 5 Cups
- Kalamata Olives- 1/3 Cup (Halved)
- Watermelon – 2 Cups (cubed)

Vinaigrette

- Salt and black Pepper – As Needed
- Extra Virgin Olive Oil – ¼ Cup
- Shallots – 1 Small (Chopped)
- Sherry Vinegar – 2 Tbsp.

Procedure:

1. Take a medium-sized bowl and add arugula, feta, olives, and cubed watermelon to prepare the salad by mixing them all together
2. Take a small measure cup and add all of the ingredients listed under vinaigrette ingredients and whisk well
3. Season with some salt and pepper
4. When you are ready to serve, whisk the vinaigrette a stir and drizzle half of the vinaigrette over the salad
5. Toss well
6. Add more vinaigrette to lightly coat up the arugula
7. Enjoy!

Storage: It can be stored in the refrigerator for 2-3 days. Alternatively, you may store it in your freezer for 2 months at most.
Nutrition value per serving: Calories: 234 kcal, Fat: 27 g, Carbs: 8 g, Protein: 8g, Sodium: 245 mg

32.6 Morning Scrambled Pesto Eggs

Preparation Time: 10 minutes
Cooking Time: 5 minutes
Servings: 2
Ingredients:

- Large Eggs – 3 Whole
- Butter – 1 Tbsp.
- Pesto – 1 Tbsp.
- Creamed Coconut Milk – 2 Tbsp.
- Salt And Pepper- As Needed

Procedure:

1. Take a bowl and crack open your egg
2. Season with a pinch of salt and pepper
3. Pour eggs into a pan
4. Add butter and introduce heat
5. Cook on low heat and gently add pesto
6. Once the egg is cooked and scrambled, remove the heat
7. Spoon in coconut cream and mix well

8. Turn on the heat and cook on LOW for a while until you have a creamy texture
9. Serve and enjoy!

Storage: It can be stored in the refrigerator for 2-3 days.
Nutrition value per serving: Calories: 35 kcal, Fat: 31 g, Carbs: 3 g, Protein: 25 g, Sodium: 245 mg

32.7 Egg And Acorn In A Hole

Preparation Time: 10 minutes
Cooking Time: 20 minutes
Servings: 4
Ingredients:

- Acorn Squash – 2 Whole
- Whole Eggs – 5 Whole
- Extra Virgin Olive Oil – 2 Tbsp.
- Salt – As Needed
- Pepper – As Needed
- Dates – 5 Whole (Pitted)
- Walnut – 8 Halves
- Parsley- A Bunch
- Maple Syrup – As Needed For Garnish

Procedure:

1. Pre-heat your oven to 375°F
2. Slice the squash crosswise and prepare 3 slices with holes in them
3. While slicing the squash, make sure that each slice has a measurement of ¾ inch thickness
4. Remove the seeds from the slices
5. Take a baking sheet and line it up with parchment paper
6. Transfer the slices to your baking sheet and season them with salt and pepper
7. Bake in your oven for 20 minutes
8. Chop the walnuts and dates on your cutting board
9. Take the baking dish out from the oven and drizzle slices with olive oil
10. Crack an egg into each of the holes in the slices and season with pepper and salt
11. Sprinkle the chopped walnuts on top
12. Bake for 10 minutes
13. Garnish with parsley and add maple syrup
14. Enjoy!

Storage: It can be stored in the refrigerator for 2-3 days. Alternatively, you may store it in your freezer for 2 months at most.
Nutrition value per serving: Calories: 200 kcal, Fat: 12 g, Carbs: 17 g, Protein: 8 g, Sodium: 245 mg

32.8 Dill And Tomato Frittata

Preparation Time: 10 minutes
Cooking Time: 30 - 40 minutes
Servings: 4
Ingredients:

- Salt And Pepper – To Taste
- Feta Cheese-½ Cup (Chopped)
- Eggs – 8 Whole
- Fresh Dill – ¼ Cup (Chopped)
- Cherry Tomatoes – 3 Cups (Quartered)
- Red Pepper – 1 Whole (Diced)
- Garlic Cloves – 2 (Minced)
- Onion – 1 Whole (Diced)
- Olive Oil – 1 Tbsp.

Procedure:

1. Preheat your oven to 350 degrees F. Grease a 9x13-inch baking dish. In a large skillet over medium heat, add olive oil and heat the oil.
2. Add the onion and garlic and cook until softened, about 5 minutes. Add the red pepper and cook for an additional 2 minutes.
3. Add the tomatoes and dill and bring to a simmer. Remove from heat. Whisk the eggs in a large bowl.
4. Gradually whisk in the tomato mixture until well combined.

5. Pour the mixture into the prepared baking dish. Sprinkle with feta cheese and salt and black pepper to taste. Bake for 30 minutes or until firm.

Storage: It can be stored in the refrigerator for 2-3 days. Alternatively, you may store it in your freezer for 2 months at most.
Nutrition value per serving: Calories: 200 kcal, Fat: 15 g, Carbs: 6 g, Protein: 9 g, Sodium: 245 mg

32.9 Fancy Olive And Cheese Loaf

Preparation Time: 10 minutes
Cooking Time: 15 minutes
Servings: 8
Ingredients:

- Soft Butter – ½ Cup
- Mayo – ¼ Cup
- Garlic Powder – 1 Tsp.
- Onion Powder – 1 Tsp.
- Mozzarella Cheese – 2 Cups
- Black Olives – ½ Cup
- French Bread – 1 Loaf (Halved)

Procedure:

1. The oven should be pre-heated at 350 degrees Fahrenheit.
2. 2. In a mixing bowl, combine the butter and mayo and whisk until well combined.
3. Add onion powder and garlic powder
4. Stir in olives and cheese
5. Spread the whole mixture over French bread
6. Place them on your baking sheet and bake for 10-12 minutes
7. Increase the heat to broil and cook until the cheese has melted until the bread is golden brown

Storage: It can be stored in BPA Free container for around 4-5 days in the refrigerator and 1-2 months in the freezer.

Nutrition value per serving: Calories: 400 kcal, Fat: 23 g, Carbs: 34 g, Protein: 13 g, Sodium: 245 mg

32.10 Savory Pistachio Balls

Preparation Time: 10 minutes
Cooking Time: 10 minutes
Servings: 4
Ingredients:

- Raisins – ½ Cup
- Fennel Seeds – ½ Tsp. (Ground)
- Dates – 1 Cup (Pitted)
- Pistachios – ½ Cup (Unsalted)
- Pepper – Just A Pinch
- Salt – Just A Pinch
- Fresh Parsley – 1 Tsp.

Procedure:

1. Preheat oven to 375 degrees F (190 degrees C).
2. Line a baking sheet with parchment paper.
3. In a medium bowl, combine pistachios, salt, raisins, dates and pepper.
4. With your hands, work the mixture into 1-inch balls.
5. In a large skillet over medium heat, heat olive oil.
6. Add onion and cook until softened, about 5 minutes.
7. Add parsley and cook for 1 minute more.
8. Remove from heat and roll pistachio balls in onion mixture until coated.
9. Place on prepared baking sheet and repeat until all ingredients are used up.
10. Bake in oven for 10 minutes until golden
11. Enjoy!

Storage: It can be stored in BPA Free container for around 4-5 days in the refrigerator and 1-2 months in the freezer.

Nutrition value per serving: Calories: 528 kcal, Fat: 2 g, Carbs: 10 g, Protein: 2 g, Sodium: 245 mg

32.11 Roasted Almonds

Preparation Time: 10 minutes
Cooking Time: 20 minutes
Servings: 4
Ingredients:

- Almonds – 2 and ½ cups
- Cayenne – ¼ tsp.
- Coriander – ¼ tsp.
- Cumin – ¼ tsp.
- Chili powder – ¼ tbsp.
- Rosemary – 1 tbsp. (chopped)
- Maple syrup – 2 and ½ tbsp.
- Salt – just a pinch

Procedure:

1. Preheat oven to 350 degrees F.
2. Spread almonds on a baking sheet and bake for 10 minutes, or until lightly browned. In a large skillet over medium heat, heat olive oil.
3. Add garlic and cook for 1 minute.
4. Add oregano and cumin; season with salt and pepper, remaining herbs and spices, to taste. Cook for 2 minutes longer.
5. Toss well to ensure that everything is mixed
6. Enjoy!

Storage: It can be stored in BPA Free container for around 4-5 days in the refrigerator and 1-2 months in the freezer.

Nutrition value per serving: Calories: 528 kcal, Fat: 2 g, Carbs: 10 g, Protein: 2 g, Sodium: 245 mg

32.12 Chocolate Matcha Balls

Preparation Time: 10 minutes
Cooking Time: 5 minutes
Servings: 4
Ingredients:

- Unsweetened Cocoa Powder – 2 Tbsp.
- Oats, Gluten-Free – 3 Tbsp.
- Pine Nuts – ½ Cup
- Almonds – ½ Cup
- Dates – 1 Cup (Pitted)
- Matcha Powder – 2 Tbsp.

Procedure:

1. Add cocoa powder, oats, pine nuts, almonds, and dates into a food processor and process until well combined.
2. Place matcha powder in a small dish.
3. Make small balls from mixture and coat with matcha powder.
4. Enjoy or store in refrigerator until ready to eat.

Storage: It can be stored in BPA Free container for around 4-5 days in the refrigerator and 1-2 months in the freezer.

Nutrition value per serving: Calories: 528 kcal, Fat: 2 g, Carbs: 10 g, Protein: 2 g, Sodium: 245 mg

33 SALADS RECIPES

33.1 Blood Orange Vinaigrette Salad

Preparation Time: 10 minutes
Cooking Time: 0 minute
Servings: 4
Ingredients:
For Blood Orange Vinaigrette

- Extra Virgin Olive Oil – 1/3 Cup
- Fresh Blood Orange Juice – ½ Cup
- Red Wine Vinegar – 2 Tbsp.
- Fresh Ginger – 1 Tbsp. (Grated)
- Garlic Powder – 1 Tsp.
- Ground Sumac – 1 Tsp.
- Salt– As Needed
- Pepper– As Needed
- Mustard Oil – 1 tsp.

For Base Salad

- Vegetable Oil – 2/3 Cup
- Sumac – ½ Tsp.
- Shallots – 2 (Sliced)
- Salt – As Needed
- Raw Unsalted Almonds – 1/3 Cup
- Raw Sliced Almonds – 1/3 Cup
- Pita Bread – 2 Loaves
- Paprika – ½ Tsp.
- Frisee Lettuce – 3 Cups (Chopped)
- Dried Apricots – 1/3 Cup (Chopped)
- Blood Oranges – 1 To 2 (Peeled And Sliced)
- 4 Cups Of Baby Spinach – 4 Cups

Procedure:

1. Cut the blood orange in half crosswise and remove the seeds. Peel and chop the flesh.
2. In a small bowl, whisk together the red wine vinegar, Dijon mustard, and olive oil until well combined. Season with salt and pepper to taste.
3. Add the chopped blood orange to the vinaigrette and stir to combine.
4. Take another bowl and mix all the ingredients listed under salad, cover with vinaigrette and toss
5. Serve and enjoy!

Storage: Can be stored in airtight BPA Safe containers for 3-4 days in the refrigerator. However, not recommended to store in the freezer for a long time as it does not stay well.
Nutrition value per serving: Calories: 528 kcal, Fat: 2 g, Carbs: 10 g, Protein: 2 g, Sodium: 245 mg

33.2 Mediterranean Tabouli Salad

Preparation Time: 10 minutes
Cooking Time: 0 minute
Servings: 4
Ingredients:

- Salt As Needed – As Needed
- Romaine Lettuce Leaves - As Needed
- Roma Tomatoes– 4 Whole(Chopped)
- Mint Leaves– 12 To 15 Leaves (Chopped)
- Lime Juice – 3 To 4 Tbsp.
- Green Onions (With White And Green Parts) – 4 Whole (Chopped)
- Fresh Parsley (Washed Up And Finely Chopped) – 2 Bunch
- Extra Virgin Olive Oil – 3-4 Tbsp.

- Extra Fine Bulgar Wheat – ½ Cup
- Cucumber – 1 Whole (Chopped)
- Kidney Beans – 1 cup (Cooked)
- Cilantro – As Deeded
- Pepper – as needed

Procedure:

1. Take a mixing bowl and add lime juice and olive oil to make the dressing
2. Take a salad bowl and add all of the remaining ingredients. Toss them well to mix thoroughly.
3. Serve chilled or at room temperature.

Storage: Can be stored in airtight BPA Safe containers for 3-4 days in the refrigerator. However, not recommended to store in the freezer for a long time as it does not stay well.
Nutrition value per serving: Calories: 528 kcal, Fat: 2 g, Carbs: 10 g, Protein: 2 g, Sodium: 245 mg

33.3 Kidney Beans Cilantro Salad

Preparation Time: 10 minutes
Cooking Time: 0 minute
Servings: 4
Ingredients:

- Kidney Beans (Drained And Rinsed) – 15 Oz.
- English Cucumber Chopped Up – ½ Cup (Chopped)
- Heirloom Tomatoes – 1 Medium Sized (Chopped)
- Fresh Cilantro Bunch (Stems Removed)
- Onion – 1 Whole (Chopped)
- Lime – 1 Whole
- Dijon Mustard – 3 Tbsp.
- Fresh Garlic Paste – ½ Tsp.
- Sumac – 1 Tsp.
- Salt -As Needed
- Pepper– As Needed

Procedure:

1. Take a medium-sized bowl and add Kidney beans, chopped-up veggies, and cilantro
2. Take a small bowl and make the vinaigrette by adding lime juice, oil, fresh garlic paste, pepper, mustard, and sumac
3. Pour the vinaigrette over the salad and give it a nice stir
4. Add some salt and pepper
5. Cover it up and allow it to chill for half an hour
6. Serve!

Storage: Can be stored in airtight BPA Safe containers for 3-4 days in the refrigerator. However, not recommended to store in the freezer for a long time as it does not stay well.

Nutrition value per serving: Calories: 528 kcal, Fat: 2 g, Carbs: 10 g, Protein: 2 g, Sodium: 245 mg

33.4 Simple Medi Salad

Preparation Time: 10 minutes
Cooking Time: 0 minute
Servings: 4
Ingredients:

- Romaine Lettuce – 1 Whole (Chopped)
- Roma Tomatoes – 3 Whole (Diced)
- English Cucumber – 1 Whole (Diced)
- Onions – 1 Whole
- Curly Parsley– ½ Cup (Chopped)
- Olive Oil – 2 Tbsp.
- Large Lemon – ½ A Lemon
- Garlic Powder – 1 Tsp.
- Salt – As Needed
- Pepper– As Needed

Procedure:

1. Wash the vegetable thoroughly
2. Prepare them as indicated in the ingredients section

3. Take a large-sized bowl and add vegetables, olive oil, spices, and lemon juice
4. Toss well and transfer them to your serving bowl
5. Enjoy fresh!

Storage: Can be stored in airtight BPA Safe containers for 3-4 days in the refrigerator. However, not recommended to store in the freezer for a long time as it does not stay well.
Nutrition value per serving: Calories: 528 kcal, Fat: 2 g, Carbs: 10 g, Protein: 2 g, Sodium: 245 mg

33.5 Tuna And Dijon Salad

Preparation Time: 10 minutes
Cooking Time: 0 minute
Servings: 4
Ingredients:
For Base recipe

- Genova Tuna Dipped In Olive Oil – 5 Oz.
- Celery Stalks– 2 And ½ Stalks (Chopped)
- English Cucumber – ½ A Cucumber (Chopped)
- Radishes- 4 To 5 Whole (Stems Removed, Chopped)
- Green Onions– 3 Whole (Chopped)
- Red Onion– ½ A Medium Sized (Chopped)
- Kalamata Olives – ½ Cup (Halved)
- Parsley– 1 Bunch (Chopped)
- Fresh Mint Leaves– 10 To 15 Sprigs (Stems Removed, Chopped)
- Heirloom Tomatoes – 5 Slices
- Pita Pockets For Serving- For Serving

For Zesty Dijon Mustard Vinaigrette

- Dijon Mustard – 2 And ½ Tsp.
- Zest Of Lime – 1 Piece (Zest)
- Juice Of Lime – 1 And ½ (Juiced)
- Olive Oil – 1/3 Cup
- Sumac – ½ Tsp.
- Salt – Pinch
- Pepper– As Needed
- Crushed Red Pepper Flakes – ½ Tsp. (Crushed)

Procedure:

1. Prepare the Zest Mustard Vinaigrette by taking a small bowl and adding all of the ingredients listed under Zesty Dijon Mustard vinaigrette. Stir well.
2. For the Tuna salad, take a large-sized bowl and add 3 cans of 5-ounce Genova Tuna (or your preferred brand) alongside the chopped vegetables, chopped up fresh parsley, mint leaves, and Kalamata olives
3. Mix well using a spoon
4. Dress the tuna salad with the prepared vinaigrette
5. Mix again until the tuna salad is properly coated with the vinaigrette
6. Cover and allow it to chill for 30 minutes
7. Once done, give the salad a toss and serve with a side of pita chips or pita bread and some sliced-up heirloom tomatoes!
8. Enjoy!

Storage: Can be stored in airtight BPA Safe containers for 3-4 days in the refrigerator. However, not recommended to store in the freezer for a long time as it does not stay well.
Nutrition value per serving: Calories: 528 kcal, Fat: 2 g, Carbs: 10 g, Protein: 2 g, Sodium: 245 mg

33.6 Arugula And Garlic Avocado Vinaigrette

Preparation Time: 10 minutes
Cooking Time: 0 minute
Servings: 4

Ingredients:

For Base recipe

- Shelled Fava Beans – 1 And ½ Cups
- Persian Cucumbers – 3 Whole (Chopped)
- Packed Grape Tomatoes – 2 Cups (Halved)
- Packed Baby Arugula -4 Cups
- Jalapeno Pepper – 1 Whole (Sliced)
- Green Onions– 4 Whole (Chopped)
- Avocado – 1 Whole

For Lemon-Honey Vinaigrette

- Salt– As Needed
- Pepper - As Needed
- Juice Of Lemon – 1 And 1/2
- Garlic Clove – 1 Clove (Chopped)
- Extra Virgin Olive Oil – ½ Cup
- Cilantro – 2 Tbsp. (Chopped)
- Chopped Fresh Mint- 2 Tbsp. (Chopped)

Procedure:

1. Prepare your ingredients as directed above
2. Take a small-sized bowl and add the ingredients listed under the vinaigrette
3. Whisk them well to prepare the vinaigrette
4. Take a large-sized mixing bowl and the remaining ingredients from the base ingredients section, except for avocado
5. Dress the salad with garlic herb vinaigrette and finely toss them
6. Peel your avocado at this point and core it up
7. Chop it up and add the avocado to the salad as well
8. Divide the whole salad among four bowls
9. Enjoy!

Storage: Can be stored in airtight BPA Safe containers for 3-4 days in the refrigerator. However, not recommended to store in the freezer for a long time as it does not stay well.

Nutrition value per serving: Calories: 528 kcal, Fat: 2 g, Carbs: 10 g, Protein: 2 g, Sodium: 245 mg

33.7 Homely Fattoush Salad

Preparation Time: 10 minutes
Cooking Time: 0 minute
Servings: 4

Ingredients:

For Base recipe

- Pita Bread – 2 Loaves
- Extra Virgin Olive Oil – As Needed
- Tsp. Of Sumac – ½ Tsp.
- Salt– As Needed
- Pepper - As Needed
- Romaine Lettuce Chopped Up – 1 Whole Heart (Chopped)
- English Cucumber – 1 Whole (Chopped)
- Roma Tomatoes – 5 Whole (Chopped)
- Onions– 5 Whole (Chopped)
- Radishes– 5 Whole (Thinly Sliced)
- Fresh Parsley Leaves (Stems Removed) – 2 Cups (Chopped)
- Fresh Mint Leaves- 1 Cup (Chopped)

For Lime Vinaigrette

- Sumac – 1 Tsp.
- Ground Allspice – ¼ Tsp.
- Ground Cinnamon – ¼ Tsp.
- Juice Of Lime – 1 And ½
- Bottle Of Extra Virgin Olive Oil – 1/3 A Bottle
- Salt– As Needed
- Pepper– As Needed

Procedure:

1. yAdd your pita bread to your toasted and toast them until they are crisp but not browned
2. Take a large-sized pan and place it over medium heat
3. Add 3 tablespoons of olive oil and heat it up

4. Break the toasted pita into pieces and add them to the oil
5. Fry until browned, making sure to toss them from time to time
6. Add salt, ½ a tsp. of sumac, and pepper
7. Remove the pita from the heat and place them on a paper towel to drain them
8. Take a large-sized mixing bowl and add chopped-up lettuce, tomatoes, cucumber, and green onions with sliced-up parsley and radish
9. Make the lime vinaigrette by taking a bowl and mixing all of the ingredients listed under vinaigrette
10. Toss the salad with vinaigrette very gently
11. Add pita chips on top and some additional sumac
12. Give it a final toss, and enjoy!

Storage: Can be stored in airtight BPA Safe containers for 3-4 days in the refrigerator. However, not recommended to store in the freezer for a long time as it does not stay well.

Nutrition value per serving: Calories: 528 kcal, Fat: 2 g, Carbs: 10 g, Protein: 2 g, Sodium: 245 mg

33.8 Roasted Beet And Kale Salad

Preparation Time: 10 minutes
Cooking Time: 30 minute
Servings: 4

Ingredients:

For Base recipe

- Seasonings: olive oil, pepper, and salt as needed
- Bunch Of Kale– 1 Bunch (Washed And Dried)
- Washed Beets– 5 Whole (Washed, Peeled, and Dried)
- Dried Rosemary – ½ Tsp.
- Garlic Powder – ½ Tsp.
- Red Onion – ¼ Medium (Thinly Sliced)
- Almonds - 2 Tbsp. (Slivered)

For Lemon-Honey Vinaigrette

- Lemon Juice – 1 And 1/2
- Garlic Powder – ¼ Tsp.
- Olive Oil – ¼ Cup
- Honey – ¼ Cup
- Dried Rosemary – 1 Tsp.
- Salt– As Needed
- Pepper– As Needed

Procedure:

1. Pre-heat your oven to a temperature of 400 degrees Fahrenheit
2. Toss kale, onion, and beets with rosemary, garlic powder, and almonds
3. Take a small-sized bowl and add the ingredients for the lemon honey vinaigrette. Mix well until you have a nice dressing. Drizzle the dressing over your prepared kale.
4. Transfer the kale to a baking sheet lined with parchment paper. Transfer to oven.
5. Roast for 20-25 minutes, stirring once, on a baking sheet. The dish can be served at room temperature or warmed to your preference.

Storage: Can be stored in airtight BPA Safe containers for 3-4 days in the refrigerator. However, not recommended to store in the freezer for a long time as it does not stay well.

Nutrition value per serving: Calories: 528 kcal, Fat: 2 g, Carbs: 10 g, Protein: 2 g, Sodium: 245 mg

33.9 Pearl Couscous Salad

Preparation Time: 10 minutes
Cooking Time: 0 minute
Servings: 4

Ingredients:

For Lemon Dill Vinaigrette

- Juice OfLarge Sized Lemon – 1 Whole (Juiced)
- Extra Virgin Olive Oil – 1/3 Cup
- Dill Weed – 1 Tsp.

- Garlic Powder- 1 Tsp.
- Salt– As Needed
- Pepper – As Needed

For Israeli Couscous

- Pearl Couscous – 2 Cups
- Extra Virgin Olive Oil – As Needed
- Red Onion – 1 Cup (Sliced)
- Cilantro – 1 Bunch (Chopped)
- Smoked Paprika – 1 Tsp.
- Salt And Black Pepper – As Needed

Procedure:

1. In a medium bowl, combine the couscous, black pepper, salt, red onion, parsley, cilantro, smoked paprika, stir to combine.
2. Prepare the lemon dill vinaigrette by taking a small-sized bowl and adding the ingredients listed under Lemon Dill Vinaigrette; stir well
3. Toss the mixture with the Israeli Couscous.
4. Serve refrigerated or at room temperature.

Storage: Can be stored in airtight BPA Safe containers for 3-4 days in the refrigerator. However, not recommended to store in the freezer for a long time as it does not stay well.

Nutrition value per serving: Calories: 528 kcal, Fat: 2 g, Carbs: 10 g, Protein: 2 g, Sodium: 245 mg

33.10 Sweet Broad Bean Pomegranate Mix

Preparation Time: 10 minutes
Cooking Time: 0 minute
Servings: 4

Ingredients:

- Pumpkin Seeds – 2 Tbsp.
- Pomegranate Seeds – 1 Cup
- Parsley – Small Bunch (Chopped)
- Mint – Small Bunch (Chopped)
- Large Handful Of Watercress- Large Handful
- Frozen Broad Beans – 1 And ½ Cups
- Fennel Bulb - 1 Whole (Core Removed, Thinly Sliced)
- Bulgar Wheat – 1 Cup

For Dressing

- Zest OfLemon – 1 Whole Lemon
- Juice OfLemon- 1 Lemon (Juiced)
- Extra Virgin Rapeseed Oil – 5 Tbsp.
- Dijon Mustard- 1 Tbsp.
- Cider Vinegar – 2 Tbsp.

Procedure:

1. Take a bowl and add Bulgar Wheat alongside a bit of salt
2. Take a kettle and heat up some water and bring to a boil
3. Pour the boiling water over the Bulgar and allow it to sit for 10 minutes
4. Lock up the lid and give it a nice shake
5. Uncover and drain
6. Tip in the Bulgar wheat into a bowl
7. Add fennel, pomegranate, herbs, pumpkin seeds and broad beans
8. Take a jar and add the ingredients listed under dressing, mix them well and pour over Bulgar.
9. Toss well
10. Top up with some salad leaves (watercress)
11. Drizzle with the dressing
12. Enjoy!

Storage: Can be stored in airtight BPA Safe containers for 3-4 days in the refrigerator. However, not recommended to store in the freezer for a long time as it does not stay well.

Nutrition value per serving: Calories: 355 kcal, Fat: 13 g, Carbs: 38 g, Protein: 11 g, Sodium: 245 mg

34 SOUPS RECIPES

34.1 Pear And Cinnamon Squash Soup

Preparation Time: 10 minutes
Cooking Time: 20 minutes
Servings: 4
Ingredients:

- Greek Yogurt – ¼ Cup
- White Kidney Beans – ½ Cup
- Salt – ½ Tsp.
- Black Pepper – ½ Tsp.
- Butternut Squash – 1 Small (Peeled Into 1 Inch Pieces)
- Pear – 1 Small (Peeled And Cored)
- Yellow Onion – 1 Small (Diced)
- Cinnamon – 1 Stick
- Dried Oregano – 1 Tsp.
- Low Sodium Chicken Stock – 2 Cups
- Garlic Cloves – 2 Large Sized
- Extra Virgin Olive Oil – 2 Tbsp.
- Oregano – 2 Tbsp.
- Parsley – 2tbsp. (Chopped)
- Walnuts – 2 Tbsp.

Procedure:

1. In a large pot or Dutch oven, heat the olive oil over medium heat.
2. Add the onion and cook until softened, about 5 minutes.
3. Add the butternut squash, pears, cinnamon, and stock. Bring to a boil and then reduce the heat to a low simmer.
4. Cook until the vegetables are tender, about 20 minutes.
5. Purée the soup in a blender or food processor until smooth. Season with salt and pepper to taste. Serve hot.
6. Season with oregano and parsley, and add some walnuts on top. Serve and enjoy!

Storage: It can be stored in BPA Safe container or pots for up to 3-4 days in the fridge and 2 months in the freezer.

Nutrition value per serving: Calories: 200 kcal, Fat: 10 g, Carbs: 12 g, Protein: 3 g, Sodium: 300 mg, Potassium:

34.2 Mediterranean Pepper Soup

Preparation Time: 10 minutes
Cooking Time: 30 minutes
Servings: 6
Ingredients:

- Uncooked Rice – ¼ Cup
- Onion – 1 Whole (Chopped)
- Green Pepper – 1 Large (Chopped)
- Tomato – 1 Large (Chopped)
- Lean Ground Beef – 1 Lb. (Ground)
- Garlic Cloves – 2 (Minced)
- Parsley (Additional For Garnish) – 2 Tbsp. (Chopped)
- Olive Oil – 2 Tbsp.
- Tomato Paste – 2 Tbsp.
- Beef Broth – 4 Cups
- Salt And Pepper – As Needed
- Oregano – 1 tbsp.
- Cumin – 1 tsp.
- Red Wine Vinegar – ¼ cup

Procedure:

1. In a large pot, sauté onions, green pepper, ground beef, garlic cloves,and garlic in olive oil over medium heat until softened. Add the tomatoes with their juice, oregano, cumin, salt and black pepper and uncooked rice.
2. Bring to a boil then reduce heat and simmer for 30 minutes. Add beef broth and red wine vinegar.

3. Simmer for 10 more minutes or until heated through. Ladle into bowls and top with parsley leaves.
4. Serve hot, and enjoy!

Storage: It can be stored in BPA Safe container or pots for up to 3-4 days in the fridge and 2 months in the freezer.
Nutrition value per serving: Calories: 162 kcal, Fat: 3 g, Carbs: 12 g, Protein: 21 g, Sodium: 250 mg

34.3 Mediterranean Tomato Soup

Preparation Time: 10 minutes
Cooking Time: 25 minute
Servings: 4
Ingredients:

- Red Pepper Flakes – ½ Tsp.
- Coconut Milk – 14 Oz.
- Tomatoes – 15 Oz. (Diced)
- Plum Tomatoes – 28 Oz. (Diced)
- Coriander – 1 Tsp. (Ground)
- Cumin – 1 Tsp. (Ground)
- Red Curry Powder – 1 Tsp.
- Salt (Extra For Taste If Needed) – 1 Tsp.
- Yellow Onions – 2 Medium (Sliced)
- Curry Powder – 2 Tsp.
- Olive Oil- 4 Tbsp.
- Water (Vegetable Broth Or Chicken Broth Also Usable) – 5 And ½ Cups

Procedure:

1. In a large pot or Dutch oven over medium heat, sauté tomatoes, plum tomatoes, and yellow onions well
2. Add oregano and thyme and other spices and stir well
3. Add broth and oil and bring the mixture to a boil
4. Lower down the heat and simmer for about 30 minutes or until the lentils are cooked through. Serve hot.

Storage: It can be stored in BPA Safe container or pots for up to 3-4 days in the fridge and 2 months in the freezer.

Nutrition value per serving: Calories: 74 kcal, Fat: 0.7 g, Carbs: 16 g, Protein: 2 g, Sodium: 300 mg

34.4 Classic Tuscan Veggie Soup

Preparation Time: 10 minutes
Cooking Time: 20 minutes
Servings: 4
Ingredients:

- Black Pepper – ¼ Tsp.
- Salt – ½ Tsp.
- Onion – ½ An Onion (Diced)
- Garlic Clove – 1 Whole (Minced)
- Zucchini – 1 Small (Diced)
- Fresh Thyme Leaves – 1 Tbsp. (Chopped)
- Olive Oil – 1 Tbsp.
- Low Sodium Cannellini Beans (Drained And Rinsed) – 15 Oz.
- Freshly Grated Parmesan – 1/3 Cup
- Tomatoes – 14 Oz. (Diced)
- Baby Spinach Leaves – 2 Cups. (Chopped)
- Carrots – 2 Whole (Diced)
- Celery – 2 Stalks (Diced)
- Fresh Sage – 2 Tsp. (Chopped)
- Low Sodium Chicken Broth – 32 Oz.

Procedure:

1. Take a small-sized bowl and mash half of your beans using the back of your spoons
2. Keep it on the side
3. Take a large-sized soup pot and place it over medium-high heat
4. Add oil and allow it to heat up

5. Add carrots, onion, celery, garlic, zucchini, thyme, ½ a tsp. of salt, sage, ¼ tsp. of pepper, and cook well for about5 minutes until the vegetables are tender
6. Add broth and tomatoes (with the juice) and bring the whole mixture to a boil
7. Add beans (both mashed and whole) alongside spinach
8. Cook for 3 minutes until the spinach has wilted
9. Serve with toppings of Parmesan
10. Enjoy!

Storage: It can be stored in BPA Safe container or pots for up to 3-4 days in the fridge and 2 months in the freezer.

Nutrition value per serving: Calories: 140 kcal, Fat: 9 g, Carbs: 21 g, Protein: 10 g, Sodium: 340 mg

34.5 Excellent Mediterranean Lemon Chicken Soup With Turmeric

Preparation Time: 10 minutes
Cooking Time: 40 minute
Servings: 4
Ingredients:

- Lemons (zest and juice) – 2 whole
- Fresh parsley – ½ Cup (Chopped)
- Fresh dill – ¼ Cup (chopped)
- Baby spinach – 2 cups
- Turmeric – 1/2 tsp.
- Aleppo pepper – 1 tsp.
- Coriander – 1 tsp.
- Carrot – 2 whole (peeled and sliced)
- Extra virgin olive oil – as needed
- Garlic cloves – 4 large (2 minced and 2 whole)
- Yellow Onion – 1 whole (Quartered)
- Chicken breast – 1 lb. (Boneless)

Procedure:

1. Take a large-sized Dutch oven and add 6 cups of water alongside the chicken.
2. Season the mix generously with salt and pepper, add Onion and garlic and bring the whole mix to a boil over medium-high heat.
3. Once the water has started to boil, lower the heat to simmer and let it cook for 15-20 minutes until the chicken is thoroughly cooked
4. Once done, remove the chicken from the pot and shred it using forks
5. Strain the remaining broth using a fine metal mesh/strainer and pour it into a large-sized bowl
6. Discard the whole garlic and Onion
7. Wipe the pot and return it back to medium heat
8. Add 2-3 tablespoons of olive oil and let it heat up
9. Add minced garlic, spices, and other vegetables except for spinach, parsley, and dill
10. Add the now shredded chicken to the pot, and stir the whole mixture well
11. Add the reserved broth and bring the mixture to a boil. Once boiling point is reached, remove the heat and cook for about 20 minutes, partly covered
12. Stir in herbs and spinach alongside the zest and juice of a lemon
13. Mix and serve!

Storage: It can be stored in BPA Safe container or pots for up to 3-4 days in the fridge and 2 months in the freezer.

Nutrition value per serving: Calories: 170 kcal, Fat: 3 g, Carbs: 9 g, Protein: 25 g, Sodium: 72 mg, Potassium: 512 mg

34.6 Homely Sweet Potato Soup

Preparation Time: 10 minutes
Cooking Time: 30 minutes

Servings: 4

Ingredients:

- Coriander – ½ Tsp. (Ground)
- Chili – ¼ Tsp. (Ground)
- Cinnamon – ¼ Tsp. (Ground)
- Salt – ¼ Tsp.
- Cumin – ½ Tsp. (Ground)
- Onion – 1 Large (Chopped)
- Sweet Potato – 1 Lb. (Peeled And Cut)
- Garlic – 2 Cloves (Crushed)
- Chicken Stock – 2 Cups
- Extra Virgin Olive Oil – 2 Tbsp.
- Coriander - As Needed For Garnish
- Freshly Parsley – As Needed For Garnish
- Low Fat Crème Fraiche- As Needed For Garnish

Procedure:

1. In a soup pot over medium heat, heat the oil. Add the onion and garlic and cook until softened, about 5 minutes.
2. Add the rest of the vegetables alongside and cook them for 2-3 minutes until crispy, making sure to add the spices as well
3. Add the broth and ring the mix to a boil
4. Simmer until the vegetables are tender when pierced with a fork, about 20 minutes. Garnish with crème Fraiche on top, and enjoy!

Storage: It can be stored in BPA Safe container or pots for up to 3-4 days in the fridge and 2 months in the freezer.

Nutrition value per serving: Calories: 300 kcal, Fat: 10 g, Carbs: 15 g, Protein: 25 g, Sodium: 347 mg

34.7 Lovely Onion Soup

Preparation Time: 10 minutes

Cooking Time:250 minute

Servings: 4

Ingredients:

- Red Wine – 1 cup
- Brandy – 1 measure
- Butter – 1 oz.
- Parmesan Cheese – 1 oz. (grated)
- Flour – 1 tbsp.
- Brown Sugar – 1 tsp.
- Provence Herbs De Provence – 1 tsp.
- Vegetable Stock – 2 cups
- Large Onions – 2 whole (sliced)
- Olive Oil – 2 tbsp.
- Strong Cheese – 4 oz. (grated)
- Stale Bread – 4 Slices
- Salt and Pepper – as needed

Procedure:

1. Place a pan on medium-high heat.
2. Allow the butter and oil to warm up before adding.
3. Add onions and sugar
4. Cook until the onions and golden brown
5. Pour brandy and flambe, making sure to keep stirring it until the flames are out
6. Add plain flour and herbs de Provence and keep stirring well
7. Add stock and red wine (not all at once, bit by bit)
8. Season well and simmer for 20 minutes, making sure to add water if the soup becomes too thick
9. Ladle the soup into bowls
10. Slices of stale bread should be placed on top.
11. Add strong cheese
12. Sprinkle some parmesan over the top.
13. Place the bowls under a hot grill or in an oven until the cheese has melted
14. Serve immediately!

Storage: It can be stored in BPA Safe container or pots for up to 3-4 days in the fridge and 2 months in the freezer.

Nutrition value per serving: Calories: 55 kcal, Fat: 20 g, Carbs: 8 g, Protein: 6 g, Sodium: 222 mg

35 BEANS RECIPES

35.1 Black Bean With Mangoes

Preparation Time: 10 minutes
Cooking Time: 10 minute
Servings: 4
Ingredients:

- Coconut Oil – 2 Tbsp.
- Onion– 1 Whole (Chopped)
- Black Beans- 15 Oz. (Drained And Rinsed)
- Chili Powder – 1 Tbsp.
- Salt – 1 Tsp.
- Freshly Ground Black Pepper – ¼ Tsp.
- Water – 1 Cup
- Mangoes– 2 Whole (Sliced)
- Fresh Cilantro, Divided- ¼ Cup (Chopped)
- Scallions, Divided – ¼ Cup (Sliced)

Procedure:

1. Preheat the oven to 375 degrees F (190 degrees C).
2. In a bowl, combine black beans, red onion, mango, and olive oil.
3. Spread mixture in a single layer on a baking sheet and roast for 20 minutes, or until vegetables are tender.
4. Stir in cumin, chili powder, and salt; lime juice to taste. Serve warm.

Nutrition value per serving: Calories: 528 kcal, Fat: 2 g, Carbs: 10 g, Protein: 2 g, Sugar: 200 mg, Potassium: 100 mg

35.2 Italian Cannellini Beans

Preparation Time: 10 minutes
Cooking Time:10 minutes
Servings: 4
Ingredients:

- Extra-Virgin Olive Oil – 2 Tsp.
- Onion – ½ Cup (Minced)
- Red Wine Vinegar – ¼ Cup
- No-Salt-Added Tomato Paste – 12 Oz.
- Raw Honey- 2 Tbsp.
- Water – ½ Cup
- Ground Cinnamon – ¼ Tsp. (Ground)
- Cannellini Beans – 15 Oz.

Procedure:

1. Heat the olive oil in a saucepan over medium heat until shimmering.
2. Add the onion and sauté for 5 minutes or until translucent.
3. Pour in the red wine vinegar, tomato paste, honey, and water.
4. Sprinkle with cinnamon. Stir to mix well.
5. Reduce the heat to low, then pour all the beans into the saucepan. Cook for 10 more minutes. Stir constantly.
6. Serve immediately.

Storage: It can be stored in airtight BPA Safe containers for around 4-5 days in the refrigerator and 4-6 months in the freezer.
Nutrition value per serving: Calories: 528 kcal, Fat: 2 g, Carbs: 10 g, Protein: 2 g, Sugar: 200 mg, Potassium: 100 mg

35.3 Mashed Beans And Cumin

Preparation Time: 10 minutes
Cooking Time: 10 minute
Servings: 4
Ingredients:

- Extra-Virgin Olive Oil, Plus Extra For Serving – 1 Tbsp.

- Garlic – 2 Cloves (Minced)
- Ground Cumin – 1 Tsp.
- Fava beans – 15 Oz.
- Tahini – 2 Tbsp.
- Lemon Juice, Plus Lemon Wedges For Serving – 2 Tbsp. (Juiced)
- Salt And Pepper – To Taste
- 1 Tomato– 1 Whole (Cored And Cut)
- Small Onion– 1 Whole (Chopped)
- Fresh Parsley – 2 Tbsp. (Chopped)

Procedure:

1. In a large bowl, combine all of the listed ingredients.
2. Bring the mix to a boil and simmer for 10-15 minutes until cooked
3. Serve warm or cold

Storage: It can be stored in airtight BPA Safe containers for around 4-5 days in the refrigerator and 4-6 months in the freezer.
Nutrition value per serving: Calories: 528 kcal, Fat: 2 g, Carbs: 10 g, Protein: 2 g, Sugar: 200 mg, Potassium: 100 mg

35.4 Turkish Canned Pinto Beans Salad

Preparation Time: 10 minutes
Cooking Time: 0 minute
Servings: 4
Ingredients:

- Olive Oil, Divided – ¼ Cup
- Garlic Cloves– 2 Cloves (Peeled and Crushed)
- Pinto Beans, Rinsed – 15 Oz.
- Water – 1 Tbsp.
- Salt And Pepper– As Needed
- Tahini – ¼ Cup
- Lemon Juice – 2 Tbsp.
- Aleppo Pepper, Plus Extra For Serving- 1 Tbsp.
- Cherry Tomatoes, Halved – 8oz. (Halved)
- Onion– ¼ An Onion (Sliced)
- Fresh Parsley Leaves – ¼ Cup
- Toasted Sesame Seeds – 1 Tbsp. (Toasted)

Procedure:

1. In a large salad bowl, combine all of the listed ingredients
2. Toss to combine. Serve chilled or at room temperature.

Storage: It can be stored in airtight BPA Safe containers for around 4-5 days in the refrigerator and 4-6 months in the freezer.

Nutrition value per serving: Calories: 528 kcal, Fat: 2 g, Carbs: 10 g, Protein: 2 g, Sugar: 200 mg, Potassium: 100 mg

35.5 Fava And Garbanzo Beans Platter

Preparation Time: 10 minutes
Cooking Time: 10 minutes
Servings: 4
Ingredients:

- Garbanzo Beans, Rinsed And Drained- 1 Lb.
- Fava Beans, Rinsed And Drained – 15 Oz.
- Water – 3 Cups
- Lemon Juice – ½ Cup
- Garlic – 3 Cloves(Peeled And Minced)
- Salt – 1 Tsp.
- Extra-Virgin Olive Oil – 2 Tbsp.

Procedure:

1. In a pot over medium heat, cook the beans in water for 10 minutes.

2. Drain the beans and transfer them to a bowl. Reserve 1 cup of the liquid from the cooked beans.
3. Add Salt, lemon juice, and chopped garlic to a bowl. Mix thoroughly.
4. About half of the beans should be mashed with a potato masher.
5. Add the prepared lemon dressing to the bowl with beans
6. Give the mixture one more stir to make sure the beans are evenly mixed.
7. Drizzle with the olive oil and serve.

Storage: It can be stored in airtight BPA Safe containers for around 4-5 days in the refrigerator and 4-6 months in the freezer.

Nutrition value per serving: Calories: 528 kcal, Fat: 2 g, Carbs: 10 g, Protein: 2 g, Sugar: 200 mg, Potassium: 100 mg

35.6 Bulgar Pilaf With Garbanzo Beans

Preparation Time: 10 minutes
Cooking Time: 20 minutes
Servings: 4
Ingredients:

- Extra-Virgin Olive Oil- 2 Tbsp.
- Onion – 1 Whole (Chopped)
- Garbanzo Beans– 1 Lb. (Rinsed And Drained)
- Bulgur Wheat - 2 Cups (Rinsed And Drained)
- Salt and pepper – 1 And ½ Tsp.
- Cinnamon – ½ Tsp.
- Water – 2 Cups
- Tomato Paste – 1 And ½Cups
- Fresh parsley – 1 tsp.
- Fresh thyme – 1 tsp.

Procedure:

1. Preheat the oven to 350 degrees F (175 degrees C).
2. In a large bowl, combine bulgur, garbanzo beans, parsley, onion, garlic, oil, and thyme; season with salt and pepper. Mix well.
3. Pour mixture into an 8x8 inch baking dish. Bake for 25 minutes or until heated through.
4. In a small saucepan over medium heat, bring broth to a boil. Add tomato paste; cook for 2 minutes or until bubbly. Pour over pilaf; serve warm.

Storage: It can be stored in airtight BPA Safe containers for around 4-5 days in the refrigerator and 4-6 months in the freezer.

Nutrition value per serving: Calories: 528 kcal, Fat: 2 g, Carbs: 10 g, Protein: 2 g, Sugar: 200 mg, Potassium: 100 mg

35.7 Mediterranean Beans And Veggie

Preparation Time: 10 minutes
Cooking Time: 0 minute
Servings: 4
Ingredients:

- Tomatoes With Juice – 14 Oz. (Diced)
- Kidney Beans, Drained And Rinsed – 15 Oz. (Cooked)
- Black Beans, Drained And Rinsed – 15 oz. (Cooked)
- Green Olives– 2 Tbsp. (Chopped)
- Vegetable Broth, Plus More As Needed – ¼ Cup
- Extra-Virgin Olive Oil – 1 Tsp.
- Garlic – 2 Cloves (Minced)
- Arugula – 2 Cups
- Freshly Squeezed Lemon Juice – ¼ Cup

Procedure:

1. In a large bowl, add all of the listed ingredients
2. Mix well to combine.

3. Cover and refrigerate for at least 2 hours or overnight.
4. Serve and enjoy!

Storage: It can be stored in airtight BPA Safe containers for around 4-5 days in the refrigerator and 4-6 months in the freezer.

Nutrition value per serving: Calories: 528 kcal, Fat: 2 g, Carbs: 10 g, Protein: 2 g, Sugar: 200 mg, Potassium: 100 mg

36 FISH AND SHELLFISH RECIPES

36.1 Pesto And Lemon Halibut

Preparation Time: 10 minutes
Cooking Time: 10 minutes
Servings: 4
Ingredients:

- Lemon Juice – 1 Tbsp.
- Lemon Rind, – 1 Tbsp.
- Garlic– 2 Cloves (Peeled)
- Olive Oil – 2 Tbsp.
- Parmesan Cheese– ¼ Cup
- Firmly Packed Basil Leaves – 2/3 Cup
- Freshly Ground Black Pepper – 1/8 Tsp.
- Salt – ¼ Tsp.
- Halibut Fillets- 4 Whole (5 Oz. Each)
- Pesto – 1 cup
- Onion – 1 whole (Diced)

Procedure:

1. In a medium bowl, combine the pesto, lemon juice, salt, and pepper. Reserve 1 tablespoon of the pesto mixture for brushing on the halibut.
2. Heat the olive oil in a large skillet over medium heat. Add the halibut and cook until browned on both sides, about 3 minutes per side. Remove from the skillet and set aside.
3. Add the onion to the skillet and cook until softened, about 5 minutes. Add the garlic and cook for 1 minute longer.
4. Add the reserved pesto mixture to the skillet and bring it to a boil. Cook for 2 minutes longer to blend the flavors. Return the halibut to the skillet and spoon some of the sauce over each fillet. Serve immediately.
5. Garnish with basil if needed

Storage: It can be stored in airtight, BPA Safe containers for up to 2-4 days on average in the fridge. If you prefer to store it in the freezer, you can go up to 4-6 months on average. However, a dish containing Shrimp, Crayfish, and Squid can be stored in the freezer for up to 18 months.

Nutrition value per serving: Calories: 528 kcal, Fat: 2 g, Carbs: 10 g, Protein: 2 g, Sugar: 245 mg, Potassium: 200 mg

36.2 Pecan Crusted Trout

Preparation Time: 10 minutes
Cooking Time: 12 minute
Servings: 4
Ingredients:

- Crushed Pecans – ½ Cup
- Fresh Ginger – ½ Tsp. (Grated)
- 1 Egg,– 1 Whole (Beaten)

- Dried Rosemary – 1 Tsp. (Crushed)
- Salt -1 Tsp.
- Trout Fillets – 4 Whole (4 Oz. Each)
- Black Pepper– As Needed
- Cooking Oil – As Needed
- Whole Wheat Flour- As Needed

Procedure:

1. Grease baking sheet lightly with cooking spray and preheat oven to 400oF.
2. In a shallow bowl, combine black pepper, salt, rosemary, and pecans. In another shallow bowl, add whole wheat flour. In a third bowl, add beaten egg.
3. To prepare fish, dip in flour until covered well. Shake off excess flour. Then dip into beaten egg until coated well. Let excess egg drip off before dipping trout fillet into pecan crumbs. Press the trout lightly onto pecan crumbs to make it stick to the fish.
4. Place breaded fish onto prepared pan. Repeat the process for the remaining fillets.
5. Pop into the oven and bake for 10 to 12 minutes or until fish is flaky.

Storage: It can be stored in airtight, BPA Safe containers for up to 2-4 days on average in the fridge. If you prefer to store it in the freezer, you can go up to 4-6 months on average. However, a dish containing Shrimp, Crayfish, and Squid can be stored in the freezer for up to 18 months.

Nutrition value per serving: Calories: 528 kcal, Fat: 2 g, Carbs: 10 g, Protein: 2 g, Sugar: 245 mg, Potassium: 200 mg

36.3 Spicy Paprika And Salmon Green Beans

Preparation Time: 10 minutes
Cooking Time: 20 minutes
Servings: 4

Ingredients:

- Olive Oil – ¼ Cup
- Cayenne Pepper – ½ Tsp.
- Smoked Paprika – 1 Tbsp.
- Green Beans – 1 Lb.
- Minced Garlic – 2 Tsp. (Minced)
- Fresh Herbs – 3 Tbsp.
- Salmon Steak -5 Oz.
- Salt And Pepper To Taste- As Needed
- Tomato – 1 Whole (Diced)
- Chili Power – 1 tsp.
- Vinegar – 1 tsp.
- Vegetable Broth – 1 Cup

Procedure:

1. In a large skillet over medium heat, sauté onion and garlic in olive oil until softened. Add the salmon, tomatoes, smoked paprika, green beans, cayenne, chili powder, salt, and black pepper;
2. Bring to a boil. Reduce heat and simmer for 10 minutes.
3. In a small bowl, whisk together the broth and vinegar. Pour into the skillet; bring to a boil. Cook for 3 minutes or until the sauce is slightly thickened. Sprinkle with parsley and rosemary before serving.

Storage: It can be stored in airtight, BPA Safe containers for up to 2-4 days on average in the fridge. If you prefer to store it in the freezer, you can go up to 4-6 months on average. However, a dish containing Shrimp, Crayfish, and Squid can be stored in the freezer for up to 18 months.

Storage: It can be stored in airtight, BPA Safe containers for up to 2-4 days on average in the fridge. If you prefer to store it in the freezer, you can go up to 4-6 months on average. However, a dish containing Shrimp, Crayfish, and Squid can be stored in the freezer for up to 18 months.

Nutrition value per serving: Calories: 528 kcal, Fat: 2 g, Carbs: 10 g, Protein: 2 g, Sugar: 245 mg, Potassium: 200 mg

36.4 Pan Fried Tuna And Herbs Meal

Preparation Time: 10 minutes
Cooking Time: 5 minutes
Servings: 4
Ingredients:

- Almonds– ¼ Cup (Chopped)
- Tangerine Juice – ¼ Cup
- Fennel Seeds– ½ Tsp.
- Ground Pepper– ½ Tsp.
- Sea Salt – ½ Tsp.
- Olive Oil – 1 Tbsp.
- Fresh Mint– 2 Tbsp. (Chopped)
- Red Onion– 2 Tbsp. (Chopped)
- Tuna Steak - 4 Whole (5 Oz. Each, Cut Int Half)

Procedure:

1. Mix fennel seeds, olive oil, mint, onion, tangerine juice, and almonds in a small bowl. Season with ¼ tsp. each of pepper and salt.
2. Season fish with the remaining pepper and salt.
3. On medium-high fire, place a large nonstick fry pan and grease with cooking spray.
4. Pan fry tuna until the desired doneness is reached or for one minute per side.
5. Transfer cooked tuna to a serving plate, drizzle with dressing and serve.

Storage: It can be stored in airtight, BPA Safe containers for up to 2-4 days on average in the fridge. If you prefer to store it in the freezer, you can go up to 4-6 months on average. However, a dish containing Shrimp, Crayfish, and Squid can be stored in the freezer for up to 18 months.

Storage: It can be stored in airtight, BPA Safe containers for up to 2-4 days on average in the fridge. If you prefer to store it in the freezer, you can go up to 4-6 months on average. However, a dish containing Shrimp, Crayfish, and Squid can be stored in the freezer for up to 18 months.

Nutrition value per serving: Calories: 528 kcal, Fat: 2 g, Carbs: 10 g, Protein: 2 g, Sugar: 245 mg, Potassium: 200 mg

36.5 Orange And Herbed Sauce White Bass

Preparation Time: 10 minutes
Cooking Time: 33 minutes
Servings: 4

Ingredients:

- Onions – ¼ Cup (Sliced)
- Orange Juice – ½ Cup
- Fresh Lemon Juice – 1 And ½ Tbsp.
- Olive Oil – 1 And ½ Tbsp.
- Onion– 1 Large Sized (Halved)
- Orange– 1 Large (Unpeeled And Sliced)
- Fresh – 3 Tbsp. (Chopped)
- Skinless White Bass Fillets – 5 Whole (3 Oz. Each, Skinless)
- Additional Unpeeled Orange Slices – As Needed
- Salt and Pepper – As Needed
- Thyme And Oregano – 1 tsp. each

Procedure:

1. Preheat the oven to 400 degrees F.
2. Season white bass with olive oil, salt, and pepper. Place on a baking sheet and roast in preheated oven for 10 minutes.
3. In a small bowl, mix together orange segments, parsley, thyme, and oregano.
4. To prepare sauce, mix the orange mixture with reserved pan juices from the fish.

5. Serve over grilled white bass.

Storage: It can be stored in airtight, BPA Safe containers for up to 2-4 days on average in the fridge. If you prefer to store it in the freezer, you can go up to 4-6 months on average. However, a dish containing Shrimp, Crayfish, and Squid can be stored in the freezer for up to 18 months.

Nutrition value per serving: Calories: 528 kcal, Fat: 2 g, Carbs: 10 g, Protein: 2 g, Sugar: 245 mg, Potassium: 200 mg

36.6 Seafood Chowder

Preparation Time: 10 minutes
Cooking Time: 10 minutes
Servings: 4
Ingredients:

- Shrimps – 2 Cups
- Salt And Pepper– As Needed
- Garlic – 1 Tbsp. (Minced)
- Coconut Milk – 3 Cups
- Clams – 3 Cups (Chopped)
- Fresh Shrimps,1 Pack (Shelled And Deveined)
- Corn,– 1 Cup (Drained)
- Potatoes – 4 (Large Sized, Diced)
- Carrots– 2 Whole (Peeled And Chopped)
- Celery Stalks- 2 Whole (Chopped)
- Onions – ½ cup (Sliced)
- Bell Pepper – 1 Whole (Sliced)

Procedure:

1. In a large pot or Dutch oven, sauté onions and peppers in olive oil over medium heat until softened.
2. Add garlic and sauté for an additional minute. Stir in remaining ingredients except for shrimp to the pot and bring the mix to a boil
3. Reduce heat to low and simmer for 30 minutes.
4. Add shrimp and simmer for an additional 5 minutes or until shrimp turn pink. Season with salt and black pepper to taste.
5. Serve hot.

Storage: It can be stored in airtight, BPA Safe containers for up to 2-4 days on average in the fridge. If you prefer to store it in the freezer, you can go up to 4-6 months on average. However, a dish containing Shrimp, Crayfish, and Squid can be stored in the freezer for up to 18 months.

Nutrition value per serving: Calories: 528 kcal, Fat: 2 g, Carbs: 10 g, Protein: 2 g, Sugar: 245 mg, Potassium: 200 mg

36.7 Lemon And Garlic Baked Halibut

Preparation Time: 10 minutes
Cooking Time: 15 minutes
Servings: 4
Ingredients:

- Olive Oil – 1 Tsp.
- Flat Leaf Parsley – 1 Tbsp. (Chopped)
- Garlic Clove,-1 Clove (Minced)
- Halibut Fillets – 2 Fillets (5 Oz. Each, Skin On)
- Lemon Zest – 2 Tsp.
- Lemon, Divided – ½ A Lemon
- Salt And Pepper - As Needed
- Honey – 1 Tsp.
- Lemon Juice – 1 Tsp.
- Tomato -1 Whole (Diced)

Procedure:

1. Place the halibut fillets in the dish and drizzle with olive oil. Sprinkle with lemon juice, honey, garlic, salt, and pepper.

2. Bake for about 20 minutes or until fish flakes easily when tested with a fork.
3. Remove from oven and sprinkle with tomatoes, parsley leaves, and any additional seasoning desired. Serve hot.

Storage: It can be stored in airtight, BPA Safe containers for up to 2-4 days on average in the fridge. If you prefer to store it in the freezer, you can go up to 4-6 months on average. However, a dish containing Shrimp, Crayfish, and Squid can be stored in the freezer for up to 18 months.

Nutrition value per serving: Calories: 528 kcal, Fat: 2 g, Carbs: 10 g, Protein: 2 g, Sugar: 245 mg, Potassium: 200 mg

36.8 Poached Trout Meal

Preparation Time: 10 minutes
Cooking Time: 10 minutes
Servings: 4
Ingredients:

- Lemon Juice – 1 Tbsp.
- Leeks, Halved – 2 (Halved)
- Trout Fillet – 1 Whole (8 Oz. , Boneless And Skin On)
- Chicken Broth Or Water – 2 Cups
- Salt And Pepper - As Needed
- Onion – 1 Whole (Sliced)
- Garlic – 1 Whole (Cloves, Sliced)
- For Garnish – Raisin, Pine Nuts etc.

Procedure:

1. In a large skillet or wok, heat the oil over high heat. Add the trout and cook for 1 minute per side or until browned. Remove from the pan and set aside.
2. In the same pan, add the leeks, onion, and garlic and stir fry for 2 minutes. Add the chicken broth and lemon juice and bring to a boil.
3. Lower the heat and simmer for 10 minutes or until the vegetables are tender.
4. Season with salt and pepper to taste.
5. Spoon the vegetables over the trout in the skillet and sprinkle with parsley, pine nuts, raisins, and any other desired garnishes. Serve immediately.

Storage: It can be stored in airtight, BPA Safe containers for up to 2-4 days on average in the fridge. If you prefer to store it in the freezer, you can go up to 4-6 months on average. However, a dish containing Shrimp, Crayfish, and Squid can be stored in the freezer for up to 18 months.

Nutrition value per serving: Calories: 528 kcal, Fat: 2 g, Carbs: 10 g, Protein: 2 g, Sugar: 245 mg, Potassium: 200 mg

36.9 Salmon And Corn Pepper Salsa

Preparation Time: 10 minutes
Cooking Time: 10-12 minute
Servings: 4
Ingredients:
For Spicy Salmon

- Garlic Clove – 1 Clove
- Mild Chili Powder – ½ Tsp.
- Ground Coriander – ½ Tsp.
- Ground Cumin – ¼ Tsp.
- Grated Zest – 1 Lime (Grated)
- Rapeseed Oil – 2 Tsp.
- Salmon Fillets – 2 Whole

For Salsa Salad

- Corn On The Cob– 1 Whole (Husk Removed)
- Red Pepper – 1 Whole (Deseeded And Chopped)
- Red Chili – 1 Whole (Halved)
- Coriander – ½ A Pack (Chopped)

- Lime Juice – 1 Tbsp.
- Lime Wedges – As Needed
- Salsa- As Needed For Serving

Procedure:

1. Take a bowl and grate up the garlic
2. Boil the corn for about 6-8 minutes until they are tender
3. Drain off and cut off the kernels
4. Take your garlic bowl and add the spices, 1 tablespoon of lime juice, and oil
5. Mix well to prepare a spice rub
6. Coat the salmon with the rub
7. Add the rest of the zest to the corn and give it a nice stir
8. Take a frying pan and place it over medium heat
9. Add salmon and cook for about 2 minutes on each side
10. Serve the cooked salmon with salsa and lime wedges!
11. Enjoy!

Storage: It can be stored in airtight, BPA Safe containers for up to 2-4 days on average in the fridge. If you prefer to store it in the freezer, you can go up to 4-6 months on average. However, a dish containing Shrimp, Crayfish, and Squid can be stored in the freezer for up to 18 months.

Nutrition value per serving: Calories: 530 kcal, Fat: 32 g, Carbs: 27 g, Protein: 29 g, Sugar: 245 mg, Potassium: 200 mg

36.10 Spicy Cajun Shrimp

Preparation Time: 10 minutes
Cooking Time: 50 minute
Servings: 4
Ingredients:
For the Dish

- Garlic – 3 Cloves (Crushed)
- Grass Fed Butter – 3 Tbsp.
- Jumbo Shrimps- 20 Pieces

For The Cajun Seasoning

- Paprika – 1 Tsp.
- Cayenne Pepper – Just A Dash
- Himalayan Sea Salt – ½ Tsp.
- Red Pepper Flakes – Just A Dash
- Garlic Granules – 1 Tsp.
- Onion Powder – 1 Tsp.

For Others

- Zucchinis – 2 Large Sized (Spiralized)
- Red Pepper – 1 Whole (Sliced)
- Onion – 1 Whole (Sliced)
- Grass Fed Butter – 1 Tbsp.
- Cilantro – For Garnish

Procedure:

1. In a large pot or Dutch oven, heat the oil over medium heat.
2. Add the onion and bell pepper and cook until softened, about 5 minutes.
3. Add the garlic and cook for 1 minute longer.
4. Add all the remaining ingredients to the pot and stir well. Bring the mixture to boil, then lower it down to a simmer. Cook for 10 minutes
5. Stir in the cilantro and serve.

Storage: It can be stored in airtight, BPA Safe containers for up to 2-4 days on average in the fridge. If you prefer to store it in the freezer, you can go up to 4-6 months on average. However, a dish containing Shrimp, Crayfish, and Squid can be stored in the freezer for up to 18 months.

Nutrition value per serving: Calories: 92 kcal, Fat: 8 g, Carbs: 2 g, Protein: 5 g, Sugar: 245 mg, Potassium: 200 mg

36.11 Asparagus Salmon Fillets

Preparation Time: 10 minutes
Cooking Time: 10 minute
Servings: 4
Ingredients:

- Salmon Fillets -2 Whole Fillets, 6 Oz Each (Skin One)
- Salt – As Needed
- Asparagus – 1 lb. (Trimmed)
- Garlic – 2 Cloves (Minced)
- Butter – 3 Tbsp.
- Parmesan Cheese – ¼ Cup (Grated)

Procedure:

1. Pre-heat your oven to 400 degree F
2. Line a baking sheet with oil
3. Pat your fish dry with a kitchen towel and season as desired.
4. Arrange the salmon around the baking sheet and the asparagus around it.
5. Place a pan over medium heat and melt butter
6. Cook for 3 minutes, or until the garlic begins to color slightly.
7. Drizzle the sauce over the salmon.
8. Bake for 12 minutes, or until the salmon appears cooked all the way through and is flaky.
9. Serve and have fun!

Storage: It can be stored in airtight, BPA Safe containers for up to 2-4 days on average in the fridge. If you prefer to store it in the freezer, you can go up to 4-6 months on average. However, a dish containing Shrimp, Crayfish, and Squid can be stored in the freezer for up to 18 months.

Nutrition value per serving: Calories: 250 kcal, Fat: 13 g, Carbs: 10 g, Protein: 27 g, Sugar: 245 mg, Potassium: 200 mg

Nutrition value per serving: Calories: 200 kcal, Fat: 12 g, Carbs: 17 g, Protein: 8 g, Sugar: 245 mg, Potassium: 200 mg

36.12 Hearty Glazed Salmon Meal

Preparation Time: 10 minutes
Cooking Time: 15 minute
Servings: 4

Ingredients:

- Salmon Fillets – 4 Pieces (5 Ounce Each)
- Coconut Aminos – 4 Tbsp.
- Olive Oil – 4 Tsp.
- Ginger – 2 Tsp. (Minced)
- Sugar-Free Ketchup – 2 Tbsp.
- Dry White Wine – 4 Tbsp.
- Red Boat Fish Sauce – 2 Tbsp.

Procedure:

1. Take a bowl and mix in coconut aminos, garlic, ginger, fish sauce, and mix
2. Add salmon and let it marinate for 15-20 minutes
3. Take a skillet/pan and place it over medium heat
4. Add oil and let it heat up
5. Add salmon fillets and cook on HIGH for 3-4 minutes per side
6. Remove dish once crispy
7. Add sauce and wine
8. Simmer for 5 minutes on low heat
9. Return salmon to the glaze and flip until both sides are glazed
10. Serve and enjoy!

Storage: It can be stored in airtight, BPA Safe containers for up to 2-4 days on average in the fridge. If you prefer to store it in the freezer, you can go up to 4-6 months on average. However, a dish containing Shrimp, Crayfish, and Squid can be stored in the freezer for up to 18 months.

Nutrition value per serving: Calories: 360 kcal, Fat: 15 g, Carbs: 12 g, Protein: 43 g, Sugar: 245 mg, Potassium: 200 mg

36.13 Traditionally Cooked Salmon

Preparation Time: 10 minutes

Cooking Time: 15 minute
Servings: 4
Ingredients:

- Garlic Cloves – 4 Cloves(Pressed)
- Balsamic Vinegar – ¼ Cup
- Olive Oil – ½ Cup
- Salmon Fillets – 4 Whole
- Salt And Pepper - 1 And ½ Tsp.
- Oregano – 1 tsp.
- Thyme – 1 tsp.
- Parsley – 1 tsp. For Garnish
- Lemon Juice – 1 Tbsp.

Procedure:

1. Preheat the oven to 350 degrees F (175 degrees C).
2. In a large skillet over medium heat, heat olive oil. Add garlic, oregano, thyme, and black pepper; cook for 1 minute.
3. Place salmon in the skillet; cook for 3 minutes per side or until browned.
4. Remove salmon from skillet; place on a baking sheet. Bake for 10 minutes or until just cooked through.
5. Remove from oven; garnish with lemon juice and parsley leaves. Serve immediately.

Nutrition value per serving: Calories: 400 kcal, Fat: 35 g, Carbs: 3 g, Protein: 15 g, Sugar: 245 mg, Potassium: 200 mg

36.14 Mediterranean Tilapia Delight

Preparation Time: 10 minutes
Cooking Time: 15 minute
Servings: 4
Ingredients:

- Tilapia – 2 Whole
- Lemon Juice – 1 Tbsp.
- Olive Oil – As Needed For Cooking
- Salt And Pepper –As Needed
- Onions -1 Whole (Sliced)
- Bell Pepper – 1 Whole (Sliced)
- Garlic – 1 Tbsp.
- Oregano –1 Tbsp.
- Tomatoes – 1 Whole (Sliced)

Procedure:

1. Preheat the oven to 375 degrees F. In a large baking dish or casserole, arrange the tilapia filets in a single layer.
2. In a small bowl, whisk together the olive oil, lemon juice, salt, and pepper.
3. Pour the mixture over the tilapia filets and toss to coat.
4. Bake in preheated oven for 18 minutes or until fish is cooked through. Meanwhile, in a medium saucepan over medium heat, sauté onions and bell peppers in olive oil until tender.
5. Add garlic and oregano and sauté for an additional minute. Add tomatoes and simmer for 10 minutes or until heated through.

Storage: It can be stored in airtight, BPA Safe containers for up to 2-4 days on average in the fridge. If you prefer to store it in the freezer, you can go up to 4-6 months on average. However, a dish containing Shrimp, Crayfish, and Squid can be stored in the freezer for up to 18 months.

Nutrition value per serving: Calories: 183 kcal, Fat: 10 g, Carbs: 18 g, Protein: 24 g, Sugar: 245 mg, Potassium: 200 mg

37 PASTA RECIPES

37.1 Lebanese Thin Pasta

Preparation Time: 10 minutes
Cooking Time: 25 minutes
Servings: 4
Ingredients:

- Sea Salt – ¼ Tsp.
- Garlic Cloves– 2 Cloves (Mashed)
- Water – ½ Cup
- Extra-Virgin Olive Oil – 1 Tbsp.
- Low-Sodium Vegetable Soup – 2 Cups
- Vermicelli -3 Oz.(Broken Down To 1 Inch Pieces)
- Cabbage – 3 Cups
- Brown Rice -1 Cup
- Red Pepper Flakes- ½ Tsp. (Crushed)
- Cilantro – ½ Cup (Chopped)
- Fresh Lemon Slices, For Serving – For Serving
- Feta Cheese – 1 cup (Shredded)
- Parsley – For Garnish

Procedure:

1. Cook the pasta according to package instructions. Drain and return it to the pot.
2. In a large skillet over medium heat, heat the olive oil. Add the onion and garlic and cook until softened, about 5 minutes. Add remaining ingredients except cheese, parsley
3. Stir in the cooked pasta and feta cheese. Top with parsley and Parmesan cheese and serve warm.

Storage: It can be stored in the fridge in an airtight BPA-free container for up to 3-4 days. Storing in a freezer is not recommended as it raises the risk of salmonella colonization.
Nutrition value per serving: Calories: 528 kcal, Fat: 2 g, Carbs: 10 g, Protein: 2 g, Sugar: 245 mg, Potassium: 200 mg

37.2 Walnut And Ricotta Spaghetti

Preparation Time: 10 minutes
Cooking Time: 10 minutes
Servings: 4
Ingredients:

- Whole-Wheat Spaghetti – 2 Cups
- Walnuts– ¼ Cup (Toasted, Chopped)
- Sea Salt And Freshly Ground- As Needed
- Ricotta Cheese – 2 Tbsp.
- Pepper, To Taste- As Needed
- Parmesan Cheese – ½ Cup (Grated)
- Garlic– 4 Cloves (Minced)
- Flat-Leaf Parsley– ¼ Cup (Chopped)
- Extra-Virgin Olive Oil- 2 Tbsp.
- Red Onion – 1 Whole (Sliced)
- Thyme – 1 Tsp.
- Sugar – 1 Tbsp.

Procedure:

1. Cook the spaghetti according to the package instructions. Drain well and return it to the pot.
2. While the pasta is cooking, heat the oil in a large skillet over medium heat. Add the walnuts and sauté for 2 minutes, stirring occasionally. Add the red onion and

garlic and cook for 5 minutes more, until everything is softened. Add the diced tomatoes, parsley, thyme, sugar, and salt and bring to a simmer. Lower the heat to low and cook for 10 minutes more, until everything is heated through.

3. Meanwhile, mix together the ricotta cheese and feta cheese in a small bowl. Once the sauce has cooked down

Storage: It can be stored in the fridge in an airtight BPA-free container for up to 3-4 days. Storing in a freezer is not recommended as it raises the risk of salmonella colonization.

Nutrition value per serving: Calories: 528 kcal, Fat: 2 g, Carbs: 10 g, Protein: 2 g, Sugar: 245 mg, Potassium: 200 mg

37.3 Butternut Squash And Zucchini Penne

Preparation Time: 10 minutes
Cooking Time: 30 minute
Servings: 4
Ingredients:

- Zucchini– 1 Whole (Diced)
- Whole-Grain Penne – 2 Cups
- Sea Salt – ½ Tsp.
- Parmesan Cheese – 2 Tbsp.
- Freshly Ground Black Pepper – ½ Tsp.
- Extra-Virgin Olive Oil – 1 Tbsp.
- Butternut Squash– 1 Large (Peeled And Diced)
- Marinara Sauce – 1 Cup

Procedure:

1. Preheat oven to 375 degrees F (190 degrees C).
2. In a large bowl, combine butternut squash and zucchini.
3. Pour marinara sauce over the top and mix well.
4. Spread mixture into an 8x8 inch baking dish.
5. Sprinkle with Parmesan cheese, salt, and pepper.
6. Bake for 30 minutes, or until vegetables are tender.
7. Meanwhile, cook spaghetti in a large pot of boiling water following package instructions.
8. Drain spaghetti and add it to the baking dish with the olive oil and salt and pepper to taste. Mix well and bake for 5 more minutes, or until cheese is melted.

Storage: It can be stored in the fridge in an airtight BPA-free container for up to 3-4 days. Storing in a freezer is not recommended as it raises the risk of salmonella colonization.
Nutrition value per serving: Calories: 528 kcal, Fat: 2 g, Carbs: 10 g, Protein: 2 g, Sugar: 245 mg, Potassium: 200 mg

37.4 Red Chicken And Spaghetti

Preparation Time: 10 minutes
Cooking Time: 42 minutes
Servings: 4
Ingredients:

- White Wine – ½ Cup
- Spaghetti – 1 Lb.
- Salt – As Needed
- Chicken Broth – 1 Cup
- Milk – 1 Cup
- Ground Chicken – 1 And ½ Lb.
- Red Pepper Flakes – ¼ Tsp.
- Tomato Paste – ¼ Cup
- Garlic Cloves – 2 Whole (Crushed)
- Carrot – 1 Whole (Minced)
- Onion – 1 Whole (Minced)
- Bacon – 6 Oz. (Cubed)
- Olive Oil – 2 Tbsp.
- Celery – 1 Cup (diced)

Procedure:

1. Take a pressure cooker and add oil, let it warm up over medium heat
2. Add bacon, fry for 5 minutes until crispy
3. Add celery, garlic, carrot, onion and cook for around 5 minutes until fragrant
4. Add red pepper flakes, tomato paste and cook for 2 minutes more
5. Break your chicken into small pieces and add them to the pot
6. Cook for 10 minutes, making sure to keep stirring until browned
7. Add wine, let it simmer for 2 minutes over low heat
8. Add chicken broth, milk
9. Place the lid on top and lock it, let it pressure cook for 10-15 minutes
10. Let the pressure release naturally, open the lid and add spaghetti
11. Lock the lid once more and let it pressure cook for 5 minutes more
12. Quick release the pressure and check the pasta for doneness, once done, serve and enjoy!

Storage

Cooked paste can be stored in an BPA safe container in the fridge for 2-3 days.

Nutrition value per serving: Calories: 477 kcal, Fat: 20 g, Carbs: 48 g, Protein: 28 g, Sodium: 270 mg, Potassium: 280 mg

37.5 Mushroom And Fettucine Platter

Preparation Time: 10 minutes
Cooking Time: 15 minutes
Servings: 4

Ingredients:

- Whole Wheat Fettuccine – 12 Oz.
- Salt – ½ Tsp.
- Mixed Mushrooms Such As Oyst4er, Cremini Etc. – 4 Cups
- Low Fat Milk – 2 Cups
- Garlic – 1 Tbsp. (Minced)
- Freshly Ground Pepper – ½ Tsp.
- Extra Virgin Olive Oil – 1 Tbsp.
- Dry Sherry- ½ Cup
- Brussels Sprouts – 4 Cups (Sliced)
- Asiago Cheese- 1 Cup (Shredded)
- All-Purpose Flour – 2 Tbsp.

Procedure:

1. Take a large sized pot and cook your pasta in boiling water for about 8-10 minutes
2. Drain the pasta and keep them on the side
3. Take a large sized skillet and place it over medium heat
4. Add oil and heat it up
5. Add mushrooms, Brussels and cook for about 8-10 minutes until the mushroom has released the liquid
6. Add garlic and cook for about 1 minute until fragrant
7. Add sherry, making sure to scrape up any brown bits
8. Bring the mix to a boil and cook for about 1 minute until evaporated
9. Take a bowl and whisk flour and milk
10. Add the mix to your skillet
11. Season with some pepper and salt
12. Cook well for about 2 minutes until the sauce begins to bubble and is thickened
13. Stir in Asiago until it has fully melted
14. Add the sauce to your pasta
15. Give it a nice toss
16. Serve with some more cheese
17. Enjoy!

Storage: It can be stored in the fridge in an airtight BPA-free container for up to 3-4 days. Storing in a freezer is not recommended as it raises the risk of salmonella colonization.

Nutrition value per serving: Calories: 384 kcal, Fat: 10 g, Carbs: 56 g, Protein: 18 g, Sugar: 245 mg, Potassium: 200 mg

37.6 Creamy And Wholesome Shrimp Pasta

Preparation Time: 10 minutes
Cooking Time: 15 minutes
Servings: 4

Ingredients:

- Whole Wheat Spaghetti -5 Oz.
- Raw Shrimp– 12 Oz.
- Asparagus- 1 Bunch (Sliced)
- Large Bell Pepper – 1 Whole (Sliced)
- Garlic – 3 Cloves (Chopped)
- Kosher Salt – 1 And ¼ Tsp.
- Non-Fat Plain Yogurt – 1 And ½ Cups
- Flat Leaf Parsley – ¼ Cup (Chopped)
- Lemon Juice – 3 Tbsp.
- Extra Virgin Olive Oil – 1 Tbsp.
- Fresh Ground Black Pepper – 12 Tsp.
- Pine Nuts- ¼ Cup (Toasted)

Procedure:

1. Take a large sized pot and bring water to a boil
2. Add your spaghetti and cook them for about 2 minutes less than the directed package instruction
3. Add shrimp, bell pepper, asparagus and cook for about 2- 4 minutes until the shrimp are tender
4. Drain the pasta and the contents well
5. Take a large bowl and mash garlic until a paste forms
6. Whisk in yogurt ,parsley, oil, pepper and lemon juice into the garlic paste
7. Add pasta mix and toss well
8. Serve by sprinkling some pine nuts!
9. Enjoy!

Storage: It can be stored in the fridge in an airtight BPA-free container for up to 3-4 days. Storing in a freezer is not recommended as it raises the risk of salmonella colonization.

Nutrition value per serving: Calories: 361 kcal, Fat: 6 g, Carbs: 53 g, Protein: 28 g, Sugar: 245 mg, Potassium: 200 mg

37.7 Hot And Enticing Lemon Garlic Sardine Fettucine

Preparation Time: 10 minutes
Cooking Time: 15 minute
Servings: 4

Ingredients:

- Whole Wheat Fettuccine – 8 Oz.
- Extra Virgin Olive Oil – 4 Tbsp.
- Garlic – 4 Cloves (Minced)
- Lemon Juice – ¼ Cup
- Freshly Ground Pepper – 1 Tsp.
- Salt – ½ Tsp.
- Sardines (Dipped In Tomato Sauce) – 8 Oz. (Boneless And Skinless)

Procedure:

1. Cook spaghetti according to package instructions. Drain well.
2. In a large skillet over medium heat, heat olive oil. Add lemon juice, garlic, salt and pepper.
3. Cook until garlic is fragrant.
4. Add sardines and cook until browned. Serve over spaghetti.

Storage: It can be stored in the fridge in an airtight BPA-free container for up to 3-4 days. Storing in a freezer is not recommended as it raises the risk of salmonella colonization.

Nutrition value per serving: Calories: 480 kcal, Fat: 21 g, Carbs: 53 g, Protein: 23 g, Sugar: 245 mg, Potassium: 200 mg

37.8 Tuna And Olive Pasta

Preparation Time: 10 minutes
Cooking Time: 15 minutes

Servings: 4

Ingredients:

- Whole Wheat Gobetti, Rotini Or Penne Pasta - 5 Oz.
- Tuna Steak– 8 Oz. (Cut)
- Garlic – 3 Cloves (Minced)
- Fresh Oregano – 2 Tsp. (Chopped)
- Fresh Ground Pepper – ¼ Tsp.
- Extra Virgin Olive Oil – 4 Tbsp.
- Divided Salt – ½ Tsp.

Procedure:

1. Cook pasta according to package instructions. Drain.
2. In a large skillet over medium heat, heat olive oil. Add tuna, garlic, salt, pepper, oregano, and thyme; cook for about 5 minutes or until tuna is cooked through.
3. Add pasta and parsley; toss to combine. Serve warm.

Storage: It can be stored in the fridge in an airtight BPA-free container for up to 3-4 days. Storing in a freezer is not recommended as it raises the risk of salmonella colonization.

Nutrition value per serving: Calories: 422 kcal, Fat: 17 g, Carbs: 42 g, Protein: 22 g, Sugar: 245 mg, Potassium: 200 mg

37.9 The Perfect Basil Pasta

Preparation Time: 10 minutes
Cooking Time: 15 minutes
Servings: 4

Ingredients:

- Red Onion– 2 Whole (Cu Into Wedges)
- Red Pepper Seeded– 2 Whole (Seeded And Cut Into Chunks)
- Mild Red Chilies– 2 Whole (Diced And Seeded)
- Garlic Cloves – 3 Cloves (Chopped)
- Golden Caster Sugar – 1 Tsp.
- Olive Oil (Plus Additional For Serving) – 2 Tbsp.
- Small Ripe Tomatoes– 2 Lb.
- Dried Pasta – 12 Oz.
- Basil Leaves - Handful
- Parmesan- 2 Tbsp.

Procedure:

1. Pre-heat your oven to a temperature of 392 degree Fahrenheit
2. Take a large sized roasting tin and scatter peppers, red onion, garlic and chilies
3. Sprinkle sugar on top
4. Drizzle olive oil and season with some salt and pepper
5. Roast the veggies for 15 minutes
6. Add tomatoes and roast for another 15 minutes
7. Take a large sized pan and cook your pasta in salted boiling water according to instructions
8. Drain them once ready
9. Remove the veggies from the oven and tip in the pasta carefully
10. Toss everything well
11. Tear the basil leaves on top
12. Sprinkle a bit of parmesan
13. Enjoy!

Storage: It can be stored in the fridge in an airtight BPA-free container for up to 3-4 days. Storing in a freezer is not recommended as it raises the risk of salmonella colonization.

Nutrition value per serving: Calories: 452 kcal, Fat: 8 g, Carbs: 88 g, Protein: 14 g, Sugar: 245 mg, Potassium: 200 mg

37.10 Mediterranean Chicken And Bacon Pasta

Preparation Time: 10 minutes
Cooking Time: 20 minute

Servings: 4

Ingredients:

- Tomatoes With Juice – 4 Oz. (Peeled And Diced)
- Salt As Needed – As Needed
- Linguine Pasta – 8 Oz.
- Feta Cheese – 1/3 Cup (Crumbled)
- Dried Rosemary – ¼ Tsp.
- Chicken Breast Half– 1 Lb. (Cooked Up And Diced)
- Black Olives – 2/3 Cup (Pitted)
- Bacon – 3 Slices
- Artichoke Hearts (6 Ounce) -5 Oz.

Procedure:

1. Take al large sized pot and fill it up with salted water
2. Bring the water to a boil and add linguine
3. Cook for 8-10 minutes until Al Dente
4. Take a large sized deep skillet and cook the Bacon until brown
5. Crumble the bacon and keep it on the side
6. Season your chicken with salt
7. Stir the chicken and bacon into a large sized skillet
8. Add tomatoes and rosemary and simmer the whole mixture for about 20 minutes
9. Stir in feta cheese, artichokes hearts, olives and cook until thoroughly heated
10. Toss the freshly cooked pasta with the breast and serve immediately!
11. Garnish with some extra feta if your heart desires

Storage: It can be stored in the fridge in an airtight BPA-free container for up to 3-4 days. Storing in a freezer is not recommended as it raises the risk of salmonella colonization.

Nutrition value per serving: Calories: 625 kcal, Fat: 26 g, Carbs: 50 g, Protein: 45 g, Sugar: 245 mg, Potassium: 200 mg

37.11 Veggie Friendly Mediterranean Pasta

Preparation Time: 10 minutes
Cooking Time: 120 minutes
Servings: 4
Ingredients:
For Sauce

- Dried Basil – 1 Tsp.
- Tomatoes – 28 Oz. (Chopped)
- Sun-Dried Tomato Paste – 1 Tbsp.
- Salt – ½ Tsp.
- Oregano – 1 Tsp.
- Onion – 1 Small (Chopped)
- Olive Oil – 1 Tbsp.
- Garlic (Finely Chopped) – 2 Small Cloves (Chopped)
- Dried Parsley – 1 Tsp.
- Freshly Ground Black Pepper – As Needed
- Dried Thyme – 1 Tsp.
- Brown Sugar – ½ Tsp.
- Bay Leaf – 1 Leaf

For Veggies

- Ripened Tomatoes- 12 Small
- Olive Oil – 2 To 3 Tbsp.
- Garlic Cloves – 2 Cloves
- Deseeded Red Peppers – 2 Whole
- Courgettes – 2 Whole
- Aubergine- 1 Whole

For serving

- pasta of your preferred shape such as gigli, conchiglie etc. – 1 lb.
- parmesan cheese -3 and ½ oz.

Procedure:

1. Cook pasta according to package instructions
2. Take a large sized skillet and heat up oil
3. Add the veggies to skillet and Saute for around 5-10 minutes until tender

4. Take another bowl and add the sauce ingredients. Cook for around 5-10 minutes until you have a thick sauce
5. Add the vegetables and pasta to the sauce, stir well
6. Serve and enjoy!

Storage: It can be stored in the fridge in an airtight BPA-free container for up to 3-4 days. Storing in a freezer is not recommended as it raises the risk of salmonella colonization.

Nutrition value per serving: Calories: 252 kcal, Fat: 17 g, Carbs: 20 g, Protein: 0 g, Sugar: 238 mg, Potassium: 243 mg

37.12 Broccoli And Carrot Pasta

Preparation Time: 10 minutes
Cooking Time: 10 minutes
Servings: 4
Ingredients:

- Whole-Wheat Pasta – 8 Oz.
- Sea Salt And Freshly Ground Pepper– As Needed
- Peeled And Shredded Carrots – 1 Cup
- Greek Yogurt – ¼ Cup
- Broccoli Florets – 2 Cups
- Onion – 1 Cup, sliced
- Garlic – 6 Cloves (Diced)
- Fresh Thyme – 1 tsp.

Procedure:

1. Preheat oven to 375 degrees F (190 degrees C).
2. Cook pasta according to package instructions; drain.
3. Heat oil in large skillet over medium heat. Add onion and garlic; cook until softened, about 5 minutes.
4. Add carrot and broccoli; cook until cabbage is tender, about 10 minutes.
5. Sprinkle with thyme and salt and pepper; add chicken broth and bring to a simmer.
6. Transfer mixture to baking dish; cover with foil and bake for 20 minutes. Uncover and bake for 5 minutes more to firm up the sauce.

Storage: It can be stored in the fridge in an airtight BPA-free container for up to 3-4 days. Storing in a freezer is not recommended as it raises the risk of salmonella colonization.

Nutrition value per serving: Calories: 252 kcal, Fat: 17 g, Carbs: 20 g, Protein: 0 g, Sugar: 238 mg, Potassium: 243 mg

38 RICE RECIPES

38.1 Creamy Millet Dish

Preparation Time: 10 minutes
Cooking Time: 10 minutes
Servings: 4
Ingredients:

- Millet – ½ Cup
- Cream Cheese- 1 Oz.
- Salt – ½ Tsp.
- Hot Water 1 And ½ Cups

Procedure:

1. Mix hot water and millet in the saucepan.
2. Boil it for 8 minutes on low heat.
3. Add cream cheese and salt.
4. Carefully stir the cooked millet.

Nutrition value per serving: Calories: 528 kcal, Fat: 2 g, Carbs: 10 g, Protein: 2 g, Sugar: 245 mg, Potassium: 200 mg

38.2 Perfect Rice Stew

Preparation Time: 10 minutes
Cooking Time: 30 minute
Servings: 4
Ingredients:

- Long Grain Rice – 5 Oz.
- Squid – 4 Oz. (Sliced)
- Jalapeno Pepper – 1 Whole (Sliced)
- Tomatoes – ½ Cup (Chopped)
- Onion – 1 Whole (Diced)
- Chicken Stock – 2 Cups
- Avocado Oil- 1 Tbsp.

Procedure:

1. Roast the onion with avocado oil in the skillet for 3-4 minutes or until the onion is light brown.
2. Add squid, jalapeno pepper, and tomatoes.
3. Cook the ingredients for 7 minutes.
4. Then cook rice with water for 15 minutes.
5. Add cooked rice in the squid mixture, stir, and cook for 3 minutes more.

Storage: It can be stored in the fridge in an airtight BPA-free container for up to 4-5 days. Storing in a freezer is not recommended as it raises the risk of salmonella colonization.

Nutrition value per serving: Calories: 528 kcal, Fat: 2 g, Carbs: 10 g, Protein: 2 g, Sugar: 245 mg, Potassium: 200 mg

38.3 Awesome Rice Rolls

Preparation Time: 10 minutes
Cooking Time: 35 minutes
Servings: 4
Ingredients:

- White Cabbage Leaves – 4 Whole
- Ground Chicken – 4 Oz. (Ground)
- Garlic Powder – ½ Tsp.
- Long Grain Rice – ½ Cup (Cooked)
- Chicken Stock – ½ Cup
- Tomatoes – ½ Cup (Chopped)

Procedure:

1. In the bowl, mix ground chicken, garlic powder, and rice.
2. Then put the rice mixture on every cabbage leaf and roll.
3. Arrange the rice rolls in the saucepan.
4. Add chicken stock and tomatoes and close the lid.
5. Cook the rice rolls for 3-5 minutes on low heat.

Storage: It can be stored in the fridge in an airtight BPA-free container for up to 4-5 days. Storing in a freezer is not recommended as it raises the risk of salmonella colonization.

Nutrition value per serving: Calories: 528 kcal, Fat: 2 g, Carbs: 10 g, Protein: 2 g, Sugar: 245 mg, Potassium: 200 mg

38.4 Seafood Rice Meal

Preparation Time: 10 minutes
Cooking Time: 30 minute
Servings: 4
Ingredients:

- Seafood Mix – ½ Cup
- Long Grain Rice – ½ Cup
- Water – 3 Cups
- Olive Oil – 1 Tbsp.
- Ground Coriander – ½ Tsp.

Procedure:

1. Boil the rice with water for 15-18 minutes or until it soaks all water.
2. Then heat olive oil in the saucepan.

3. Add seafood mix and ground coriander. Cook the ingredients for 10 minutes on low heat.
4. Then add rice, stir well, and cook for 5 minutes more.
5. Serve and enjoy once ready.

Nutrition value per serving: Calories: 528 kcal, Fat: 2 g, Carbs: 10 g, Protein: 2 g, Sugar: 245 mg, Potassium: 200 mg

38.5 Salsa Rice Meal

Preparation Time: 10 minutes
Cooking Time: 15 minutes
Servings: 4
Ingredients:

- Long Grain Rice – 9 Ounces
- Chicken Stock – 4 Cups
- Salsa – 1 Cup
- Avocado Oil- 2 Tbsp.

Procedure:

1. Mix chicken stock and rice in the saucepan.
2. Cook the rice for 15 minutes on medium heat.
3. Then cool it to the room temperature and mix with avocado oil and salsa.
4. Serve and enjoy!

Storage: It can be stored in the fridge in an airtight BPA-free container for up to 4-5 days. Storing in a freezer is not recommended as it raises the risk of salmonella colonization.

Nutrition value per serving: Calories: 528 kcal, Fat: 2 g, Carbs: 10 g, Protein: 2 g, Sugar: 245 mg, Potassium: 200 mg

38.6 Rice And Fish Cakes

Preparation Time: 10 minutes
Cooking Time: 10 minutes
Servings: 4
Ingredients:

- Salmon– 6 Oz. (Shredded)
- Basmati Rice – ¼ Cup (Cooked)
- Cilantro – 1 Tsp. (Dried)
- Chili Flakes – ½ Tsp.
- Organic Canola Oil – 1 Tbsp.
- Egg – 1 Whole (Beaten)

Procedure:

1. Mix salmon with egg, basmati rice, dried cilantro, and chili flakes.
2. Heat the organic canola oil in the skillet.
3. Make the small cakes from the salmon mixture and put in the hot oil.
4. Roast the cakes for 2 minutes per side or until they are light brown.

Storage: It can be stored in the fridge in an airtight BPA-free container for up to 4-5 days. Storing in a freezer is not recommended as it raises the risk of salmonella colonization.

Nutrition value per serving: Calories: 528 kcal, Fat: 2 g, Carbs: 10 g, Protein: 2 g, Sugar: 245 mg, Potassium: 200 mg

38.7 Rice And Prunes

Preparation Time: 10 minutes
Cooking Time: 20 minutes
Servings: 4
Ingredients:

- Basmati Rice – 1 And ½ Cups
- Organic Canola Oil – 3 Tbsp.
- Prunes – 5 Whole (Chopped)
- Cream Cheese – ¼ Cup
- Cups Water – 3 And ½ Cups
- Salt - ½ Tsp.

Procedure:

1. Mix water and basmati rice in the saucepan and boil for 15 minutes on low heat.

2. Then add cream cheese, salt, and prunes.
3. Stir the rice carefully and bring it to boil.
4. Add organic canola oil and cook for 1 minute more.

Storage: It can be stored in the fridge in an airtight BPA-free container for up to 4-5 days. Storing in a freezer is not recommended as it raises the risk of salmonella colonization.

Nutrition value per serving: Calories: 528 kcal, Fat: 2 g, Carbs: 10 g, Protein: 2 g, Sugar: 245 mg, Potassium: 200 mg

39 PIZZA RECIPES

39.1 Fried Cauliflower Pizza

Preparation Time: 10 minutes
Cooking Time: 0 minute
Servings: 4
Ingredients:

- Extra-Virgin Olive Oil – 1 Tbsp.
- Salt – ¼ Tsp.
- Cauliflower – 1 Medium Sized Head(Cut Into Small Florets)
- Lemon – 1 Large Sized
- Sun-Dried Tomatoes – 6 Whole (Chopped)
- Olives – 1/3 Cup (Pitted And Sliced)
- Eggs – 1 Whole (Lightly Beaten)
- Mozzarella Cheese – 1 Cup (Shredded And Partly Skimmed)
- Oregano – ½ Tsp (Dried)
- Freshly Ground Pepper – 1 Tsp.
- Fresh Basil – ¼ Cup (Chopped)

Procedure:

1. Pre-heat your oven to a temperature of 450 degree Fahrenheit
2. Line up a pizza pan with parchment paper
3. Take a food processor and add cauliflower and pulse them well to rice size crumbles
4. Transfer it to a large sized non-stick skillet and place it over medium heat
5. Add 1 tablespoon of oil and salt
6. Cook the cauliflower for about 8-10 minutes until they are soft
7. Transfer it to a large sized bowl and allow it to cool for 10 minutes
8. Take a sharp knife and skin the white pith from your lemon
9. Discard it
10. Work all the way round the segments from the membranes allow the segments to fall onto a bowl
11. Remove the seeds if needed
12. Drain the juice from the segments
13. Add tomatoes and olive to the lemon segments
14. Toss well to combine everything
15. Add egg, oregano and cheese to the cooled cauliflowers
16. Give it a nice stir to combine everything well
17. Spread the mix onto prepped baking sheet

18. Shape the whole mixture into an 10 inch round pizza pan
19. Drizzle 1 tsp. of oil all over
20. Bake the pizza for about 10-14 minutes
21. Scatter the lemon and olive mix on top
22. Season with some pepper and bake for another 8-14 minutes until it is nicely browned all over
23. Scatter some basil on top
24. Slice the pizza into wedges
25. Enjoy!

Storage: It can be stored in air-tight containers for 3-4 days in the refrigerator and 1-2 months in the freezer.

Nutrition value per serving: Calories: 356 kcal, Fat: 10 g, Carbs: 12 g, Protein: 10 g, Sodium: 250 mg

39.2 Hearty Chicken And Olives Pizza

Preparation Time: 10 minutes
Cooking Time: 0 minute
Servings: 4
Ingredients:
For Pizza Dough

- Olive Oil – ¼ Cup
- Instant Yeast – 1 Tsp.
- Sugar – 1 Tsp.
- All-Purpose Flour – 4 And ½ Cups
- Kosher Salt – 1 And ¾ Tsp.
- Ice Cold Water – 1 And 13/4 Cups

For Pizza

- Olive Oil – 2 Tbsp.
- Fresh Basil – 2 Tbsp (Chopped)
- Mozzarella Cheese – ¾ Cup (Shredded)
- Rotisserie Chicken – ½ Cup (Chopped)
- Roasted Red Bell Pepper – ¼ Cup (Sliced)
- Assorted Olives – 9 (Sliced)
- Tomato– 1 Whole (Sliced Into Thin Wedges)
- Sliced Sun Dried Tomatoes – ¼ Cup (Sliced)
- Artichokes– ½ Cup (Cut Into Thin Wedges)
- Spinach – ½ Cup
- Feta – ½ Cup (Crumbled)
- Fresh Oregano – 2 Tbsp. (Chopped)
- Roasted Garlic – 10-12 Cloves

Procedure:

1. Prepare the pizza dough by taking a mixer with hook attachment and mixing flour, sugar, salt and yeast
2. Slowly blend it and keep mixing olive oil until fully combined
3. Drizzle some cold water
4. Once everything is well mixed, reduce the speed to medium and mix for another 6 minutes.
5. After that, transfer the flour to a floured surface and roll it into small balls.
6. Place the balls on a flour-dusted baking sheet (lined up with parchment paper)
7. Pour a bit of olive oil on top of each of the balls
8. Wrap the pan with foil and allow it to chill overnight
9. Roll out the dough once done on a flour dusted surface using your hands and knuckles
10. Once the dough is rolled out, brush more olives
11. Spread the mozzarella cheese on top followed by the vegetables, chicken and chopped up herbs
12. Transfer it to a sheet pan or pizza stone and dust with corn meal
13. Bake at 500 degree Fahrenheit in your oven for about 8-12 minutes
14. Once done, top with some more fresh herbs
15. Enjoy by cutting it up into slices!

Storage: It can be stored in air-tight containers for 3-4 days in the refrigerator and 1-2 months in the freezer.

Nutrition value per serving: Calories: 253 kcal, Fat: 10 g, Carbs: 14 g, Protein: 10 g, Sodium: 300 mg

39.3 Fresh Pesto Pizza

reparation Time: 10 minutes
Cooking Time: 0 minute
Servings: 4

Ingredients:
For Pesto

- Extra Virgin Olive Oil – 1 Cup
- Whole Blanched Toasted Almonds – ½ Cup
- Brined Capers – 2 Tbsp.
- Garlic – 3 Cloves
- Firmly Packed Fresh Basil Leaves – 1 Cup
- Firmly Packed Fresh Oregano Leaves – ½ Cup
- Feta Cheese – 4 Oz. (Crumbled)
- Kalamata Olives- 1 Oz. (Chopped)
- Fresh Lemon Juice – 1 Tbsp.
- Black Pepper – 1 Tsp.
- Freshly Packed Fresh Flat Parsley Leaves – ½ Cup

For Pizza

- Inch Greek Pita Flatbreads – 2 Whole (6 Inches)
- Mozzarella Cheese – ½ Cup
- Tomatoes – 2 Small (Chopped)
- Kalamata Olives – 8 Whole (Pitted)
- Onion – 1 Whole (Sliced)
- Parsley – For Garnish

Procedure:

1. Preheat oven to 350 degrees F (175 degrees C).
2. Take a bowl and mix the ingredients listed under pesto using an immersion blender to make the pesto sauce
3. Spread pesto over pizza crust.
4. Add mozzarella cheese, tomatoes, parsley and onion.
5. Bake in preheated oven for 20 minutes or until cheese is melted and bubbly.

Storage: It can be stored in air-tight containers for 3-4 days in the refrigerator and 1-2 months in the freezer.
Nutrition value per serving: Calories: 440 kcal, Fat: 20 g, Carbs: 15 g, Protein: 20 g, Sodium: 254 mg

40 BRUSCHETTA RECIPES

40.1 Avocado And Chimichurri Bruschetta

Preparation Time: 10 minutes
Cooking Time: 0 minute
Servings: 4
Ingredients:

- Whole Grain Ciabatta Bread – 6 Whole Pieces (1/2 Inch Thick, Toasted)
- Salt – ¾ Tsp.
- Red Wine Vinegar – 2 Tbsp.
- Red Pepper Flakes – ½ Tsp.

- Olive Oil – ¼ Cup
- Lemon Juice – 2 Tbsp.
- Garlic – 3 Cloves (Minced)
- Fresh Parsley – ¼ Cup (Chopped)
- Dried Oregano – ½ Tsp.
- Cilantro – ¼ Cup (Chopped)
- Black Pepper – ¼ Tsp.
- Avocado – 2 Whole Pieces (Pitted And Cubed)

Procedure:

1. Take a bowl and add lemon juice, garlic, vinegar, salt, and pepper flakes
2. Mix and add oregano and black pepper
3. Whisk in oil and stir in the cilantro and parsley
4. Fold in avocado cubes
5. Toss well
6. Spoon the whole mixture onto toasted bread slices and enjoy!

Storage: It can be stored in the fridge for 3-4 days. Not suitable for long-term storage in the freezer.

Nutrition value per serving: Calories: 247 kcal, Fat: 17 g, Carbs: 20 g, Protein: 5 g, Sodium: 245 mg

40.2 Tomato Bruschetta

Preparation Time: 10 minutes
Cooking Time: 10 minutes
Servings: 4

Ingredients:

- Olive Oil – 1 Tsp.
- Baguette – 1 Whole (Sliced)
- Tomatoes – 6 Whole (Cubed)
- Salt And Black Pepper – Just A Pinch
- Store bought/home made pesto sauce – 1 cup
- Mozzarella cheese – 1 cup (Shredded)
- Parsley – as needed (chopped)

Procedure:

1. Preheat the oven to 350 degrees F (175 degrees C).
2. On a baking sheet, spread out the sliced Italian bread (baguette) .
3. Spread pesto over the top of the bread slices.
4. Arrange the diced tomatoes over the top of the pesto.
5. Sprinkle shredded mozzarella cheese and chopped parsley over the tomatoes.
6. Bake in the preheated oven for 10-15 minutes, until the cheese is melted and bubbly and the bread is golden brown on top.

Storage: It can be stored in the fridge for 3-4 days. Not suitable for long-term storage in the freezer.

Nutrition value per serving: Calories: 528 kcal, Fat: 2 g, Carbs: 10 g, Protein: 2 g, Sodium: 245 mg

40.3 Chicken Bruschetta Burgers

Preparation Time: 10 minutes
Cooking Time: 16 minutes
Servings: 4

Ingredients:

- Sun-Dried Tomatoes Packed In Olive Oil- 2 Tbsp. (Minced)
- Salt and pepper – ¼ Tsp. each
- Onion – 2 Tbsp. (Minced)
- Olive Oil – 1 Tbsp.
- Mozzarella Balls, Minced – 2 Whole Small Sized (Minced)
- Chicken Breast- 8 Oz. (Ground)
- Basil – 1 Tsp. (Dried)
- Bread crumbs – ½ cup
- Fresh parsley – 1 tsp.
- Fresh thyme – 1 tsp.
- Fresh rosemary – 1 tsp.

Procedure:

1. Preheat oven to 400 degrees F (200 degrees C). Grease a baking sheet.

2. In a bowl, combine ground chicken, bread crumbs, parsley, rosemary, thyme and pepper. Mix well.
3. Shape mixture into 8 burgers. Heat olive oil in a large skillet over medium heat. Add burgers and cook until browned on both sides, about 3 minutes per side.
4. Place burgers on the prepared baking sheet and bake for 10 minutes. Sprinkle with minced cheese and tomato slices and serve on buns.

Storage: It can be stored in the fridge for 3-4 days. Not suitable for long-term storage in the freezer.

Nutrition value per serving: Calories: 528 kcal, Fat: 2 g, Carbs: 10 g, Protein: 2 g, Sodium: 245 mg

41 SIDES AND SMALL PLATES RECIPES

41.1 Excellent Tuna Croquettes

Preparation Time: 40 minutes + 4 Hours Chill Time
Cooking Time: 25 minutes
Servings: 12
Ingredients:

- Extra-Virgin Olive Oil – 6 Tbsp.
- Heavy Cream – 1 And ¼ Cups
- Red Onion – 1 Tbsp. (Chopped)
- Almond Flour – 5 Tbsp.
- Yellow Fin Tuna – 4 Oz.
- Dried Dill – ½ Tsp.
- Panko Breadcrumbs – 1 Cup
- Capers – 2 Tsp. Minced
- Eggs – 2 (Whole)
- Fresh Black Pepper – ¼ Tsp.

Procedure:

1. Take a large sized skillet and add 6 tbsp of oil, let the oil heat up over medium-low heat
2. Add 5 tbsp of almond flour, cook gently for 2-3 minutes until you have a thin paste and the flour browns slightly
3. Increase heat to medium-high and gently add the heavy cream, carefully whisking for 5 minutes as you keep on adding
4. Remove the heat and stir in tuna, capers, red onion, dill and pepper
5. Pour the mixture into a 8 inch square baking dish (Coated with olive oil), let it cool down to room temperature
6. Cover the mix and let it chill for 4 hours
7. Take 3 separate bowls, in one bowl add eggs (Beaten). In another, add remaining almond flour while in the third add panko
8. Line a baking sheet with parchment
9. Add 1 tbsp of cold dough into flour mix, roll well. Shake off any excess and use your hand to form oval shape
10. Dip the croquette into eggs, and then in panko
11. Place it on the baking sheet, repeat with remaining dough
12. Take a small sized saucepan and add 1-2 cups of olive oil over medium high heat
13. Once the oil is hot, add croquettes and fry them until golden brown

Storage

Since this is a fried item, it is ideal that you consume it right away. However, you may still store it in fridge for 1-2 days in an air tight box, but the taste will deteriorate.

Nutrition value per serving: Calories: 92 kcal, Fat: 5 g, Carbs: 10 g, Protein: 10 g, Sodium: 300 mg, Potassium: 230 mg

41.2 Fancy Wrapped Plums

Preparation Time: 10 minutes
Cooking Time: 0 minute
Servings: 4

Ingredients:

- Prosciutto – 2 Oz. (Cut Into 16 Pieces)
- Plums,– 4 Whole (Quartered)
- Chives – 1 Tbsp. (Chopped)
- Red Pepper Flakes- Just A Pinch (Crushed)
- Salt And Pepper – As Needed

Procedure:

1. Preheat oven to 400 degrees F (200 degrees C).
2. Cut prosciutto into small pieces.
3. Mix prosciutto, salt, and pepper in a Bowl.
4. Place plums on a baking sheet lined with foil and top with prosciutto mixture.
5. Bake for 30 minutes or until plum is soft.
6. Serve and enjoy!

Storage: It can be stored in BPA Free container for around 4-5 days in the refrigerator. Storage in the Freezer is not recommended

Nutrition value per serving: Calories: 528 kcal, Fat: 2 g, Carbs: 10 g, Protein: 2 g, Sugar: 245 mg, Potassium: 200 mg

41.3 Simple Cheese Mug

Preparation Time: 10 minutes
Cooking Time: 2-5 minute
Servings: 4

Ingredients:

- 2 ounces roast beef slices
- 1 and ½ tablespoons green chilies, diced
- 1 and ½ ounces pepper jack cheese, shredded
- 1 tablespoon sour cream

Procedure:

1. Layer roast beef on the bottom of your mug, making sure to break it down into small pieces
2. Add half a tablespoon of sour cream, add half tablespoon green Chile and half an ounce of pepper jack cheese
3. Keep layering until all ingredients are used
4. Microwave for 2 minutes
5. Server warm and enjoy!

Storage: It can be stored in BPA Free container for around 4-5 days in the refrigerator. Storage in the Freezer is not recommended.

Nutrition value per serving: Calories: 5 kcal, Fat: 2 g, Carbs: 10 g, Protein: 2 g, Sugar: 245 mg, Potassium: 200 mg

41.4 Stuffed Avocado Meal

Preparation Time: 10 minutes
Cooking Time: 0 minute
Servings: 4

Ingredients:

- Basil– 1 Tbsp (Chopped)
- Pine Nuts– 2 Tsp. (Toasted And Chopped)
- Salt And Black Pepper– To Taste
- Black Olives– 2 Tbsp. (Chopped And Pitted)
- Basil Pesto – 1 And ½ Tbsp.
- Sun-Dried Tomatoes – 2 Tbsp. (Chopped)

- Tuna– 10 Oz. (Drained)
- Avocado– 1 Whole (Halved And Pitted)

Procedure:

1. Cut the avocados in half and remove the pit. Scoop out the flesh and place it in a bowl.
2. Into the bowl, add remaining ingredients and mix them thoroughly
3. Stuff the avocados with the mixture and serve immediately.

Storage: It can be stored in BPA Free container for around 4-5 days in the refrigerator. Storage in the Freezer is not recommended.

Nutrition value per serving: Calories: 528 kcal, Fat: 2 g, Carbs: 10 g, Protein: 2 g, Sugar: 245 mg, Potassium: 200 mg

41.5 Yogurt And Banana Bowls

Preparation Time: 10 minutes
Cooking Time: 10 minute
Servings: 4

Ingredients:

- Bananas– 2 Whole (Sliced)
- Nutmeg – ½ Tsp. (Ground)
- Flaxseed Meal – 3 Tbsp.
- Creamy Peanut Butter – ¼ Cup
- Greek Yogurt – 4 Cups

Procedure:

1. Divide Greek yogurt between 4 serving bowls and top with sliced bananas.
2. Add peanut butter in microwave-safe bowl and micro- wave for 30 seconds.
3. Drizzle 1 tbsp. of melted peanut butter on each bowl on top of the sliced bananas.
4. Sprinkle cinnamon and flax meal on top and serve.

Storage: It can be stored in BPA Free container for around 4-5 days in the refrigerator. Storage in the Freezer is not recommended.

Nutrition value per serving: Calories: 528 kcal, Fat: 2 g, Carbs: 10 g, Protein: 2 g, Sugar: 245 mg, Potassium: 200 mg

41.6 Quick Cashew Energy Bites

Preparation Time: 10 minutes + 1 Hour Chill Time
Cooking Time: 0 minute
Servings: 4

Ingredients:

- Cashew Nuts – 2 Cups
- Cinnamon – ¼ Tsp.
- Lemon Zest – 1 Tsp.
- Dates – 4 Tbsp. (Chopped)
- Unsweetened Coconut – 1/3 Cup (Shredded)
- Dried Apricots – ¾ Cups

Procedure:

1. Preheat oven to 350 degrees F (175 degrees C).
2. Spread cashews in a single layer on a baking sheet and roast for 8 minutes, or until lightly browned.
3. When cashews are done roasting, let cool for 5 minutes.
4. Take a medium bowl add cashew, cinnamon, lemon zest, dates, shredded coconut and apricots. Toss them well and enjoy!

Storage: It can be stored in a BPA Free container for around 7-12 days in the refrigerator and 8-12 months in the freezer.

Nutrition value per serving: Calories: 528 kcal, Fat: 2 g, Carbs: 10 g, Protein: 2 g, Sugar: 245 mg, Potassium: 200 mg

41.7 Chia Almond Butter Pudding

Preparation Time: 10 minutes
Cooking Time: 5 minutes
Servings: 4

Ingredients:

- Chia Seeds – ¼ Cup
- Unsweetened Almond Milk – 1 Cup
- Maple Syrup – 1 And ½ Tbsp.
- Almond Butter - 2 And ½ Tbsp.
- Cinnamon – 1 tsp.
- Applesauce – ½ cup
- Salt – as needed
- Coconut oil – 1 tbsp.
- Sugar - 1 cup
- Plain Flour – ½ cup

Procedure:

1. Preheat oven to 375 degrees F (190 degrees C). Grease a 9x13 inch baking dish.
2. In a medium bowl, combine chia seeds, almond butter, applesauce, cinnamon and salt. Mix well.
3. Pour mixture into the prepared baking dish.
4. Bake for 20 minutes or until set. Cool on a wire rack before serving.
5. In a small saucepan over low heat, melt coconut oil or butter. Add sugar and stir until dissolved. Add flour and stir until blended. Cook for 2 minutes longer, stirring constantly. Remove from heat and stir in vanilla extract.
6. Drizzle over pudding when serving.

Storage: It can be stored in BPA Free container for around 4-5 days in the refrigerator and 1-2 months in the freezer. However, if you feel like it smells bad or has an odd texture, then better not to consume it.
Nutrition value per serving: Calories: 528 kcal, Fat: 2 g, Carbs: 10 g, Protein: 2 g, Sugar: 245 mg, Potassium: 200 mg

42 POULTRY RECIPES

42.1 Almond Crusted Chicken Tenders With Honey

Preparation Time: 10 minutes
Cooking Time: 20 minutes
Servings: 4

Ingredients:

- Honey - 1 Tbsp.
- Dijon Mustard – 1 Tbsp.
- Freshly Ground Black Pepper – ¼ Tsp.
- Kosher Or Sea Salt – ¼ Tsp.
- Chicken Breast Tenders Or Tenderloins – 1 Lb.
- Almond Flour – 1 Cup(Chopped)
- Olive Oil – As Needed
- Parsley And Thyme – For Garnish

Procedure:

1. Preheat oven to 400 degrees F (200 degrees C).
2. Place chicken tenders on baking sheet.
3. In a shallow dish, combine almond flour and salt. Dredge chicken tenders in flour mixture until coated.
4. In a large skillet over medium heat, heat olive oil and honey until warm.
5. Add chicken tenders to skillet; cook for 3 minutes per side or until golden brown and cooked through.

6. Garnish with chopped parsley and thyme; serve hot.

Storage: Can be properly stored in a BPA-free plastic/glass container box for 2 days in the refrigerator and 2-3 months in the freezer.
Nutrition value per serving: Calories: 528 kcal, Fat: 2 g, Carbs: 10 g, Protein: 2 g, Sodium: 245 mg

42.2 Coconut Chicken Tenders

Preparation Time: 10 minutes
Cooking Time: 0 minute
Servings: 4

Ingredients:

- Garlic Powder -1 Tsp
- Boneless Chicken Tenders – 4 Pieces
- Black Pepper – As Needed
- Salt – As needed
- Yogurt – 1 Cup
- Honey – 1 Tbsp.
- Lemon Juice – 1 Tsp.
- Coconut Milk – 1 Cup

Procedure:

1. Preheat oven to 400 degrees F (200 degrees C).
2. Heat olive oil in a large baking dish.
3. Sprinkle chicken with garlic powder, salt, and black pepper; coat well with yogurt mixture.
4. Bake for 20 minutes or until tender.
5. In a small bowl, whisk together honey, lemon juice, and coconut milk; pour over chicken.
6. Serve warm or cold.

Storage: Can be properly stored in a BPA-free plastic/glass container box for 2 days in the refrigerator and 2-3 months in the freezer.
Nutrition value per serving: Calories: 528 kcal, Fat: 2 g, Carbs: 10 g, Protein: 2 g, Sodium: 245 mg

42.3 Parsley & Dijon Chicken Potatoes

Preparation Time: 10 minutes
Cooking Time: 22 minute
Servings: 4

Ingredients:

- Garlic – 3 Cloves (Minced)
- Freshly Squeezed Lemon Juice – 1 Tbsp. (Freshly Juiced)
- Freshly Ground Black Pepper – ¼ Tsp.
- Yukon Gold Potatoes- 1 And ½ Lb. (Cut Into ½ Inch Cubes)
- Skinless Chicken Thighs – ½ Lb. (Cut Into 1 Inch Cubes)
- Kosher Or Sea Salt – ¼ Tsp.
- Fresh Flat-Leaf (Italian) Parsley, Including Stems
- Extra-Virgin Olive Oil -1 Tbsp.
- Dijon Mustard – 1 Tbsp.
- Cup Dry White Wine – ¼ Cup
- Almond Flour – 1 Cup
- Dill – 1 Tsp.
- Vinegar – 1 Tsp.

Procedure:

1. Preheat oven to 375 degrees.
2. Season the chicken with salt and pepper before dredging it in flour. In a large pan over medium heat, heat the olive oil. Cook until the chicken is golden brown, about 4 minutes per side. Transfer to a baking dish and bake for 25 minutes.
3. Meanwhile, in a large pot of boiling water, add potatoes and 1/2 tsp. salt. Cook until tender, about 15 minutes.
4. Drain potatoes and return them to the pot. Add parsley, dill, vinegar, and

remaining salt and pepper; stir well to combine.

5. To serve, divide potatoes among 4 plates. Top with chicken and serve immediately

Storage: Can be properly stored in a BPA-free plastic/glass container box for 2 days in the refrigerator and 2-3 months in the freezer.

Nutrition value per serving: Calories: 528 kcal, Fat: 2 g, Carbs: 10 g, Protein: 2 g, Sodium: 245 mg

42.4 Parmesan Baked Chicken

Preparation Time: 10 minutes
Cooking Time: 20 minutes
Servings: 4

Ingredients:

- Fresh Black Pepper- As Needed
- Pink Salt- As Needed
- Chicken Breast – 2 Whole (Boneless, Skinless)
- Ghee – 2 Tbsp.
- Mayonnaise – ½ Cup
- Parmesan Cheese- 1/2 Cup (Grated)
- Italian Seasoning – 1 Tbsp.
- Pork Rinds – ¼ Cup (Crushed)

Procedure:

1. Pre-heat your oven to 425 degree F
2. Take a large baking dish and coat with ghee
3. Pat chicken breasts dry and wrap with towel
4. Season with salt and pepper
5. Place in baking dish
6. Take a small bowl and add mayonnaise, parmesan cheese, Italian seasoning
7. Slather mayo mix evenly over chicken breast
8. Sprinkle crushed pork rinds on top
9. Bake for 20 minutes until topping is browned
10. Serve and enjoy!

Storage: Can be properly stored in a BPA-free plastic/glass container box for 2 days in the refrigerator and 2-3 months in the freezer.

Nutrition value per serving: Calories: 528 kcal, Fat: 2 g, Carbs: 10 g, Protein: 2 g, Sodium: 245 mg

42.5 Almond Breaded Chicken Delight

Preparation Time: 10 minutes
Cooking Time: 15 minutes
Servings: 4

Ingredients:

- Sunflower Seeds– Just To Taste
- Low-Fat Chicken Broth – 2/3 Cup
- Low Sugar Raspberry Preserve – ½ Cup
- Balsamic Vinegar – 1 And ½ Tbsp.
- Arrowroot- 1 And ½ Tsp.
- Almond Flour – ¼ Cup
- 3 Boneless Chicken Breast– 3 Whole Chicken Breast

Procedure:

1. Discard skin from chicken breasts and season with seeds.
2. To begin, coat each piece of poultry in flour and shake off any excess before frying.
3. Heat a nonstick frying pan to medium-high heat.
4. Serve over rice and steamed broccolini and simmer for 15 minutes, stirring halfway through.
5. Remove the chicken to a serving plate and keep warm.
6. Toss in the arrowroot powder, broth, and raspberry jam to the pan and heat through.
7. For a few minutes, mix in balsamic vinegar and decrease the heat.

8. Return the chicken to the sauce and simmer for a further 15 minutes, stirring occasionally.
9. Serve and savor your meal!

Storage: Can be properly stored in a BPA-free plastic/glass container box for 2 days in the refrigerator and 2-3 months in the freezer.

Nutrition value per serving: Calories: 528 kcal, Fat: 2 g, Carbs: 10 g, Protein: 2 g, Sodium: 245 mg

42.6 Simple Stir Fried Chicken

Preparation Time: 10 minutes
Cooking Time: 12 minutes
Servings: 4
Ingredients:

- Chicken Breast – 2 Large (Boneless)
- Lemon Juice – 1/3 Cup
- Almond Meal – 1 And ½ Cups
- Coconut Oil – 2 Tbsp.
- Lemon Pepper – As Needed
- Parsley – As Needed

Procedure:

1. Cut the chicken breast in half.
2. Pound each half until it is 14 inch thick.
3. Place a pan over medium heat, add oil, and heat it up.
4. Allow each chicken breast slice to soak in lemon juice for 2 minutes.
5. Turn over and allow the other side to settle for 2 minutes.
6. Coat both sides with the almond meal.
7. Fry the coated chicken in the oil for 4 minutes per side, making sure to liberally sprinkle with lemon pepper.
8. Repeat with the remaining chicken until all of them are fried.Garnish with parsley and enjoy!

Storage: Can be properly stored in a BPA-free plastic/glass container box for 2 days in the refrigerator and 2-3 months in the freezer.

Nutrition value per serving: Calories: 528 kcal, Fat: 2 g, Carbs: 10 g, Protein: 2 g, Sodium: 245 mg

42.7 Blackberry Chicken Wings

Preparation Time: 10 minutes
Cooking Time: 30 minute
Servings: 4
Ingredients:

- Chicken Wings – 3 Lb. (20 Pieces)
- Blackberry Chipotle Jam – ½ Cup
- Salt And Pepper – To Taste
- Water – ½ Cup

Procedure:

1. Add water and jam to a bowl and mix well
2. Place chicken wings in a zip bag and add two-thirds of marinade
3. Season with salt and pepper
4. Let it marinate for 30 minutes
5. Pre-heat your oven to 400 degree F
6. Prepare a baking sheet and wire rack, place chicken wings in wire rack and bake for 15 minutes
7. Brush remaining marinade and bake for 30 minutes more
8. Enjoy!

Storage: Can be properly stored in a BPA-free plastic/glass container box for 2 days in the refrigerator and 2-3 months in the freezer.

Nutrition value per serving: Calories: 237 kcal, Fat: 5 g, Carbs: 17 g, Protein: 30 g, Sodium: 245 mg

42.8 Amazing Chicken Sheekh Kebab

Preparation Time: 10 minutes
Cooking Time: 10 minute
Servings: 4

Ingredients:

- Wooden Skewers – 6 Pieces
- White Vinegar - ¼ Cup
- Salt – ¼ Tsp.
- Olive Oil – ¼ Cup
- Lemon Juice – ¼ Cup
- Ground Cumin – 1 Tsp. (Ground)
- Ground Black Pepper – ¼ Tsp.
- Green/Red Bell Peppers– 2 Large (Cut Into 1 Inch Pieces)
- Garlic Cloves – 2 Cloves (Minced)
- Fresh Mushrooms- 12 Whole
- Dried Thyme – ½ Tsp.
- Dried Oregano – 1 Tsp. (Ground)
- Cherry Tomatoes – 12 Whole
- Boneless And Skinless Chicken– 2 Lb. (Cut Into 1 And ½ Inch Pieces)

ForSauce

- Tahini Sauce – 1 Cup
- Lemon Juice – 1 Tbsp.
- Garlic Powder – 1 Tsp.

Procedure:

1. Preheat your grill to medium heat.
2. Brush the chicken breast with some olive oil or cooking spray and season it with the spices and herbs listed above
3. Thread the chicken into skewers, alternative between the meat and vegetables
4. Grill the chicken for about 3-5 minutes per side or until cooked through.
5. Remove from the grill and let cool slightly before slicing into thin strips.
6. In a bowl, mix together tahini sauce, lemon juice and garlic powder until well combined.
7. Serve immediately and enjoy with the sauce mix

Storage: Can be properly stored in a BPA-free plastic/glass container box for 2 days in the refrigerator and 2-3 months in the freezer.

Nutrition value per serving: Calories: 290 kcal, Fat: 13 g, Carbs: 10 g, Protein: 33 g, Sodium: 245 mg

42.9 Awesome Chicken Bell Pepper Platter

Preparation Time: 10 minutes
Cooking Time: 30 minute
Servings: 4

Ingredients:

- Water – ½ Cup
- Tomato– 1 Whole.
- Skinless And Boneless Diced Chicken Breast Halves – 6 Halves (Skinless, Boneless, Diced)
- Salt And Pepper – As Needed
- Red Onion – 1 Whole (Diced)
- Olive Oil – 3 Tbsp.
- Red Bell Pepper– 1 (Whole)
- Dried Oregano, Rosemary, Thyme, Garlic Powder– 2 Tsp. Each

Procedure:

1. Preheat oven to 375 degrees F. In a small bowl, combine garlic, rosemary, thyme and pepper. Rub mixture all over chicken breasts.
2. Heat a large skillet over medium heat.
3. Add oil and swirl to coat.
4. Add chicken breasts and cook for about 3 minutes per side or until browned.
5. Transfer to a baking dish and bake for about 20 minutes or until cooked through. Meanwhile, in a medium bowl,

combine tomatoes, red onion and bell pepper.

6. Drizzle with olive oil and sprinkle with salt and parsley leaves. Serve the chicken atop the vegetables.

Storage: Can be properly stored in a BPA-free plastic/glass container box for 2 days in the refrigerator and 2-3 months in the freezer.

Nutrition value per serving: Calories: 336 kcal, Fat: 10 g, Carbs: 26 g, Protein: 35 g, Sodium: 245 mg

42.10 Cheesy Chicken Nuggets

Preparation Time: 10 minutes
Cooking Time: 5 minutes
Servings: 4

Ingredients:

- Chicken Breast – 1 Whole (Pre-Cooked)
- Parmesan Cheese – ½ Oz. (Grated_
- Almond Flour – 2 Tbsp.
- Baking Powder – ½ Tsp.
- Egg – 1 Whole
- Water – 1 Tbsp.

Procedure:

1. Cut breast into bite sized portions
2. Take a bowl and add parmesan, flour, baking powder, water
3. Mix well
4. Cover chicken pieces in batter
5. Take a skillet and place it over medium heat, add oil and let it heat up
6. Add chicken nuggets and fry until golden brown
7. Serve and enjoy!

Storage: Can be properly stored in a BPA-free plastic/glass container box for 2 days in the refrigerator and 2-3 months in the freezer.

Nutrition value per serving: Calories: 230 kcal, Fat: 6 g, Carbs: 2 g, Protein: 28 g, Sodium: 245 mg

42.11 Simple And Wholesome Baked Chicken Breast

Preparation Time: 10 minutes
Cooking Time: 40 minute
Servings: 4

Ingredients:

- Skinless And Boneless Chicken Breast – 2 Whole (8 Ounces Each, Skinless And Boneless)
- Salt– As Needed
- Olive Oil – ¼ Cup
- Ground Black Pepper – As Needed
- Freshly Squeezed Lemon Juice – ¼ Cup
- Dried Thyme - ¼ Tsp.
- Dried Oregano - ½ Tsp.
- Chicken Broth – 1 Cup
- Vinegar – 1 Tsp.
- Honey – 1 Tsp.
- Parsley – 1 Tsp.

Procedure:

1. In a small bowl, whisk together the oil, oregano, thyme, salt and pepper. Rub the mixture all over the chicken breast.
2. Place in a baking dish. Pour the chicken broth over the chicken and bake for 25 minutes, or until cooked through. Let cool for 5 minutes before serving.
3. Stir in the vinegar and honey and garnish with parsley leaves.

Storage: Can be properly stored in a BPA-free plastic/glass container box for 2 days in the refrigerator and 2-3 months in the freezer.

Nutrition value per serving: Calories: 501 kcal, Fat: 32 g, Carbs: 3 g, Protein: 47 g, Sodium: 245 mg

42.12 Chicken And Basil Zucchini Noodles

Preparation Time: 10 minutes
Cooking Time: 10 minutes
Servings: 4
Ingredients:

- Zucchini – 1 Whole (Shredded)
- Garlic- 1 Clove (Peeled And Minced)
- Coconut Milk – ¼ Cup
- Basil – ½ Cup (Chopped)
- Tomatoes – 1 Lb. (Diced)
- Ghee – 2 Tbsp.
- Chicken Fillets – 2 Whole (Cubed)

Procedure:

1. Saute cubed chicken in ghee until no longer pink
2. Add tomatoes and season with salt
3. Simmer and reduce liquid
4. Prepare your zucchini Noodles by shredding zucchini in food processor
5. Add basil, garlic, coconut milk to chicken and cook for a few minutes
6. Add half of the zucchini Zoodles to a bowl and top with creamy tomato basil chicken
7. Enjoy!

Storage: Can be properly stored in a BPA-free plastic/glass container box for 2 days in the refrigerator and 2-3 months in the freezer.
Nutrition value per serving: Calories: 724 kcal, Fat: 26 g, Carbs: 81 g, Protein: 3 g, Sodium: 245 mg

42.13 Bacon And Chicken Garlic Wrap

Preparation Time: 10 minutes
Cooking Time: 10 minutes
Servings: 4
Ingredients:

- Chicken Fillet- 1 Whole (Cut Into Small Cubes)
- Bacon Slices –8-9 Slices (Cut Into Cubes)
- Garlic – 6 Cloves (Minced)

Procedure:

1. Pre-heat your oven to 400 degree F
2. Line a baking tray with aluminum foil
3. Add minced garlic to a bowl and rub each chicken piece with it
4. Wrap bacon piece around each garlic chicken bite
5. Secure with toothpick
6. Transfer bites to baking sheet, keeping a little bit of space between them
7. Bake for about 15-20 minutes until crispy
8. Serve and enjoy!

Storage: Can be properly stored in a BPA-free plastic/glass container box for 2 days in the refrigerator and 2-3 months in the freezer.

Nutrition value per serving: Calories: 724 kcal, Fat: 26 g, Carbs: 81 g, Protein: 3 g, Sodium: 245 mg

42.14 Hearty Chicken Breast Salad

Preparation Time: 10 minutes
Cooking Time: 30-40 minutes
Servings: 4
Ingredients:

- Spinach – 2 Tbsp.
- Olive Oil – 2 Tbsp.
- Lettuces – 1 And ¾ Oz.
- Lemon Juice To Taste – To Taste
- Chicken Breast – 3 And ½ Oz.
- Bell Pepper – 1 Whole

Procedure:

1. Boil chicken breast without adding salt cut the meat into small strips

2. Put the spinach in boiling water for a few minutes, cut into small strips
3. Cut pepper in strips as well
4. Add everything to a bowl and mix with juice and oil
5. Serve!

Storage: Can be properly stored in a BPA-free plastic/glass container box for 2 days in the refrigerator and 2-3 months in the freezer.
Nutrition value per serving: Calories: 724 kcal, Fat: 26 g, Carbs: 81 g, Protein: 3 g, Sodium: 245 mg

43 RED MEAT DISHESRECIPES

43.1 Cool Medi Grilled Lamb Chops

Preparation Time: 10 minutes
Cooking Time: 10 minutes
Servings: 4
Ingredients:

- Olive Oil – ½ Cup
- Lamb Shoulder Chops – 4 Whole (8 Ounces Each)
- Ground Black Pepper – ¼ Tsp.
- Garlic – 1 Tbsp.
- Fresh Basil – 2 Tbsp.
- Balsamic Vinegar – 2 Tbsp.
- Dijon Mustard – 2 Tbsp.

Procedure:

1. Pat the lamb chops dry first and arrange them on a shallow glass baking dish
2. Take a bowl and whisk in Dijon mustard, garlic, balsamic vinegar and pepper
3. Mix them well
4. Whisk oil slowly into the marinade until it is smooth
5. Stir in basil
6. Pour the whole marinade over the lamb chops, making sure to coat both sides
7. Cover and allow the chops to marinate for 1-4 hours
8. Bring the chops to room temperature and leave them for 30 minutes
9. Pre-heat your grill to medium heat and oil up your grate
10. Grill the lamb chops until they are nicely browned (giving 5-10 minutes) per side
11. Grill until the center read 145 degree Fahrenheit
12. Enjoy!

Storage: Can be properly stored in a BPA-free plastic/glass container box for 2 days in the refrigerator and 2-3 months in the freezer.

Nutrition value per serving: Calories: 528 kcal, Fat: 2 g, Carbs: 10 g, Protein: 2 g, Sugar: 245 mg, Potassium: 255 mg

43.2 Foil Ala Pork

Preparation Time: 10 minutes
Cooking Time: 25 minutes
Servings: 4
Ingredients:

- Salt And Pepper To Taste – As Needed
- Raw Ham – 4 Slices
- Pork Chops– 4 Whole (2 Oz. Each)
- Onion – 1 Oz.
- Olive Oil To Taste – As Needed
- Garlic – 1 Clove
- Cooking Cream – 4 Tbsp.

- Champignon Mushrooms – 10 Oz.

Procedure:

1. Wash and dry the pork ribs.
2. Remove the earthy part of the mushrooms and then wash them and dry them then chop them finely.
3. Peel and wash the garlic clove and onion and then chop them.
4. Put a little olive oil in a non-stick pan, and brown for 2 minutes on each side, season with salt and pepper and then set aside.
5. In the same pan, sauté the garlic and onion, stir and as soon as they are golden, add the mushrooms.
6. Cut the ham into strips and then add it to the mushrooms.
7. Season with salt and pepper and cook for 10 minutes.
8. Arrange the pork ribs in 4 aluminum sheets. Brush them with the cooking cream and cover with the mixture of mushrooms and ham.
9. Close the packets and place them in the oven to cook at 356 ° F for 25 minutes.
10. As soon as the pork is cooked, take them out of the oven, let the meat rest for 5 minutes and then remove them from the foil.
11. Put the meat on individual serving plates and serve sprinkled with the mushroom mix and the cooking juices as an accompanying sauce

Storage: Can be properly stored in a BPA-free plastic/glass container box for 2 days in the refrigerator and 2-3 months in the freezer.

Nutrition value per serving: Calories: 528 kcal, Fat: 2 g, Carbs: 10 g, Protein: 2 g, Sugar: 245 mg, Potassium: 255 mg

43.3 Pomegranate Sauce And Pork Fillet

Preparation Time: 10 minutes
Cooking Time: 65 minutes
Servings: 4

Ingredients:

- Salt And Pepper– As Needed
- Rosemary– As Needed
- Pork Tenderloin – 21 Oz.
- Pomegranate Juice Extract – 1 Cup
- Laurel– As Needed
- Garlic- - 1 Clove
- Cornstarch – 2 Tbsp.
- Brown Sugar – 2 Tbsp.
- Bay Leaf – 1-2 whole

Procedure:

1. Wash and dry the fillet with kitchen paper.
2. Wash all the aromatic herbs and peel the garlic clove.
3. Macerate the fillet in pomegranate juice with garlic, rosemary, bay leaf, and pepper.
4. Cover with plastic wrap and place in the fridge for about 2 hours, turning it from time to time.
5. In a pan, heat two tablespoons of olive oil and brown the fillet.
6. Wet it often with the cooking juices.
7. Now, prepare the sauce by filtering the marinating juice, add the sugar and corn starch. Put the sauce on the fire and let it thicken.
8. Place the fillet in a pan brushed with olive oil.
9. Put the baking pan in the oven and cook at 356 °F for about 20 minutes.
10. After 25 minutes, turn the meat and continue cooking for another 20 minutes.

11. As soon as it is cooked, remove the fillet from the oven and let it rest for 5 minutes.
12. Then cut the fillet into slices and place it on serving plates.
13. Drizzle with the pomegranate sauce and serve.

Storage: Can be properly stored in a BPA-free plastic/glass container box for 2 days in the refrigerator and 2-3 months in the freezer.

Nutrition value per serving: Calories: 528 kcal, Fat: 2 g, Carbs: 10 g, Protein: 2 g, Sugar: 245 mg, Potassium: 255 mg

43.4 Juicy Pork Fillet With Aromatic Crust

Preparation Time: 10 minutes
Cooking Time: 10 minute
Servings: 4

Ingredients:

- Speck – 3 And ½ Oz. (Thinly Sliced)
- Salt And Pepper To Taste – As Needed
- Rosemary – 2 Sprigs
- Pork Tenderloin – 21 Oz.
- Parsley – 10 Leaves
- Olive Oil To Taste – As Needed
- Mustard – 2 Tbsp.
- Marjoram -2 Whole
- Extra Virgin Olive Oil – 2 tbsp.

Procedure:

1. Wash and dry the parsley, rosemary and marjoram and then chop and put them in a bowl.
2. Chop the speck and put it in the bowl with the aromatic herbs.
3. Add the mustard and mix until you get a homogeneous mixture.
4. Wash and dry the pork fillet and then brush the entire surface of the meat with the emulsion.
5. Heat two tablespoons of olive oil in a pan and, when hot, brown the fillet.
6. Brown for 2 minutes on each side, then put the lid on the pan and continue cooking for another 20 minutes.
7. Season with salt and pepper, turn off and let the meat rest for 10 minutes.
8. Now cut the fillet into slices.
9. Put the fillet slices on serving plates, sprinkle them with the cooking juices and serve.

Storage: Can be properly stored in a BPA-free plastic/glass container box for 2 days in the refrigerator and 2-3 months in the freezer.
Nutrition value per serving: Calories: 528 kcal, Fat: 2 g, Carbs: 10 g, Protein: 2 g, Sugar: 245 mg, Potassium: 255 mg

43.5 Grape Sauce And Pork Fillet

Preparation Time: 10 minutes
Cooking Time: 65 minutes
Servings: 4
Ingredients:

- White Grapes – 5 And ½ Oz.
- Thyme – 3 Sprigs
- Thinly Sliced Speck – 2 Oz.
- Salt And Pepper To Taste – As Needed
- Pork Tenderloin – 2 Whole (8 Oz. Each)
- Olive Oil To Taste – As Needed
- Garlic – 2 Cloves
- Black Grapes – 5 And ½ Oz.
- Red Wine – 1 cup

Procedure:

1. Wash and dry the pork tenderloin and remove all excess fat. Season the meat with salt and pepper.
2. Peel and wash the garlic cloves and then chop them.

3. Wash and let the grapes drain.
4. Heat 3 tablespoons of olive oil in a pan and, when hot, brown the garlic cloves.
5. Add the fillet and brown it for two minutes on each side.
6. Brush a baking pan with olive oil and, when the fillet is golden on the outside, put it in the baking pan with all the cooking juices.
7. Wash and dry the thyme and put it in the baking pan with the meat.
8. Wet the meat with the wine, put the baking pan in the oven and cook at 320 ^{0} F for 35 minutes.
9. After cooking, remove the baking pan from the oven.
10. Remove the meat from the baking pan and wrap it in aluminum foil.
11. Put the pork juices in a pan.
12. Add the minced speck and brown it until crisp.
13. Now add the grapes and sauté for 4 minutes.
14. Now cut the fillet into slices and place it on serving plates.
15. Sprinkle with the grape sauce and serve.

Storage: Can be properly stored in a BPA-free plastic/glass container box for 2 days in the refrigerator and 2-3 months in the freezer.

Nutrition value per serving: Calories: 528 kcal, Fat: 2 g, Carbs: 10 g, Protein: 2 g, Sugar: 245 mg, Potassium: 255 mg

43.6 Pork With Gorgonzola Sauce

Preparation Time: 10 minutes
Cooking Time: 65 minutes
Servings: 4

Ingredients:

- Vegetable Cream – 1 Glass
- Sprig Rosemary – 1 Sprig
- Speck – 8 Slices
- Salt And Pepper To Taste – As Needed
- Pork Tenderloin In One Piece – 2 Whole (8 Oz. Each)
- Olive Oil To Taste – As Needed
- Gorgonzola –2 Whole (8 Oz Each)

Procedure:

1. Wash and dry the pork fillet and then massage the entire surface of the meat with salt and pepper.
2. Cut the fillet into 4 slices of the same size.
3. Wrap the meat with the slices of speck and then tie the meat with kitchen string.
4. Wash the sprig of rosemary and divide it into four parts.
5. Put the rosemary between the kitchen string and the meat.
6. Brush the surface of the meat with olive oil and then put it in a baking pan brushed with olive oil.
7. Cook the fillets at 356 ° for 20 minutes, then turn the fillets and continue cooking for another 35 minutes.
8. Once cooked, remove the baking pan from the oven and let the meat rest for 10 minutes.
9. Then move on to prepare the accompanying sauce.
10. Cut the gorgonzola into cubes and put it in a saucepan with the cream.
11. Put the saucepan on the stove and cook until the cheese has completely melted, and the sauce has taken on a thick and homogeneous consistency.
12. At this point, remove the kitchen string and cut the meat into slices.
13. Put the meat on serving plates, sprinkle them with the gorgonzola sauce and serve.

Storage: Can be properly stored in a BPA-free plastic/glass container box for 2 days in the refrigerator and 2-3 months in the freezer.

Nutrition value per serving: Calories: 528 kcal, Fat: 2 g, Carbs: 10 g, Protein: 2 g, Sugar: 245 mg, Potassium: 255 mg

43.7 Fennel And Figs Lamb

Preparation Time: 10 minutes
Cooking Time: 40 minutes
Servings: 4
Ingredients:

- Swerve – 1 Tbsp.
- Apple Cider Vinegar – 1/8 Cup
- Figs – 4 (Cut In Half)
- Olive Oil – 2 Tbsp.
- Salt And Pepper – As Needed
- Fennel Bulbs – 2 Whole, Sliced
- Lamb Rack – 12 Oz.

Procedure:

1. Toss fennel, figs, vinegar, swerve, and oil in a mixing dish.
2. Place in a baking dish
3. Season with salt and pepper to taste.
4. Bake for 15 minutes at 400°F.
5. Season the lamb with salt and pepper and place it in a hot skillet over medium-high heat.
6. For a few minutes, cook
7. Bake the lamb in a baking dish with the fennel for 20 minutes.
8. Serve on individual plates.
9. Enjoy!

Storage: Can be properly stored in a BPA-free plastic/glass container box for 2 days in the refrigerator and 2-3 months in the freezer.

Nutrition value per serving: Calories: 528 kcal, Fat: 2 g, Carbs: 10 g, Protein: 2 g, Sugar: 245 mg, Potassium: 255 mg

43.8 Spicy Paprika Lamb Chops

Preparation Time: 10 minutes
Cooking Time: 15 minutes
Servings: 4
Ingredients:

- Chili Powder – 1 Tsp.
- Cumin Powder – ¾ Cup
- Paprika – 3 Tbsp.
- Salt And Pepper- As Needed
- Lamb Racks – 2 Whole (Cut Into Chops)

Procedure:

1. Take a bowl and add paprika, cumin, chili, salt, pepper and stir
2. Add lamb chops and rub the mixture
3. Heat grill over medium-temperature and add lamb chops, cook for 5 minutes
4. Flip and cook for 5 minutes more, flip again
5. Cook for 2 minutes, flip and cook for 2 minutes more
6. Serve and enjoy!

Storage: Can be properly stored in a BPA-free plastic/glass container box for 2 days in the refrigerator and 2-3 months in the freezer.

Nutrition value per serving: Calories: 528 kcal, Fat: 2 g, Carbs: 10 g, Protein: 2 g, Sugar: 245 mg, Potassium: 255 mg

43.9 Coconut And Almond Beef

Preparation Time: 10 minutes
Cooking Time: 50 minutes
Servings: 4
Ingredients:

- Parsley – For Garnish
- Cumin – 1 Tsp.
- Chili Powder – 1Tsp.
- Sugar Free Coconut Milk – 2 Cups
- Shallot – 1 Whole
- Salt And Pepper To Taste – As Needed
- Olive Oil To Taste – As Needed
- Beef Fillet – 2 Whole (8 Oz. Each, Ground)

- Almonds – ¼ cup (Sliced)

Procedure:

1. Preheat oven to 350 degrees F (175 degrees C).
2. In a large bowl, combine ground beef, coconut milk, olive oil, cumin, chili powder, and salt. Mix well until all ingredients are well combined.
3. Transfer mixture to a baking dish and bake for 30-35 minutes, or until beef is cooked through.
4. Garnish with parsley and almonds before serving. Enjoy!

Storage: Can be properly stored in a BPA-free plastic/glass container box for 2 days in the refrigerator and 2-3 months in the freezer.

Nutrition value per serving: Calories: 528 kcal, Fat: 2 g, Carbs: 10 g, Protein: 2 g, Sugar: 245 mg, Potassium: 255 mg

43.10 Beef And Red Onion Stew

Preparation Time: 10 minutes + 2 Hours Of Marinating
Cooking Time: 2 hours
Servings: 4

Ingredients:

- White Wine – 1 Glass
- Salt And Pepper To Taste – As Needed
- Red Onions – 2 Whole
- Olive Oil To Taste – As Needed
- Carrot – 1 Whole
- Beef Rump – 2 Whole (8 Oz. Each)
- Basil Leaves – 4 Leaves, Chopped

Procedure:

1. First you can peel and wash the carrot and then chop it.
2. Wash and dry the rump of beef, then tie it with kitchen twine.
3. Massage the meat with salt and pepper and then put it in a bowl.
4. Add the carrot, chopped basil and white wine
5. Put the bowl in the refrigerator and let it marinate for 2 hours.
6. After this time, remove the bowl from the fridge and bring it back to room temperature.

Storage: Can be properly stored in a BPA-free plastic/glass container box for 2 days in the refrigerator and 2-3 months in the freezer.

Nutrition value per serving: Calories: 528 kcal, Fat: 2 g, Carbs: 10 g, Protein: 2 g, Sugar: 245 mg, Potassium: 255 mg

43.11 Beef Sirloin With Juniper

Preparation Time: 10 minutes
Cooking Time: 10 minutes
Servings: 4

Ingredients:

- Salt And Pepper To Taste – As Needed
- Olive Oil To Taste – As Needed
- Juniper Berries – 2 Oz.
- Garlic – 3 Cloves
- Beef Sirloin – 2 Whole (8 Oz. Each)
- Balsamic Vinegar – 2 Tbsp.

Procedure:

1. sprinkle it with salt and pepper.
2. Peel and wash the garlic cloves and then chop them.
3. Heat two tablespoons of olive oil and when it is hot, put the garlic to fry.
4. Add the juniper berries, balsamic vinegar, salt, and pepper, stir, and then turn off.
5. Place the sirloin in a bowl and cover it with the marinade.
6. Cover the bowl and leave to marinate for an hour.

7. After the hour, heat a grill and when it is hot, put the meat to grill.
8. Cook for 4 minutes on each side, then remove it from the grill and put it to rest on a cutting board.
9. Cut the sirloin into slices and place them on serving plates.
10. Sprinkle with the marinating liquid and serve.

Storage: Can be properly stored in a BPA-free plastic/glass container box for 2 days in the refrigerator and 2-3 months in the freezer.

Nutrition value per serving: Calories: 528 kcal, Fat: 2 g, Carbs: 10 g, Protein: 2 g, Sugar: 245 mg, Potassium: 255 mg

44 SAUCES, DIPS AND DRESSING RECIPES

44.1 Classic Basil Pesto

Preparation Time: 10 minutes
Cooking Time: 10 minute
Servings: 1 cup
Ingredients:

- Salt – A Pinch
- Pine Nuts - ¼ Cups (Raw And Unsalted)
- Parmesan Cheese – ¾ Cups (Shredded)
- Garlic - 2 Cloves (Peeled And Halved)
- Extra-Virgin Olive Oil – 5 Tbsp.
- Black Pepper – A Pinch
- Basil Leaves– 1 And 1/2 Cups

Procedure:

1. In a food processor, combine all of the ingredients except parmesan cheese and parsley
2. Process until ingredients are finely chopped.
3. Mix in Parmesan cheese and parsley.
4. Serve with pasta or use as a condiment for grilled meats or fish.

Storage: Ideally, the sauce can be stored in a container for up to 5-6 days. And it can be stored properly in the freezer for up to 6 months, as long as it does not contain any ingredients such as cheese or eggs.

Nutrition value per serving: Calories: 528 kcal, Fat: 2 g, Carbs: 10 g, Protein: 2 g, Sugar: 245 mg, Potassium: 200 mg

44.2 Pesto Rosso

Preparation Time: 10 minutes
Cooking Time: 5 minutes
Servings: 1 and ½ cups
Ingredients:

- Salt - Pinch
- Black Pepper – Pinch
- Extra Virgin Olive Oil – ¾ Cup
- Garlic– 3 Cloves (Peeled And Halved)
- Sun Dried Tomatoes- 1 Cup
- Almond – 1/3 Cup (Roasted And Unsalted)
- Fresh Rosemary – 1 Tbsp.
- Basil Leaves – 1 Cup (Chopped)

Procedure:

1. In a food processor, pulse the listed ingredients thoroughly until you have a fine mix
2. Pour pesto into a small serving bowl and enjoy.

Storage: Ideally, the sauce can be stored in a container for up to 5-6 days. And it can be stored properly in the freezer for up to 6 months, as long as it does not contain any ingredients such as cheese or eggs.

Nutrition value per serving: Calories: 528 kcal, Fat: 2 g, Carbs: 10 g, Protein: 2 g, Sugar: 245 mg, Potassium: 200 mg

44.3 Leafy Green Pesto

Preparation Time: 10 minutes
Cooking Time: 5 minutes
Servings: 1 cup
Ingredients:

- Salt – Pinch
- Parmesan– ½ Cup (Shredded)
- Kale – 1 Cup
- Garlic– 3 Cloves (Peeled And Halved)
- Extra-Virgin Olive Oil – ½ Cup
- Black Pepper - Pinch
- Baby Spinach Leaves – 1 Cup
- Almonds– ¼ Cup (Raw And Unsalted)

Procedure:

1. Place all the ingredients into a food processor, pulse until smooth, then serve.

Storage: Ideally, the sauce can be stored in a container for up to 5-6 days. And it can be stored properly in the freezer for up to 6 months, as long as it does not contain any ingredients such as cheese or eggs.

Nutrition value per serving: Calories: 528 kcal, Fat: 2 g, Carbs: 10 g, Protein: 2 g, Sugar: 245 mg, Potassium: 200 mg

44.4 Authentic Tomato Sauce

Preparation Time: 10 minutes
Cooking Time: 60 minutes
Servings: 1 cup
Ingredients:

- Sugar – 1 Tsp.
- Salt – Pinch
- Plum Tomatoes, – 4 Lb. (Quartered)
- Green/Red Bell Pepper – 1 Whole (Diced)
- Garlic– 4 Cloves (Peeled And Diced)
- Extra-Virgin Olive Oil -Tbsp.
- Black Pepper – Pinch
- Onion – 1 Whole (Diced)
- Fresh Oregano – 1 Tbsp.
- Fresh Lime Juice – 1 Tsp.

Procedure:

1. In a large pot or Dutch oven, heat the oil over medium heat. Add the onion and bell pepper and cook until softened, about 5 minutes.
2. Add the garlic and sugar and cook for 1 minute longer.
3. Stir in the tomatoes with their juice, oregano, black pepper, and lime juice. Bring to a simmer and cook until thickened, about 10 minutes. Serve hot.

Storage: Ideally, the sauce can be stored in a container for up to 5-6 days. And it can be stored properly in the freezer for up to 6 months, as long as it does not contain any ingredients such as cheese or eggs.

Nutrition value per serving: Calories: 528 kcal, Fat: 2 g, Carbs: 10 g, Protein: 2 g, Sugar: 245 mg, Potassium: 200 mg

44.5 Avocado Cream

Preparation Time: 10 minutes
Cooking Time: 10 minute
Servings: 1 cup
Ingredients:

- Salt – Pinch
- Garlic – 3 Cloves (Minced)

- Fresh Lime Juice – 3 Tbsp. (Fresh)
- Black Pepper – Pinch
- 2 Avocados– 2 Whole (Halved And Pitted)
- Full-Fat Greek Yogurt – 1 Cup

Procedure:

1. Add all the ingredients into a food processor. Pulse until evenly combined and smooth, then serve.

Storage: Ideally, the sauce can be stored in a container for up to 5-6 days. And it can be stored properly in the freezer for up to 6 months, as long as it does not contain any ingredients such as cheese or eggs.

Nutrition value per serving: Calories: 528 kcal, Fat: 2 g, Carbs: 10 g, Protein: 2 g, Sugar: 245 mg, Potassium: 200 mg

44.6 Original Tzatziki

Preparation Time: 10 minutes
Cooking Time: 15 minutes
Servings: 1 cup

Ingredients:

- Salt - Pinch
- White Pepper - Pinch
- Black Pepper - Pinch
- White Wine Vinegar -1 Tsp.
- Garlic – 4 Cloves (Minced)
- English Cucumber – 1 Medium
- Full-Fat Greek Yogurt – 2 Cups

Procedure:

1. Grate the cucumber and place it into a strainer. Over the kitchen sink, press the cucumber down with a spoon, so any extra liquid can drain. Then, transfer onto a kitchen towel.
2. Combine the remaining ingredients and then add the cucumber. Seal in an airtight container and allow to chill in the refrigerator for two hours.
3. Remove from the refrigerator and then serve.

Storage: Ideally, the sauce can be stored in a container for up to 5-6 days. And it can be stored properly in the freezer for up to 6 months, as long as it does not contain any ingredients such as cheese or eggs.

Nutrition value per serving: Calories: 528 kcal, Fat: 2 g, Carbs: 10 g, Protein: 2 g, Sugar: 245 mg, Potassium: 200 mg

44.7 The Salsa Verde Classic

Preparation Time: 10 minutes
Cooking Time: 5 minutes
Servings: 1 cup

Ingredients:

- Salt – Pinch
- Black Pepper – Pinch
- Extra-Virgin Olive Oil – 8 Tbsp.
- Lemon Juice – 1 And ½ Tbsp.
- Dijon Mustard – 1 Tsp.
- Garlic – 1 Clove
- Capers, Drained And Rinsed – 3 Tbsp.
- Mint Leaves– 1 And ½ Oz. (Diced)
- Flat-Leaf Parsley– 1 And ½ Oz. (Diced)

Procedure:

1. Place the garlic, capers, mint, and parsley onto a chopping board. Using a sharp knife, dice together until a rough paste is formed.
2. Scoop the paste into a bowl and add the salt, pepper, olive oil, lemon juice, and mustard. Combine, then serve.

Storage: Ideally, the sauce can be stored in a container for up to 5-6 days. And it can be stored properly in the freezer for up to 6 months, as long as it does not contain any ingredients such as cheese or eggs.

Nutrition value per serving: Calories: 528 kcal, Fat: 2 g, Carbs: 10 g, Protein: 2 g, Sugar: 245 mg, Potassium: 200 mg

44.8 Harissa

Preparation Time: 10 minutes
Cooking Time: 5 minutes
Servings: ½ cup
Ingredients:

- Tomato Puree – 1 Tsp.
- Salt – Pinch
- Saffron Threads - Pinch
- Red Pepper – 1 Whole (Roasted)
- Red Chilis-2 Whole (Deseeded And Diced)
- Ground Coriander - Pinch
- Cayenne Pepper - Pinch
- Black Pepper – Pinch

Procedure:

1. Add all the ingredients into a food processor, pulse until smooth, then serve.

Storage: Ideally, the sauce can be stored in a container for up to 5-6 days. And it can be stored properly in the freezer for up to 6 months, as long as it does not contain any ingredients such as cheese or eggs.

Nutrition value per serving: Calories: 528 kcal, Fat: 2 g, Carbs: 10 g, Protein: 2 g, Sugar: 245 mg, Potassium: 200 mg

44.9 Trapanese

Preparation Time: 10 minutes
Cooking Time: 5 minutes
Servings: 1 cup
Ingredients:

- Salt - Pinch
- Parmesan Cheese – ½ Cup (Shredded)
- Garlic, Diced – 1 Clove (Diced)
- Extra-Virgin Olive Oil – ½ Cup
- Cherry Tomatoes – 1 Cup
- Black Pepper – Pinch
- Basil Leaves – 2 And ½ Cups
- Almonds– ¼ Cup (Raw And Unsalted)

Procedure:

1. In a small frying pan over medium heat, add the almonds. Toast them for one minute, then remove from heat.
2. Add the almonds and garlic into a food processor and pulse until smooth.
3. Add the tomatoes and basil to the mixture and pulse. As the machine is pulsing, slowly add in the olive oil until smooth.
4. Follow by adding in the salt, pepper, and Parmesan. Pulse until smooth.
5. Remove from the food processor and serve.

Storage: Ideally, the sauce can be stored in a container for up to 5-6 days. And it can be stored properly in the freezer for up to 6 months, as long as it does not contain any ingredients such as cheese or eggs.

Nutrition value per serving: Calories: 528 kcal, Fat: 2 g, Carbs: 10 g, Protein: 2 g, Sugar: 245 mg, Potassium: 200 mg

44.10 Almond Butter Chocolate Dip

Preparation Time: 10 minutes
Cooking Time: 0 minute
Servings: 4
Ingredients:

- Vanilla- 1 Tsp.
- Plain Greek Yogurt – 1 Cup
- Honey – 1 Tbsp.
- Chocolate Hazelnut Spread – 1/3 Cup

- Almond Butter – ½ Cup

Procedure:

1. Take a medium sized microwave proof bowl, add the listed ingredients and gently stir
2. Microwave the mixture for around 1-2 minutes until everything has melted
3. Mix again and enjoy!

Storage: Ideally, the sauce can be stored in a container for up to 5-6 days. And it can be stored properly in the freezer for up to 6 months, as long as it does not contain any ingredients such as cheese or eggs.

Nutrition value per serving: Calories: 115 kcal, Fat: 8 g, Carbs: 15 g, Protein: 4 g, Sodium: 245 mg

45 DESSERTS

45.1 Black Tea Cake

Preparation Time: 10 minutes
Cooking Time: 35 minutes
Servings: 4

Ingredients:

- Vanilla Extract – 2 Tsp.
- Stevia- 2 Cups
- Eggs – 4 Whole
- Black Tea Powder – 6 Tbsp.
- Baking Soda – 1 Tsp.
- Baking Powder- 3 Tsp.
- Avocado Oil – 1 Cup
- Almond Milk– 2 Cups
- Almond Flour – 3 And ½ Cups

Procedure:

1. Preheat oven to 350 degrees F. Grease and flour an 8x8 inch baking pan. Sift together the flour, baking powder and salt.
2. In a large bowl using an electric mixer on medium speed, beat together the butter and sugar until light and fluffy.
3. Add the eggs one at a time, beating well after each addition.
4. Stir in the tea and raisins. Gradually add the dry ingredients to the wet ingredients, mixing just until combined. Pour batter into the prepared pan.
5. Bake for 30 minutes or until a toothpick inserted into the center comes out clean. Cool cake in pan for 10 minutes before transferring to a wire rack to cool completely.

Storage: It can be stored in BPA Free container for around 4-5 days in the refrigerator and 1-2 months in the freezer. However, if you feel like it smells bad or has an odd texture, it is better not to consume it.
Nutrition value per serving: Calories: 528 kcal, Fat: 2 g, Carbs: 10 g, Protein: 2 g, Sugar: 245 mg, Potassium: 222 mg

45.2 Tasty Figs Pie

Preparation Time: 10 minutes
Cooking Time: 60 minutes
Servings: 4

Ingredients:

- Figs – 6 whole (cut in quarters) -
- Eggs – 4 (whisked)
- Almond flour – 1 cup

- Vanilla extract – ½ tsp.
- Sugar – 1 cup
- Cinnamon – 1 tsp.

Procedure:

1. Preheat oven to 375 degrees F (190 degrees C).
2. In a medium bowl, combine figs, sugar, flour, cinnamon, nutmeg and salt. Toss until coated.
3. Pour mixture into the pie crust.
4. Dot with butter and oil. Bake for 15 minutes or until the filling is bubbly. Let cool before serving.

Storage: It can be stored in BPA Free container for around 4-5 days in the refrigerator and 1-2 months in the freezer. However, if you feel like it smells bad or has an odd texture, it is better not to consume it.

Nutrition value per serving: Calories: 528 kcal, Fat: 2 g, Carbs: 10 g, Protein: 2 g, Sugar: 245 mg, Potassium: 222 mg

45.3 Dark Chocolate Mousse

Preparation Time: 10 minutes
Cooking Time: 10 minute
Servings: 4

Ingredients:

- Unsweetened Dark Chocolate– 3 And ½ Oz (Grated)
- Vanilla – ½ Tsp.
- Honey – 1 Tbsp.
- Greek Yogurt – 2 Cups
- Unsweetened Almond Milk – ¾ Cup
- Fresh Raspberries – For Garnish

Procedure:

1. Add chocolate and almond milk in a saucepan and heat over medium heat until just chocolate melted. Do not boil.
2. Once the chocolate and almond milk combined then add vanilla and honey and stir well.
3. Add yogurt in a large mixing bowl.
4. Pour chocolate mixture on top of yogurt and mix until well combined.
5. Pour chocolate yogurt mixture into the serving bowls and place in refrigerator for 2 hours.
6. Top with fresh raspberries and serve.

Storage: It can be stored in a BPA Free container for around 4-5 days in the refrigerator and 1-2 months in a freezer. However, if you feel like it smells bad or has an odd texture, then better not to consume it.

Nutrition value per serving: Calories: 528 kcal, Fat: 2 g, Carbs: 10 g, Protein: 2 g, Sugar: 245 mg, Potassium: 200 mg

45.4 Apple And Plum Cake

Preparation Time: 10 minutes
Cooking Time: 40 minutes
Servings: 4

Ingredients:

- Zest Of Lemon– 1 Whole (Grated)
- Warm Almond Milk – 3 Oz.
- Stevia – 5 Tbsp.
- Plums– 2 Lb. (Pitted And Cut Into Sections)
- Egg– 1 Whole (Whisked)
- Walnuts – ½ cup (slived)
- Baking Powder – 1 Tsp.
- Apples - 2 Whole (Cored And Chopped)
- Almond Flour – 7 Oz.
- Sugar – 1 cup
- Flour – 1 cup
- Olive oil – as needed

Procedure:

1. Preheat oven to 350 degrees F (175 degrees C).
2. Grease and flour one 9x13 inch baking pan.

3. In a medium bowl, whisk together the sugar, flour, baking powder,and salt; set aside.
4. In a large bowl, combine the oil, eggs and apples; mix well. Add the flour mixture to the apple mixture, mixing well until well combined.
5. Stir in the plums and nuts.
6. Pour batter into prepared pan. Bake for 30 minutes or until a toothpick inserted into center comes out clean.
7. Cool cake in pan for 10 minutes before removing to a wire rack to cool completely.

Storage: It can be stored in BPA Free container for around 4-5 days in the refrigerator and 1-2 months in the freezer. However, if you feel like it smells bad or has an odd texture, it is better not to consume it.

Nutrition value per serving: Calories: 528 kcal, Fat: 2 g, Carbs: 10 g, Protein: 2 g, Sugar: 245 mg, Potassium: 222 mg

45.5 Cinnamon And Chickpea Cookies

Preparation Time: 10 minutes
Cooking Time: 0 minute
Servings: 4
Ingredients:

- Stevia – ½ Cup
- Raisins – 1 Cup
- Egg– 1 Whole (Whisked)
- Coconut– 1 Cup
- Cinnamon Powder – 1 Tsp.
- Chickpeas– 1 Cup (Drained, Rinsed And Mashed)
- Baking Powder – 1 Tsp.
- Avocado Oil – 1 Cup
- Almond Flour – 2 Cups
- Almond Extract – 2 Tsp.
- Vanilla Extract – 1 Tsp.

Procedure:

1. Preheat oven to 350 degrees F (175 degrees C). Line a baking sheet with parchment paper.
2. In a food processor, blend chickpeas until they are smooth. In a medium bowl, whisk all ingredients except vanilla extract
3. Pour chickpea mixture into the bowl and blend until just combined. With the food processor still running, add oil or butter and egg.
4. Blend until dough forms. Add vanilla extract and mix until well combined. Drop dough by rounded tablespoons onto prepared baking sheet. Bake for 12 minutes, or until cookies are golden brown around the edges.
5. Allow cookies to cool on baking sheet for 5 minutes before transferring to a wire rack to cool completely. Enjoy!

Storage: It can be stored in BPA Free container for around 12-14 days in the refrigerator and 1-2 months in the freezer

Nutrition value per serving: Calories: 528 kcal, Fat: 2 g, Carbs: 10 g, Protein: 2 g, Sugar: 245 mg, Potassium: 222 mg

45.6 Hearty Lemon Mousse

Preparation Time: 10 minutes
Cooking Time: 10 minutes +Chill Time
Servings: 4
Ingredients:

- 1 cup coconut cream
- 8 ounces cream cheese, soft
- ¼ cup fresh lemon juice
- 3 pinches salt
- 1 teaspoon lemon liquid stevia

Procedure:

1. Pre-heat your oven to 350-degree F

2. Grease a ramekin with butter
3. Beat cream, cream cheese, fresh lemon juice, salt and lemon liquid stevia in a mixer
4. Pour batter into ramekin
5. Bake for 10 minutes then transfer mouse to serving glass
6. Let it chill for 2 hours and serve
7. Enjoy!

Storage: It can be stored in BPA Free container for around 4-5 days in the refrigerator and 1-2 months in the freezer. However, if you feel like it smells bad or has an odd texture, it is better not to consume it.

Nutrition value per serving: Calories: 528 kcal, Fat: 2 g, Carbs: 10 g, Protein: 2 g, Sugar: 245 mg, Potassium: 222 mg

45.7 Spicy Poached Pears

Preparation Time: 10 minutes
Cooking Time: 17minute
Servings: 4
Ingredients:

- Whole Star Anise- 1 Whole
- Whole Garlic Cloves – 2 Cloves
- Water – 3 And ½ Cups
- Vanilla Extract – 1 Tsp.
- Semi Ripe Pears (Preferably Barlett Pears) – 3 Whole (Semi Ripe)
- Rind Of Lemon – 1
- Juice Of Lemon – 1
- Granulated Sugar – 3 Cups
- Cinnamon Sticks – 2 Sticks

Procedure:

1. Peel the pears well and keep them on the side
2. Take a pot of water and add vanilla, lemon juice, sugar, lemon rind, cinnamon sticks, cloves and star anise
3. Place it over medium heat and allow the sugar to dissolve
4. Add pears
5. Lower down the heat to low and simmer for another 15-20 minutes
6. Once the pears are ready, transfer to a Tupperware alongside the cooking liquid
7. Allow it to cool
8. Enjoy!

Storage: It can be stored in BPA Free container for around 12-14 days in the refrigerator and 1-2 months in the freezer.

Nutrition value per serving: Calories: 740 kcal, Fat: 4 g, Carbs: 18 g, Protein: 4 g, Sugar: 245 mg, Potassium: 222 mg

45.8 Pineapple And Ginger Sherbet

Preparation Time: 10 minutes
Cooking Time: 0 minute
Servings: 4
Ingredients:

- Pineapple Chunks – 8 Oz.
- Ground Ginger – ¼ Tsp.
- Vanilla – ¼ Tsp.
- Orange Sections – 11 Oz.
- Pineapple, Lemon Or Lime Sherbet – 2 Cups
- Cornstarch – 1 tsp.
- Ginger – 1 tsp. (grated)
- Sugar – ½ cup
- Cinnamon – 1 tsp. (ground)
- Salt and pepper – as needed

Procedure:

1. Combine pineapple, ginger, sugar, cornstarch, cinnamon and salt in a blender; blend until smooth.
2. Pour mixture into a saucepan over medium heat; bring to a boil.
3. Cook for 2 minutes or until thickened.
4. Add cold water and lemon sherbet; stir well. Serve immediately.

Storage: Can be stored in juice/drinks container for 2-3 days.

Nutrition value per serving: Calories: 267 kcal, Fat: 1 g, Carbs: 65 g, Protein: 2 g, Sugar: 245 mg, Potassium: 222 mg

45.9 Awesome Peach And Raspberry Trifle

Preparation Time: 10-20 minutes
Cooking Time: 0 minutes
Servings: 4

Ingredients:

- Trifle Sponge Cake– 1 Whole (Cut Into Pieces)
- Punnet Fresh Raspberries – 5 Oz.
- Peaches- 28 Oz.
- Mascarpone – 2 And ½ Cups
- Limoncello Liqueur, Sherry Or Brandy – ½ Cup
- Hazlenuts- 14 Cup (Chopped)
- Custard – 2 Cups

Procedure:

1. Take a bowl and add custard and mascarpone
2. Place about half of your sponge cake piece into the large serving bowl
3. Drizzle ¼ cup of sherry, Limoncello or brandy
4. Cover with drained up peach slices
5. Add half of the custard mix
6. Keep repeating the process (making the layers) until the mixture has been used up
7. Keep in mind that you are to end with the mascarpone layer
8. Chill and serve!
9. Top with some peaches, raspberries of hazelnut if you wish
10. Enjoy!

Storage: It can be stored in BPA Free container for around 4-5 days in the refrigerator and 1-2 months in the freezer. However, if you feel like it smells bad or has an odd texture, it is better not to consume it.

Nutrition value per serving: Calories: 472 kcal, Fat: 34 g, Carbs: 40 g, Protein: 8 g, Sugar: 245 mg, Potassium: 222 mg

45.10 Five Berry Compote

Preparation Time: 10 minutes
Cooking Time: 10 minute
Servings: 4

Ingredients:

- Water – ½ Cup
- Vanilla- 1 Tsp.
- Sugar – 2/3 Cup
- Strawberries– 1 Cup
- Sprig Fresh Mints – 3 Sprigs
- Sauvignon Blanc – 1 Bottle
- Red Raspberries – 1 Cup
- Pomegranate Juice – ½ Cup
- Orange Pekoe Tea Bags – 3 Bags
- Golden Raspberries – 1 Cup
- Fresh Sweet Cherries – 1 Cup (Pitted And Halved)
- Fresh Mint Sprigs
- Fresh Blueberries – 1 Cup
- Fresh Black Berries – 1 Cup

Procedure:

1. Take a small saucepan and add water
2. Bring the water to a boil and add tea bags, 3 mint sprigs
3. Stir well
4. Cover pan and remove the heat
5. Allow it to stand for 10 minutes
6. Take a large sized bowl and add strawberries, red raspberries, golden raspberries, blueberries, blackberries, cherries. Keep it on the side

7. Take a medium sized saucepan and add wine, sugar, pomegranate juice
8. Pour the infusion (tea mixture) through a fine mesh sieve and into the pan with wine
9. Squeeze the bags to release the liquid
10. Discard the mint sprigs and tea bags
11. Cook well until the sugar has completely dissolved
12. Remove the heat
13. Stir in vanilla and allow it to chill for 2 hours
14. Pour the mix over the fruits
15. Serve by garnishing with some mint sprigs
16. Enjoy!

Storage: It can be stored in BPA Free container for around 4-5 days in the refrigerator and 1-2 months in the freezer. However, if you feel like it smells bad or has an odd texture, it is better not to consume it.

Nutrition value per serving: Calories: 203 kcal, Fat: 0 g, Carbs: 34 g, Protein: 1 g, Sugar: 245 mg, Potassium: 222 mg

45.11 Dreamy Hot Fudge

Preparation Time: 10 minutes
Cooking Time: 5- 10 minutes
Servings: 4
Ingredients:

- ½ cup salted butter
- 4 ounces dark chocolate
- 2 tablespoons unsweetened cocoa powder
- 1 cup swerve
- 1 cup heavy whip cream
- 2 teaspoons vanilla extract
- Pinch of salt

Procedure:

1. Take a medium saucepan and place it over medium heat
2. Add butter and chocolate and melt
3. Add cocoa powder and sweetener
4. Whisk for 3-5 minutes until everything dissolves
5. Add cream and bring to a boil
6. Stir
7. Lower down heat to low and add vanilla and salt
8. Remove heat
9. Let it sit for 5 minutes
10. Serve hot and enjoy!

Storage: It can be stored in BPA Free container for around 4-5 days in the refrigerator and 1-2 months in the freezer. However, if you feel like it smells bad or has an odd texture, it is better not to consume it.
Nutrition value per serving: Calories: 256 kcal, Fat: 20 g, Carbs: 17 g, Protein: 6 g, Sugar: 245 mg, Potassium: 222 mg

45.12 Perfect Frozen Strawberry Yogurt

Preparation Time: 10 minutes
Cooking Time: 2-4 Hours
Servings: 4
Ingredients:

- Vanilla – 2 Tsp.
- Sugar – 1 Cup
- Strawberries- 1 Cup (Sliced)
- Salt – 1/8 Tsp.
- Greek Low-Fat Yogurt – 3 Cups
- Freshly Squeeze Lemon Juice – ¼ Cup

Procedure:

1. Take a medium sized bowl and add yogurt, lemon juice, sugar, vanilla and salt
2. Whisk the whole mixture well
3. Freeze the yogurt mix in a 2 quart ice cream maker according to the given instructions
4. Make sure to add sliced strawberries during the final minute
5. Transfer the yogurt to an air tight container

6. Freeze for another 2-4 hours
7. Allow it to stand for about 5-15 minutes
8. Serve and enjoy!

Storage: It can be stored in BPA Free container for around 4-5 days in the refrigerator and 1-2 months in the freezer. However, if you feel like it smells bad or has an odd texture, it is better not to consume it.

Nutrition value per serving: Calories: 86 kcal, Fat: 1 g, Carbs: 16 g, Protein: 86 g, Sugar: 245 mg, Potassium: 222 mg

45.13 Simple Chocolate Parfait

Preparation Time: 10 minutes +2 Hours
Cooking Time: 0 minute
Servings: 4
Ingredients:

- Cocoa Powder – 2 Tbsp.
- Almond Milk – 1 Cup
- Chia Seeds – 1 Tbsp.
- Vanilla Extract – ½ Tsp.

Procedure:

1. Take a bowl and add vanilla extract, chia seeds, almond milk, cocoa powder and stir
2. Place in a dessert glass and refrigerate for 2 hours.
3. Serve and enjoy!

Storage: It can be stored in BPA Free container for around 4-5 days in the refrigerator and 1-2 months in the freezer. However, if you feel like it smells bad or has an odd texture, it is better not to consume it.

Nutrition value per serving: Calories: 157 kcal, Fat: 6 g, Carbs: 18 g, Protein: 9 g, Sugar: 245 mg, Potassium: 222 mg

45.14 Perfect Blueberry Muffins

Preparation Time: 10 minutes
Cooking Time: 30 minutes
Servings: 4
Ingredients:

- Almond Flour – 1 Cup
- Salt – A Pinch
- Baking Soda – 1/8 Tsp.
- Egg- 1 Whole
- Coconut Oil – 2 Tbsp, Melted
- Coconut Milk – ½ Cup
- Fresh Blueberries – ¼ Cup

Procedure:

1. Preheat the oven to 350 degrees F.
2. Line a muffin pan with muffin cups.
3. In a mixing dish, combine almond flour, salt, and baking soda; set aside.
4. In a separate bowl, whisk together the egg, coconut oil, and coconut milk.
5. Add to flour mixture and gently combine until combined.
6. Fill the cupcake tins halfway with batter, then top with blueberries.
7. 22 minutes in the oven
8. Enjoy!

Storage: It can be stored in BPA Free container for around 4-5 days. Storage in the freezer is not recommended.

Nutrition value per serving: Calories: 250 kcal, Fat: 8 g, Carbs: 27 g, Protein: 3 g, Sugar: 245 mg, Potassium: 222 mg

46 SNACKS RECIPES

46.1 Hearty Almond Cracker

Preparation Time: 15 minutes
Cooking Time: 15 minute
Servings: 4
Ingredients:

- Salt – ¼ tsp.
- Salt And Pepper – Taste
- Almond Flour – 1 Cup
- Baking Soda – ¼ tsp.
- Black Pepper – 1/8 Tsp.
- Sesame Seeds – 3 Tbsp.
- Egg – 1 Whole (Beaten)

Procedure:

1. Preheat the oven to 350 degrees F.
2. Line two baking sheets with parchment paper and set aside.
3. In a large mixing basin, combine the dry ingredients and add the egg, stirring thoroughly to form a dough.
4. Form the dough into two balls.
5. Roll the dough out between two sheets of parchment paper.
6. Transfer the crackers to a baking sheet that has been preheated.
7. Cook for 15-20 minutes.
8. Repeat until all of the dough is gone.
9. Allow the crackers to cool before serving.
10. Enjoy!

Nutrition value per serving: Calories: 137 kcal, Fat: 10 g, Carbs: 10 g, Protein: 3 g, Sodium: 245 mg

46.2 Baby Braised Artichokes

Preparation Time: 10 minutes
Cooking Time: 30 minutes
Servings: 6
Ingredients:

- Olive Oil -6 Tbsp.
- Baby Artichokes – 2 Lb.
- Lemon Juice – ½ Cup
- Garlic Cloves – 4 Cloves (Sliced)
- Salt And Pepper – ½ Tsp.
- Tomatoes – 1 And ½ Lb. (Seeded And Diced)
- Almonds- ½ Cup (Sliced)
- Oregano – 1 tbsp.

Procedure:

1. Preheat oven to 400 degrees.
2. Cut off the top of each artichoke and cut in half lengthwise.
3. Drop artichokes into boiling water for one minute to shock them.
4. Drain artichokes and place in a large baking dish.
5. Pour chicken broth over artichokes and sprinkle with black pepper, olive oil, lemon juice, oregano, thyme, salt and pepper.
6. Bake for 30 minutes or until artichokes are tender when pierced with a fork.
7. Garnish with sliced almonds
8. Enjoy!

Storage: It can be stored in BPA Free container for around 4-5 days in the refrigerator and 1-2 months in the freezer.

Nutrition value per serving: Calories: 220 kcal, Fat: 18 g, Carbs: 15 g, Protein: 4 g, Sodium: 245 mg

46.3 Kale And Mozzarella Egg Bake

Preparation Time: 10 minutes
Cooking Time: 36 minutes
Servings: 4
Ingredients:

- Salt And Pepper – To Taste
- Spike Seasoning – 1 Tsp.
- Eggs – 8 Whole
- Green Onion – 1/3 Cup, Sliced
- Mozzarella Cheese – 1 And ½ Cup (Grated)

Procedure:

1. Pre-heat your oven to 375 degree F
2. Prepare a casserole dish by greasing lightly with olive oil
3. Take a skillet and place it over medium heat, let it get hot
4. Add kale and cook for 3 minutes
5. Add kale to prepared casserole dish
6. Spread it well
7. Top kale with onions, cheese
8. Crack eggs into medium bowl and season with salt and pepper, spike seasoning
9. Whisk well and pour into casserole dish
10. Stir
11. Bake in your oven for 35 minutes until eggs set and become golden brown
12. Serve and enjoy!

Storage: It can be stored in BPA Free container for around 4-5 days in the refrigerator and 1-2 months in the freezer.

Nutrition value per serving: Calories: 124 kcal, Fat: 8 g, Carbs: 4 g, Protein: 10 g, Sodium: 200 mg

46.4 Crunchy And Delicious Fougasse

Preparation Time: 10 minutes
Cooking Time: 30 minutes
Servings: 4
Ingredients:

- Bread Flour – 3 And 2/3 Cups
- Olive Oil – 3 And ½ Tbsp.
- Bread Yeast – 1 And 2/3 Tbsp.
- Black Olives– 1 And ½ Cups (Chopped)
- Oregano – 1 Tsp.
- Salt – ½ Tbsp.
- Water - 1 Cup

Procedure:

1. Take a bowl and add flour
2. Form a volcano in the center by making a well and add the remaining ingredients (alongside water)
3. Knead the dough well until it becomes slightly elastic
4. Mold it into a ball and let it stand for about 1 hour
5. Divide the pastry into four pieces of equal portions
6. Flatten the balls using a rolling pin
7. Place the balls on a floured baking tray
8. Make incisions on the bread as shown in the picture
9. Allow them to rest for about 30 minutes
10. Pre-heat your oven to a temperature of 428 Fahrenheit
11. Brush the Fougasse with olive oil and allow it to bake for 20 minutes
12. Turn the oven off and allow it to rest for 5 minutes
13. Remove and allow it to cool
14. Enjoy!

Storage: It can be stored in BPA Free container for around 4-5 days in the refrigerator and 1-2 months in the freezer. However, if you feel like it smells bad or has an odd texture, it is better not to consume it.

Nutrition value per serving: Calories: 560 kcal, Fat: 18 g, Carbs: 30 g, Protein: 57 g, Sodium: 245 mg

46.5 Italy's Fan Favorite Herb Bread

Preparation Time: 10 minutes
Cooking Time: 40 minutes
Servings: 25
Ingredients:

- Active Dry Yeast – 2 And ½ Tsp.
- All-Purpose Flour – 3 And ½ Cups
- Rye Flour – 2 And ¼ Cups
- Salt – 1 Tsp.
- Olive Oil – 2 Tbsp.
- Flat Leaf Parsley – 1 Tbsp.
- Fresh Thyme– 10 Sprigs
- Garlic- 1 Whole (Peeled And Chopped)
- Black Olives – ¼ Cup (Pitted And Chopped)
- Jalapenos - 3 Whole (Chopped And Deseeded)
- Sun Dried Tomatoes– ¾ Cup (Drained And Chopped)

Procedure:

1. Take a bowl of lukewarm water (temperature of 105°F) and dissolve 1 and a 2/3 cups of yeast
2. Add flour, yeast, water and salt to another bowl
3. Mix well to prepare the dough using a mixer or with your hands
4. Take a large-sized clean bowl and add the dough to the bowl. Allow it to rest covered for 2 hours
5. Transfer it to your lightly floured surface and knead the dough (alongside parsley, garlic, olives, thyme, tomatoes, and chilies) and knead well to mix everything
6. Place the kneaded dough onto an 8 and a ½ inch bread proofing basket
7. Cover it and allow it to rest for about 60 minutes
8. Pre-heat your oven to a temperature of 400 degrees Fahrenheit
9. Line up a baking sheet with parchment paper
10. Bake for about 30-40 minutes
11. Enjoy once done!

Storage: It can be stored in BPA Free container for around 4-5 days in the refrigerator and 1-2 months in the freezer.

Nutrition value per serving: Calories: 90 kcal, Fat: 2 g, Carbs: 16 g, Protein: 2 g, Sodium: 245 mg

46.6 Cheesy And Creamy Broccoli And Cauliflower

Preparation Time: 10 minutes
Cooking Time: 10 minutes
Servings: 4
Ingredients:

- Sour Cream – 4 Tsp.
- Salt And Pepper – As Needed
- Parmesan Cheese- 5 Oz. (Shredded)
- Cauliflower – 8 Oz. (Chopped)
- Butter – 2 Oz.
- Broccoli – 1 Lb. (Chopped)

Procedure:

1. Take a large skillet and melt butter
2. Stir in all the vegetables
3. Sauté until it turns into golden brown over medium-high heat
4. Add all the remaining ingredients to the vegetable
5. Mix well and cook until the cheese melts

6. Serve warm, and enjoy!

Storage: It can be stored in BPA Free container for around 4-5 days in the refrigerator and 1-2 months in the freezer.
Nutrition value per serving: Calories: 244 kcal, Fat: 10 g, Carbs: 5 g, Protein: 6 g, Sodium: 200 mg

46.7 Classic Focaccia

Preparation Time: 40 minutes
Cooking Time: 40 minute
Servings: 4
Ingredients:

- Flour – 3 And ½ Cups
- Warm Water – 1 And ¼ Cups
- Olive Oil – 2 Tbsp.
- Baker's Yeast – 2 Tsp. + Salt And Sugar To Activate The Yeast
- Tsp. Of Salt- 1 And ½ Tsp.
- Black Olives – 14 Oz. (Chopped)
- Sea Salt– As Needed
- Olive Oil– As Needed
- Butter – 1 Cup

Procedure:

1. Preheat the oven to 375 degrees F (190 degrees C). Grease a baking sheet and dust with flour.
2. Take a glass and add warm water, add yeast and let it sit for 10 minutes to activate it with a bit of salt and sugar
3. In a large bowl, mix together the flour and salt, olive oil, black olive. Cut in the butter until the mixture resembles coarse crumbs. Stir in the water until a soft dough forms.
4. Turn out the dough onto a lightly floured surface and knead for about 5 minutes. Place the dough in a greased bowl, turning it to coat with oil. Cover with plastic wrap and let rise in a warm place for 30 minutes.
5. Punch down the dough and divide into 12 equal parts. Shape each part into a 6-inch round loaf, tucking the ends under as you go. Place on the prepared baking sheet and let rise for another 20 minutes.
6. Bake for 25 minutes, until golden brown. Let cool on a wire rack before slicing into thick slices.

Storage: It can be stored in BPA Free container for around 4-5 days in the refrigerator and 1-2 months in the freezer.
Nutrition value per serving: Calories: 510 kcal, Fat: 13 g, Carbs: 86 g, Protein: 11 g, Sodium: 245 mg

46.8 Tasty Zucchini Chips

Preparation Time: 10 minutes
Cooking Time: 15 minute
Servings: 4

Ingredients:

- Olive oil – 1 tbsp.
- Salt – 1 tsp.
- Black pepper – ¼ tsp.
- Parmesan cheese – ¼ cup
- Romano cheese – ¼ cup
- Zucchini – 1 whole (cut into thin chips)
- Panko bread crumbs – ½ cup

Procedure:

1. Preheat the oven to 400 degrees F.
2. In a large bowl, mix together the salt, black pepper, Parmesan cheese, and Romano cheese.
3. Add the zucchini chips and olive oil and mix until combined. Spread mixture onto a baking sheet and bake for 18 minutes, or until golden brown.
4. Remove from oven and let cool for 5 minutes before topping with panko bread crumbs. Enjoy!

Storage: It can be stored in the refrigerator for 2-3 days. Alternatively, you may store it in your freezer for 2 months at most.

Nutrition value per serving: Calories: 528 kcal, Fat: 2 g, Carbs: 10 g, Protein: 2 g, Sodium: 245 mg

47 MEAL PLAN

I prepared a meal plan for 10 weeks which is about 2 1/2 months. Repeating this meal plan 5-6 times throughout the year, starting from the first week after the tenth, you will have concluded your annual nutrition plan. To ensure the habit of this diet and the results, we recommend applying it for 3 years, consequently for a total of 1000 days.

47.1 Week 1

Days	Breakfast	Lunch	Dinner	Dessert
1	Bacon And Brie Omelet Wedges	Kidney Beans And Cilantro Salad	Homely Fattoush Salad	Black Tea Cake
2	Vegetarian Shepherd's Pie	Mediterranean Pepper Soup	Lovely Onion Soup	Hearty Lemon Mousse
3	Fresh Watermelon And Arugula Meal	Mashed Beans And Cumin	Black Bean With Mangoes	Pineapple And Ginger Sherbet
4	Dill And Tomato Frittata	Bulgar Pila With Garbanzo Bean	Turkish Canned Pinto Bean Salad	Spicy Poached Pears
5	Classic Focaccia	Pecan Crusted Trout	Spicy Cajun Shrimp	Cinnamon And Chickpea Cookies
6	Tasty Zucchini Chips	Lebanese Thin Pasta	Mushroom And Fettucine Platter	Dark Chocolate Mousse
7	Eggs And Acorn In A Hole	Creamy Millet Dish	Tuna And Olive Pasta	Apple And Plum Cake

47.2 Week 2

Days	Breakfast	Lunch	Dinner	Dessert
1	Fresh Watermelon And Arugula Meal		Salsa Rice Meal	Tasty Figs Pie
2	Morning Scrambled Pesto Salad	Stuffed Avocado Meal	Fried Cauliflower Pizza	Frozen Strawberry Yogurt
3	Italy's Favorite Herb Bread	Parmesan Baked Chicken	Tomato Bruschetta	Perfect Blueberry Muffin
4	Tasty Zucchini Chips	Simple Stir Fried Chicken	Yogurt And Banana Bowl	Simple Chocolate Parfait
5		Foil Ala Pork	Chia And Almond Butter Pudding	Apple And Plum Cake
6	Black Olive Breakfast Loaf	Coconut And Almond Beef	Awesome Chicken Bell Pepper Platter	Tasty Figs Pie
7	Vegetarian Shepherd's Pie	Spicy Poached Pears	Bacon And Chicken Garlic Wrap	Awesome Peach And Raspberry Trifle

47.3 Week 3

Days	Breakfast	Lunch	Dinner	Dessert
1	Crunchy And Delicious Fougasse	Beef Sirloin With Juniper		Cinnamon And Chickpea Cookies
2	Dill And Tomato Frittata	Spicy Paprika Lamb	Coconut Almond Beef	Spicy Poached Pears
3	Egg And Acorn In A Hole	Blackberry Chicken Wings	Simple Stir Fried Chicken	Dreamy Hot Fudge
4	Tasty Zucchini Chips		Tuna And Olive Pasta	Perfect Frozen Strawberry Yogurt
5	Fancy Olive And Cheese Loaf	Creamy Rice Millet Dish	Red Chicken Spaghetti	Perfect Blueberry Muffins
6	Morning Scrambled Pesto Eggs	Pesto And Lemon Halibut	Pecan Crusted Trout	Five Berry Compote
7	Fresh Watermelon And Arugula Meal	Orange And Herbed Sauce White Bass	One-Pot Seafood Chowder	Pineapple And Ginger Sherbet

47.4 Week 4

Days	Breakfast	Lunch	Dinner	Dessert
1	Fresh Watermelon And Arugula Meal	Avocado And Chimichurri Bruschetta	Salsa Rice Meal	Tasty Figs Pie
2	Morning Scrambled Pesto Salad	Stuffed Avocado Meal		Frozen Strawberry Yogurt
3	Italy's Favorite Herb Bread	Parmesan Baked Chicken	Tomato Bruschetta	Perfect Blueberry Muffin
4	Tasty Zucchini Chips		Yogurt And Banana Bowl	Simple Chocolate Parfait
5	Dill And Tomato Frittata	Foil Ala Pork	Chia And Almond Butter Pudding	Apple And Plum Cake
6	Black Olive Breakfast Loaf	Coconut And Almond Beef	Awesome Chicken Bell Pepper Platter	Tasty Figs Pie
7	Vegetarian Shepherd's Pie	Spicy Poached Pears	Bacon And Chicken Garlic Wrap	Awesome Peach And Raspberry Trifle

47.5 Week 5

Days	Breakfast	Lunch	Dinner	Dessert
1	Bacon And Brie Omelet Wedges	Kidney Beans And Cilantro Salad	Homely Fattoush Salad	Black Tea Cake
2	Vegetarian Shepherd's Pie	Mediterranean Pepper Soup		Hearty Lemon Mousse
3	Fresh Watermelon And Arugula Meal		Black Bean With Mangoes	Pineapple And Ginger Sherbet
4	Dill And Tomato Frittata	Bulgar Pila With Garbanzo Bean	Turkish Canned Pinto Bean Salad	Spicy Poached Pears
5	Classic Focaccia	Pecan Crusted Trout	Spicy Cajun Shrimp	Cinnamon And Chickpea Cookies
6	Tasty Zucchini Chips	Lebanese Thin Pasta	Mushroom And Fettucine Platter	Dark Chocolate Mousse
7	Eggs And Acorn In A Hole	Creamy Millet Dish	Tuna And Olive Pasta	Apple And Plum Cake

47.6 Week 6

Days	Breakfast	Lunch	Dinner	Dessert
1	Crunchy And Delicious Fougasse	Beef Sirloin With Juniper	Grape Sauce And Pork Fillet	Cinnamon And Chickpea Cookies
2	Dill And Tomato Frittata		Coconut Almond Beef	Spicy Poached Pears
3	Egg And Acorn In A Hole	Blackberry Chicken Wings	Simple Stir Fried Chicken	Dreamy Hot Fudge
4	Tasty Zucchini Chips	Chicken Bruschetta Burgers	Tuna And Olive Pasta	
5	Fancy Olive And Cheese Loaf	Creamy Rice Millet Dish	Red Chicken Spaghetti	Perfect Blueberry Muffins
6	Morning Scrambled Pesto Eggs	Pesto And Lemon Halibut	Pecan Crusted Trout	Five Berry Compote
7	Fresh Watermelon And Arugula Meal	Orange And Herbed Sauce White Bass	One-Pot Seafood Chowder	Pineapple And Ginger Sherbet

47.7 Week 7

Days	Breakfast	Lunch	Dinner	Dessert
1	Fresh Watermelon And Arugula Meal	Avocado And Chimichurri Bruschetta	Salsa Rice Meal	Tasty Figs Pie
2	Morning Scrambled Pesto Salad		Fried Cauliflower Pizza	Frozen Strawberry Yogurt
3	Italy's Favorite Herb Bread	Parmesan Baked Chicken	Tomato Bruschetta	Perfect Blueberry Muffin
4	Tasty Zucchini Chips	Simple Stir Fried Chicken	Yogurt And Banana Bowl	Simple Chocolate Parfait
5	Dill And Tomato Frittata	Foil Ala Pork	Chia And Almond Butter Pudding	
6	Black Olive Breakfast Loaf		Awesome Chicken Bell Pepper Platter	Tasty Figs Pie
7	Vegetarian Shepherd's Pie	Spicy Poached Pears	Bacon And Chicken Garlic Wrap	Awesome Peach And Raspberry Trifle

47.8 Week 8

Days	Breakfast	Lunch	Dinner	Dessert
1	Crunchy And Delicious Fougasse	Beef Sirloin With Juniper	Grape Sauce And Pork Fillet	Cinnamon And Chickpea Cookies
2	Dill And Tomato Frittata		Coconut Almond Beef	Spicy Poached Pears
3	Egg And Acorn In A Hole	Blackberry Chicken Wings	Simple Stir Fried Chicken	Dreamy Hot Fudge
4	Tasty Zucchini Chips	Chicken Bruschetta Burgers	Tuna And Olive Pasta	Perfect Frozen Strawberry Yogurt
5	Fancy Olive And Cheese Loaf	Creamy Rice Millet Dish	Red Chicken Spaghetti	Perfect Blueberry Muffins
6	Morning Scrambled Pesto Eggs	Pesto And Lemon Halibut	Pecan Crusted Trout	Five Berry Compote
7	Fresh Watermelon And Arugula Meal	Orange And Herbed Sauce White Bass		Pineapple And Ginger Sherbet

47.9 Week 9

Days	Breakfast	Lunch	Dinner	Dessert
1	Fresh Watermelon And Arugula Meal	Avocado And Chimichurri Bruschetta	Salsa Rice Meal	Tasty Figs Pie
2	Morning Scrambled Pesto Salad	Stuffed Avocado Meal	Fried Cauliflower Pizza	Frozen Strawberry Yogurt
3	Italy's Favorite Herb Bread	Parmesan Baked Chicken	Tomato Bruschetta	Perfect Blueberry Muffin
4	Tasty Zucchini Chips	Simple Stir Fried Chicken	Yogurt And Banana Bowl	Simple Chocolate Parfait
5	Dill And Tomato Frittata	Foil Ala Pork	Chia And Almond Butter Pudding	Apple And Plum Cake
6	Black Olive Breakfast Loaf	Coconut And Almond Beef	Awesome Chicken Bell Pepper Platter	Tasty Figs Pie
7	Vegetarian Shepherd's Pie	Spicy Poached Pears	Bacon And Chicken Garlic Wrap	Awesome Peach And Raspberry Trifle

47.10 Week 10

Days	Breakfast	Lunch	Dinner	Dessert
1	Bacon And Brie Omelet Wedges	Kidney Beans And Cilantro Salad	Homely Fattoush Salad	Black Tea Cake
2	Vegetarian Shepherd's Pie	Mediterranean Pepper Soup	Lovely Onion Soup	Hearty Lemon Mousse
3	Fresh Watermelon And Arugula Meal	Mashed Beans And Cumin	Black Bean With Mangoes	Pineapple And Ginger Sherbet
4	Dill And Tomato Frittata	Bulgar Pila With Garbanzo Bean	Turkish Canned Pinto Bean Salad	Spicy Poached Pears
5	Classic Focaccia	Pecan Crusted Trout	Spicy Cajun Shrimp	Cinnamon And Chickpea Cookies
6	Tasty Zucchini Chips	Lebanese Thin Pasta	Mushroom And Fettucine Platter	Dark Chocolate Mousse
7	Eggs And Acorn In A Hole	Creamy Millet Dish	Tuna And Olive Pasta	Apple And Plum Cake

48 MEASUREMENT CONVERSION CHART

Weight volumes

US STANDARD	EU STANDARD
½ oz.	15 g
1 oz.	30 g
2 oz.	60g
3 oz.	90 g
4oz.	125g
6 oz.	175g
8 oz.	250g
10 oz.	300g
12 oz.	375 g
13 oz.	400 g
14 oz.	425 g
1 lb	500 g
1½ lb	750 g
2 lb	1 kg

Liquid volume

US STANDARD	US STANDARD (OUNCES)	METRIC (APPROX.)
2 tablespoons	1 fl. oz.	30 mL
1/4 cup	2 fl. oz.	60 mL
1/2 cup	4 fl. oz.	120 mL
1 cup	8 fl. oz.	240 mL
1 1/2 cup	12 fl. oz.	355 mL
2 cups or 1 pint	16 fl. oz.	475 mL
4 cups or 1 quart	32 fl. oz.	1 L
1 gallon	128 fl. oz.	4 L

Dry Volumes

US STANDARD	EU STANDARD
1/8 teaspoon	0.5 mL
1/4 teaspoon	1 mL
1/2 teaspoon	2 mL
3/4 teaspoon	4 mL
1 teaspoon	5 mL
1 tablespoon	15 mL
1/4 cup	59 mL
1/2 cup	118 mL
3/4 cup	177 mL
1 cup	235 mL
2 cups	475 mL
3 cups	700 mL
4 cups	1 L

Temperature

US STANDARD	EU STANDARD
225 °F	107 °C
250 °F	120 °C
275 °F	135 °C
300 °F	150 °C
325 °F	160 °C
350 °F	180 °C
375 °F	190 °C
400 °F	205 °C
425 °F	220 °C
450 °F	235 °C
475 °F	245 °C
500 °F	260 °C

49 CONCLUSION

I would like to thank you for taking the time and reading this book through to the end. I sincerely hope that you found the information within this book to be interesting and valuable. The Mediterranean Diet is a diet that combines foods from the regions of the Mediterranean, including Greece, Turkey, and Lebanon. This diet is one of the best for overall health and weight loss. The diet is low in saturated fat, high in monounsaturated fats, and low in sodium. The diet includes lots of fruits, vegetables, whole grains, olive oil, and fish. This diet has risen in popularity, and for a good reason. This diet is known for its health benefits, including lower heart disease and cancer rates, improved mental health, and reduced stress levels. It is also low in calories, which can help you lose weight or maintain a healthy weight. The diet also benefits pregnant women and young children by providing enough essential nutrients and calories to stay healthy. The diet's focus on fruits and vegetables, whole grains, legumes, cheese, and seafood, is linked with a lower risk of heart disease. The diet has been linked with a lower risk of stroke, hypertension, arthritis, diabetes, and death from any cause. In addition, the diet is good for your blood sugar control and can help improve your cholesterol levels. And those are just the tip of the iceberg because, as you know now, the diet not only focuses on healthy eating but also helps you to develop a healthy lifestyle by encouraging you to engage in more social activities with friends and families while partaking in a physical workout every day. In short, the Mediterranean diet is the complete package for anyone who wants to lead a hassle-free healthy life while not having to sacrifice the awesome and delicious foods of life. Keeping that in mind, I wish you all the best for the journey ahead! Stay safe, stay healthy, and God Bless!

BONUS: Scanning the following QR code will take you to a web page where you can access 5 fantastic bonuses after leaving your email contact: Body Fat Calculator, Body Mass Index Calculator, Daily Caloric Needs Calculator, 2 mobile apps for iOS and Android.

https://BookHip.com/NJAVBJC

Manufactured by Amazon.ca
Bolton, ON